LITTLE BIGHORN REMEMBERED

THE UNTOLD INDIAN STORY OF CUSTER'S LAST STAND

HERMAN J. VIOLA

TIMES [T] BOOKS

TIMES BOOKS

Pages ii–iii: View of the Little Bighorn
Battlefield from the top of Monument Hill.
John Warner

Pages iv–v: Northern Cheyenne Victory Dance,
Little Bighorn Battlefield, June 25, 1996.
John Warner

This page: Crazy Horse Singers, Pine Ridge
Indian Reservation, South Dakota.
Eric Haase

Library of Congress Cataloging–in–Publication Data

Viola, Herman J.
Little Bighorn remembered : the untold Indian story of
Custer's last stand / Herman J. Viola.
p.   cm.
Includes bibliographical references and index.
ISBN 0–8129–3256–0 (hardcover)
1. Little Bighorn, Battle of the, Mont., 1876.   2. Dakota
Indians—Wars, 1876   3. Cheyenne Indians—Wars, 1876.
I. Title.
E83.876.V563 1999
973.8'2—dc21   99–19919

Developed by Rivilo Books
David Jeffery, Editor
Felix C. Lowe, Project Manager

Book design by Alex Castro

Random House website address: www.atrandom.com
Printed in the United States of America on acid-free paper
24689753
First Edition

Foreword

GERARD BAKER

Former Superintendent, Little Bighorn Battlefield National Monument

I am an enrolled member of the Three Affiliated Tribes, the Mandan, Hidatsa, and Arikara, who share the Fort Berthold Reservation in North Dakota. Although my ancestry is primarily Hidatsa-Mandan, growing up on Fort Berthold I knew several of the old Arikaras who had served as scouts for Custer, and his "last stand" was never far from our consciousness. Still, never in my wildest dreams did I imagine that one day I would be responsible for the day-to-day management of that tragic piece of ground. It was both an honor and a challenge for me to be one of the first Indians—after Barbara Satir Booher—to serve as superintendent, because the Battle of the Little Bighorn represents the end of a way of life for the Indian people.

When Indians visit the battlefield today, some cry. Many get angry. They are upset for the loss of the way of life, the freedom they once enjoyed. It's something we Indian people will never retrieve. That is what the battlefield means to us. That's why as its superintendent I tried to make it a welcoming place for Indians as well as non-Indians.

No one should demean Custer's soldiers, who made the ultimate sacrifice here for their government and their way of life. But visitors should also be aware that the battlefield is on an Indian reservation and that the Seventh Cavalry was here to force the last independent Indians to give up their freedom and become wards of the government, a decision in which they had no voice or choice.

Visitors should also realize that the Battle of the Little Bighorn was not simply a conflict between whites and Indians. It was also a fight between Indian tribes. It was Crow and Arikara against Lakota and Cheyenne. The Crow and Arikara were allies of the government, and some of their young men were at Custer's side in the conflict. To them, it was a matter of survival against their age-old enemies, the Lakota and Cheyenne. So even though they had been decimated by smallpox, cholera, and other introduced illnesses, even though their population was a shadow of its former strength, even though their warriors were few and unarmed, the Arikaras and Crows felt compelled to help the Army fight the strong, aggressive, and heavily armed Lakota.

In 1876, the choice for Custer's Indian allies seemed simple and clear-cut. Today, however, even non-Indians seem to question their participation on behalf of the government.

This attitude, I believe, emerged in the 1960s as a by-product of the Red Power movement. Indian youngsters were taught to put their Indianness first. They needed to be united against all white people, all white things, all white values. The youngsters

Tourists at Monument Hill.
Glen Swanson

growing up in the sixties, however, failed to realize that a century ago pan-Indianism did not exist on the Northern Plains. Tribes like the Crow, Arikara, Hidatsa, and Mandans worked with the government in order to survive. They needed government help to fight their traditional enemies—the Lakota, Cheyenne, the Blackfeet, and others. As a result of Red Power rhetoric, Indians today often look back at Little Bighorn and see only the harmful results of the Indian alliance with the U.S. Army. Hindsight is always twenty-twenty, but our ancestors did not have crystal balls.

My people—the Mandans, Hidatsa, and Arikara—were led to believe that if we supported the government and helped the military, we would all live in peace and nothing more would be taken from us. Our people firmly believed that we Indians would have everything we wanted forever under the terms of the friendship treaties we signed with the United States. At the time, it seemed to be a wise decision. Our people retained part of their ancestral lands for their reservation; so did the Crows. Then that land was suddenly ripped away from us because the government chose to build the Garrison Dam on the Missouri River. The dam flooded a large part of our homeland on the Fort Berthold Reservation, displacing 90 to 95 percent of our population.

Gerard Baker at the monument over the mass grave containing the remains of the enlisted personnel who perished in the Battle of the Little Bighorn.
Larry Mayer

That bureaucratic decision caused considerable anguish. It hit me personally as a child growing up on the reservation. Sometimes, when I went to Sacagawea Lake to fish and picnic, old people would come to the bluffs around the lake to cry and wail. They would look out over the water and cry for the loss of the graves of their ancestors and for their lost homeland, lost way of life, and community.

I am reminded of this every time I visit my mother, who still lives on the reservation. She is nearly ninety, and was one of thirteen brothers and sisters. They are all gone now: She's the last one left of her generation and one of the oldest members of the tribe living on the reservation. She still finds it too painful to go to the lake. She says, "It hurts too much to go there." She gets mad just thinking about it. "We helped those soldiers," she says. "When they came to our country we treated them like family. Then they turned around and did this to us. It was like waving candy in front of a child and then luring him into a building. Once inside, the candy is taken away and the child is beat up."

The great irony is that Custer became a hero figure, while each of the four tribes that fought in the battle, whether as friends or enemies of Custer, suffered. We still suffer. But we cannot afford to express bitterness, or anger, or regret at the actions of the past. We Indian people have to put that behind us, otherwise it will perpetuate the negativity that surrounds Indian youngsters today. We did it for a reason; it was done. That's the reality of the way things were back then, but now we must go on and work together for a better future.

Books like this one by Herman Viola, a scholar who cares and who understands us, are important because the Indian side of the story needs to be told. Since the establishment of the Little Bighorn Battlefield National Monument, scholarship and popular culture have focused on Custer. Now, at last *we* are getting the opportunity to explain what happened. Soon visitors to the battlefield will even be able to see a monument to the Indians who fought there. I think it shows how far we have come that the team whose design was selected for the monument was non-Indian. If non-Indian visitors leave with even just a little better understanding of what this place means to Indian people and to themselves, we will have done our duty.

Acknowledgments

Publication of *Little Bighorn Remembered* fulfills a cherished hope held for more than two decades. It began with stories about Custer's Crow scouts I heard from Joseph Medicine Crow, who adopted me as his brother "One Star" and who has been my friend and adviser since we first met at the National Anthropological Archives in 1972. Through Dr. Medicine Crow, I met descendants of Crow and Cheyenne veterans of the Battle of the Little Bighorn, including Dan Old Elk and Jimmy King.

I especially value the friendship of Dennis Limberhand, whose ancestor Limber Bones was one of the Northern Cheyennes who died at Little Bighorn. Through Dennis I befriended numerous Cheyenne descendants who assisted with this book, including the Reverend Joseph Walks Along, Sr.; Dr. Alonzo Spang, the president of Dull Knife Memorial College; Florence Whiteman; Alberta Fisher; James Blackwolf; and Bill Tall Bull.

Another valued friend is Michael Her Many Horses, whom I met at the Smithsonian when he was one of the first interns in my Native American Cultural Resources Program. It was Michael who urged that the Indian side of Little Bighorn be told, and it was Michael who collected most of the Lakota stories.

I greatly appreciate the assistance of my partners in Rivilo Books, David Jeffery and Felix Lowe, who accompanied me to the Crow and Northern Cheyenne reservations as I collected material for the book—and later struggled with me to develop the material. David Jeffery then lent his considerable editorial skills to shaping several of the chapters and improving the captions.

Thanks are also due to Charlotte White, Lieutenant William Van Wyck Reily's great-great-niece, to whom the ill-fated officer is still known as "Uncle Willie." I first met Charlotte when she was a student in my archival science class at the Catholic University of America in 1983. She asked me if I knew anything about "Custer's Last Stand" because her Uncle Willie was killed there and the family still had the three letters he'd sent his mother while a member of the Seventh Cavalry. The rest, as is so often said, is history. Thanks are due to her family for waiting patiently as I tried to get the young officer's story into print.

I also thank Brian C. Pohanka, who generously shared with me the considerable information he had already found about Lieutenant Reily.

Others to whom thanks are due:

Michael Sullivan, a high school teacher in northern Virginia, who researched the records of the Crow and Arikara scouts for me at the National Archives.

Robert Kvasnicka, archivist at the National Archives, whose knowledge of the Indian and War Department records was often timely and invaluable.

Jan Shelton Danis, who has edited my work for thirty years, and who has been my partner in most of my publications.

Kitty Belle Deernose, archivist at the Little Bighorn Battlefield National Monument.

Gerard Baker, former superintendent of the Little Bighorn Battlefield National Monument, who introduced me to the descendants of the Arikara scouts on Fort Berthold Reservation and who provided invaluable assistance in my search for stories from descendants of battle veterans.

This book benefited immensely from the generous support of Glen Swanson, whose collection of Custer memorabilia, documents, and photographs is unparalleled. Glen and his wife, Joanne, have been exceptionally generous with their time and encouragement, and in permitting me to publish—often for the first time—Little Bighorn–related items from their exceptionally rich and remarkable collection of Western Americana. Not only is the collection exceptional, but so is Glen's skill with a camera. As his many photographic credits attest, he is one of the major contributors of this book's imagery.

At the National Museum of Natural History, my thanks go to Jake Homiak, Paula Fleming, and Vyrtis Thomas of the National Anthropological Archives. At the National Museum of American History, I am indebted to Margaret Vining, whose knowledge of the museum's military collection is unequaled; to Harry Hunter and Sarah J. Rittgers, ordnance specialists; and to James Hutchins, Curator Emeritus of Military History, who shared with me not only his remarkable Curtis story but also his large collection of Custer-related photographs and publications.

Vic Krantz, retired photographer from the National Museum of Natural History, took many of the photographs that appear in this book. Other photographers whose work appears here are Eric Haase, who did the Sioux portraits, and John Warner, who photographed the Cheyennes. The two original maps were created by David Chandler. Elie S. Rogers assisted with picture editing.

George Chalou of the National Archives and Ralph Ehrenberg of the Library of Congress have been my archival companions for three decades, and they have patiently listened to my Custer stories, for which they deserve thanks, but it is for their key assistance at crucial moments in the research and publication process that I am especially grateful.

At Random House and Times Books, I am thankful to former publisher Harold Evans and to Walter Weintz, who saw the value in this book when the idea was first broached to them—and for their patience as the book missed one deadline after another; to Kate Humphreys, Walter's cheerful assistant; to Kathy Rosenbloom, the production manager; and to Benjamin Dreyer, the production editor.

Credit for the brilliant design of the book goes to Alex Castro, for whom this project was a labor of love. Thanks are also due to his assistant Kevin Meadowcroft.

Finally, thanks are due to my wife, Susan; our sons, Joseph, Paul, and Peter; and their wives, Allison, Janice, and Veronique; who have assisted me in various ways with this project, especially with regards to mastering the computer. As youngsters, each of my sons accompanied me on my many trips to Indian country—to the Crow, the Nez Perce, the Cheyenne and Arapaho, the Lakota, and the Makah.

Many other individuals and institutions assisted in the preparation of this book. I am grateful to them, and I regret the lack of space to list them here.

Sitting Bull assemblage, including his photograph and items that once belonged to him.
Glen Swanson Collection

Contents

LITTLE BIGHORN REMEMBERED

The Trail to Little Bighorn

HERMAN J. VIOLA

The Battle of the Little Bighorn has contributed much to the romantic lore of the West. The story of "Custer's Last Stand" has been told and retold in countless books and movies. What remains largely untold is the story of the Indians at Little Bighorn. Lost in all the fascination about Custer and his doomed command are the Arikara and Crow warriors who rode at his side that day. Along with Sitting Bull and Crazy Horse, the Indians who defeated Custer have fared poorly in the romantic literature. Here is their story.

Few people fought harder to maintain their traditional way of life than the Indians of the Great Plains. But courage could not overcome the railroad, the telegraph, and, above all, the extermination of the bison. As long as Plains Indians could live off the land, they were invincible. Nobody knew this better than the soldiers chasing them. That is one reason western army officers issued free ammunition to the hide hunters who, along with diseases introduced into the buffalo herds by domesticated livestock, helped the United States solve its "Indian problem."

Another important factor in the defeat of the western Indians was their inability to put aside tribal differences to organize against a common enemy. Indeed, it was not uncommon for Indians to assist the U.S. Army against members of their own tribes. At the Little Bighorn, for example, several of the Arikara scouts riding with the Seventh Cavalry were actually Sioux men married to Arikara women.

The events of 1876 need to be understood in the context of the rapid changes that overtook the West after the American Civil War. Following Lee's surrender at Appomattox, a tide of white settlement surged across the Great Plains. What helped fuel the migration was the Homestead Act of 1862, which dispensed public land to settlers for a nominal fee after five years of residence; the transcontinental railroad, which carried passengers and freight from coast to coast safely and conveniently in a mere six days; and an incredible influx of European immigrants—of the thirty-eight million people living in the United States in 1870, approximately five million were foreign-born. All these pressures conspired to further reduce Indian landholdings and increase tensions between the races that flared into hostilities on the Northern and Southern Plains.

Deer Medicine Rock. The day before its rendezvous with Sitting Bull at Little Bighorn, Custer's column passed this striking sandstone formation, located a few miles north of the town of Lame Deer on the Northern Cheyenne Reservation. It was here, ten days before the battle, that Sitting Bull underwent the Sun Dance in which he saw "dead soldiers falling into camp." Deer Medicine Rock, which is on private property, remains sacred to the Northern Cheyennes.
Glen Swanson

Previous pages:
The Little Bighorn battlefield at sunset.
David Jeffery

3

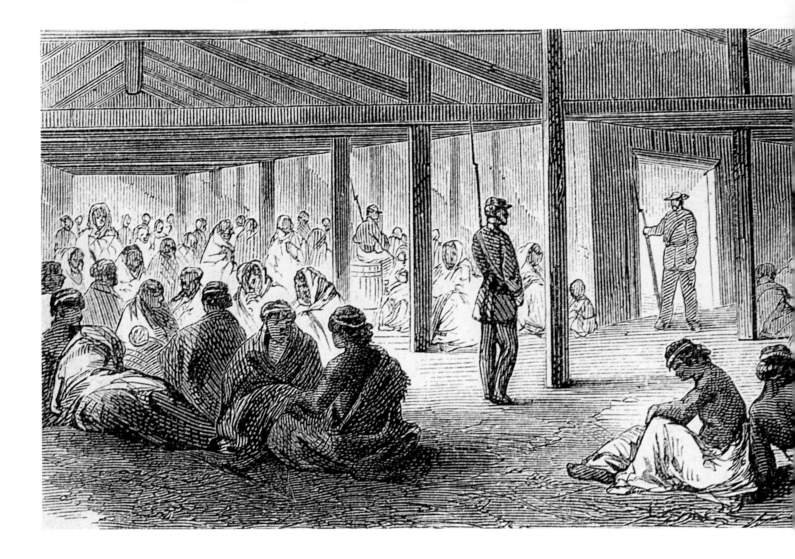

Condemned Santee Sioux prisoners awaiting execution for crimes committed during the Minnesota uprising, 1862.
Herman J. Viola Collection

Two brutal incidents set the stage for the violence that engulfed the Plains in the 1870s. In Minnesota, the Santee or Eastern Sioux, having witnessed the steady erosion of their lands to white settlement, were greatly agitated by rumors that their annuities would be cut off and their rations reduced. When tribal leaders asked a local trader for more food, he told them to eat grass. In August 1862, this emotionally charged climate encouraged four young Indian men to kill a white family. Fearing a massive retaliation by the U.S. Army, tribal leaders persuaded Chief Little Crow to strike first. Although Little Crow had visited Washington, D.C., a few years earlier and knew his people had no hope of victory, he agreed to lead the uprising. The fighting claimed the lives of more than five hundred Minnesotans, including a trader whose mouth was stuffed with grass.

The U.S. Army responded swiftly and ruthlessly. In command was General John Pope, who had just suffered an embarrassing defeat at the Second Battle of Bull Run. Perhaps hoping to win back some lost laurels, Pope was merciless. "It is my purpose," he informed his superiors, "to utterly exterminate the Sioux if I have the power to do so.... They are to be treated as maniacs or wild beasts, and by no means as people with whom treaties or compromises can be made." Within a month of his taking command, the Sioux war was over, but it was another year before a starving Little Crow was killed by a Minnesota farmer who found the chief and his son picking berries. In the meantime, a military commission had condemned 303 of his followers to death. It is to Abraham Lincoln's credit that, despite intense pressure from the Minnesota con-

gressional corps, he commuted the death sentences of all but thirty-eight of the condemned Indians, who were executed in a mass hanging in the public square of Mankato on December 26, 1862. Despite Lincoln's caution not to punish innocent Indians, at least one of those executed that day had actually saved white lives. In fact, the reason the insurgents had not taken more lives was due to the number of Santee who had warned white friends to seek safety.

The Santee survivors were forced from Minnesota. Most of them eventually accepted a reservation in present-day Nebraska, but some of the displaced Santees chose instead to seek refuge among their western kinsmen. They were among the thousands of people in Sitting Bull's camp on the Little Bighorn that fateful June day in 1876.

The second tragedy occurred in Colorado Territory, which had experienced phenomenal growth because of the gold and silver rushes of the 1850s. As many as one hundred thousand miners had elbowed their way into the mineral fields, dislocating and angering the Cheyennes and Arapahos, who seized the opportunity offered them by the reduced military garrisons during the Civil War to attack wagon trains, mining camps, and stagecoach lines. One white family was killed within twenty miles of Denver.

To stem the mounting violence, the governor of Colorado Territory called out the militia. Its commander was Colonel J. M. Chivington, a former clergyman whose compassion for his fellow man did not extend to Indians. Having chased the elusive hostiles for several weeks with little more than saddle sores to show for his troubles, Chivington decided to attack the village of Chief Black Kettle, whose people had in fact been involved in some of the disturbances but were then camped on Sand Creek under what they thought was the protective custody of the commander at Fort Lyon, some forty miles away.

Chivington and his men charged the sleeping camp at dawn, the morning of November 28, 1864. Black Kettle rushed from his tent and raised first an American flag and then a white flag, but Chivington wanted a victory, not prisoners. Men, women, and children were hunted down and shot. "Nits make lice," Chivington was quoted by one of his soldiers at a subsequent military inquiry when asked why children had been killed.

An interpreter living in the village later testified: "They were scalped, their brains knocked out; the men used their knives, ripped open women, clubbed little children, knocked them in the head with their guns, beat their brains out, mutilated their bodies in every sense of the word." As many as 450 of the 700 Indians in the village that day were killed. Black Kettle was not one of them, however. He survived, only to be killed in November 1868, when George Armstrong Custer carried out a similar attack on an unsuspecting Cheyenne village in winter camp along the banks of the Washita River.

The Sand Creek Massacre outraged easterners, but it pleased the people of Colorado Territory. Chivington later appeared on a Denver stage, where he regaled delighted audiences with his "war" stories and displayed one hundred Indian scalps.

If Chivington hoped to bring peace by destroying Black Kettle's village, he failed. Instead, it ignited a fire of revenge among the Plains tribes. The U.S. Army, on the other hand, felt confident about its ability to stamp out any Indian unrest. Western citizens, who had little sympathy for a policy that appeared to coddle Indians, supported the Army attitude. Graffiti found scrawled on Indian skulls, such as "I am on the reservation at last," succinctly expressed the racist feelings of most westerners toward their Indian neighbors. Indians had to give way peacefully or face the consequences.

The soldier charged with pacifying the militants among the Plains tribes was General John Pope. His uncompromising treatment of the Santee Sioux in Minnesota had endeared him to both westerners and his military superiors. In command of the entire western theater, Pope launched a massive assault against the Plains Indians in spring 1865. Fully six thousand combat troops comprising three separate armies were hurled against the Comanches and Kiowas on the Southern Plains and the Arapahos, Cheyennes, and Sioux on the Central and Northern Plains.

The campaign did little except anger the Indians and embarrass the U.S. Army, which learned a valuable lesson. Feeding and supporting the unwieldy military columns absorbed so much energy that there was little time to pursue Indians. Inhospitable weather further hampered military effectiveness. One unit not only lost most of its horses and mules to the inclement weather, but came perilously close to losing a large number of its personnel.

Meanwhile, the Indians chased by Pope's forces had little difficulty locating and eluding their pursuers. Arapaho, Cheyenne, and Sioux war parties on the Central Plains revenged the atrocities at Sand Creek in dramatic fashion as they burned ranches and stage stations, disrupted telegraph service, twice terrorized the town of Julesburg, Colorado, and generally played havoc with any unwary travelers who came their way. One war party, for instance, derailed a steam engine employed by construction crews on the transcontinental railroad.

Another party, according to a story still told by Southern Cheyennes, killed a telegraph operator. Aware that white people somehow talked over the wire, members of the war party shoved a piece of it through his head from ear to ear "so he could hear better in the afterlife."

Determined to bring the Southern Plains tribes to heel, the Army launched a three-pronged campaign reminiscent of the ill-fated strategy that led to the debacle at Little Bighorn a decade later. One of the columns was led by George Armstrong Custer, who pushed south from Fort Dodge, Kansas, and found the winter camp of Black Kettle. This star-crossed chief had survived Sand Creek and was now sincere in his hopes to live in peace with the white man. Custer, as he was to do at Little Bighorn, divided his forces and assaulted the sleeping village from four sides. According to Captain Albert Barnitz, a company commander in the Seventh Cavalry,

> We had just reached the edge of a shallow ravine beyond which we could see the clustered tepees . . . when a shot was fired in the village, and instantly we heard the band on the ridge beyond it strike up the familiar air "Garry Owen" and the answering cheers of the men, as Custer and his legion came thundering down the long divide, while nearer at hand on our right came Benteen's squadron, crashing through the frozen snow, as the troops deployed into line at a gallop, and the Indian village rang with unearthly war-whoops, the quick discharge of fire-arms, the clamorous barking of dogs, the cries of infants, and the wailing of women.

Custer quickly captured the village, but almost as quickly found himself under attack from growing numbers of angry warriors pouring from nearby villages also wintering in the Washita valley. The Seventh Cavalry managed to extricate itself with little loss—five troopers killed (including the grandson of Alexander Hamilton) and fifteen missing. Their mutilated bodies were later found in a setting again reminiscent of Little Bighorn, but this time Custer triumphed. He left Black Kettle's village in ashes. His troopers shot the entire Cheyenne pony herd—nine hundred animals—and killed dozens of men, women, and children including Black Kettle and his wife, who, double mounted on a pony, were cut down as they tried to escape the slaughter. To many easterners, the so-called Battle of the Washita was little more than another Sand Creek Massacre, but it enhanced Custer's reputation as a dashing cavalier and launched his reputation as an Indian fighter.

Meanwhile, there was a growing sentiment among the people of the United States to stop the bloodshed even if it meant that certain Indians went unpunished for their "crimes." In fact, in spring 1866, government officials had already begun extending olive branches to the militants on the Northern Plains by asking them to assemble for a grand conference at Fort Laramie in order to establish "a lasting peace."

Foremost among the militants was Red Cloud, the Oglala war chief whose name, along with those of Crazy Horse and Sitting Bull, was to become a household word in the decades following the Civil War. When news went out that government officials wished to talk of peace and were promising presents and badly needed food, Red

In 1867, Congress established the United States Peace Commission, comprised of civilian and military leaders with interest and competence in Indian affairs. Members of the commission included Generals Alfred H. Terry, later Custer's superior officer on the march to the Little Bighorn, William Tecumseh Sherman of Civil War fame, Christopher C. Augur, and William S. Harney. The goal of the commission was to bring peace to the West by locating the tribes on reservations. The Fort Laramie Treaty of 1868 kept the lid on things for several years but also laid the groundwork for the Sioux wars of 1867–81. Shown here are Generals Harney (with white beard), Sherman (to his left), Augur (with muttonchops), and (to Augur's left) Terry. *National Anthropological Archives*

James E. Taylor

Custer's dawn attack on Black Kettle's Cheyenne village on the Washita, November 27, 1868, as depicted by artist James E. Taylor, from his scrapbook titled *Our Wild Indians in Peace and War*. Images such as this added luster to Custer's reputation as a dashing cavalier and Indian fighter.
National Anthropological Archives

Cloud and several thousand Sioux and Cheyenne assembled at Fort Laramie in June 1866 to meet with the Great Father's representatives, led by Commissioner E. B. Taylor.

The government did not wish to purchase their country, the Indians were told. It simply wanted to make peace and obtain permission for white travelers to use the Bozeman Trail, a new road through the Powder River country. A promise that all travelers would stay on the road and not do any hunting was, one official later admitted, "well calculated, and . . . designed to deceive."

Red Cloud was not fooled. Travelers were already using the road, and he suspected the worst when Colonel Henry B. Carrington and a battalion of infantry marched into Fort Laramie in the midst of the proceedings. Carrington, in fact, had orders to build a string of posts along the Bozeman Trail to protect emigrants from Indian attack. When Carrington appeared at the conference, Red Cloud refused an introduction. According to witnesses, he rebuked Carrington for being a party to deceit: "The Great Father sends us presents and wants us to sell him the road, but the White Chief goes with soldiers to steal the road before the Indians say yes or no!" With that, Red Cloud stalked from the treaty grounds, taking most of the militants with him.

Commissioner Taylor continued with the conference and persuaded the remaining chiefs to sign an agreement for use of the Bozeman Trail. He did not seem concerned that the signatories were primarily "Laramie Loafers"—friendly Indians who spent most of the time lounging around the fort—and a handful of leaders not affected by the proposed right-of-way. "Satisfactory treaty concluded with the Sioux and

Although the Oglala chief Red Cloud refused to sign the 1866 Treaty of Fort Laramie, he did sign the 1868 treaty, which supposedly guaranteed the integrity of the Black Hills. The 1868 treaty also created the Great Sioux Reservation and permitted the Indians to continue hunting around the Powder River in Montana and Wyoming. The Indians in this 1868 photograph are, left to right, Packs His Drum, Old Man Afraid of His Horses, and Red Bear. The white men are, left to right, unidentified, John Finn, Amos Bettelyoun (standing), W. G. Bullock and Benjamin Mills (seated), and James Bordeau. Photograph by Alexander Gardner.
National Anthropological Archives

Cheyennes," he immediately wired his superiors in Washington. "Most cordial feelings prevail."

The extent of the "cordial feelings" soon became evident as Red Cloud's war parties harassed travelers and the garrisons building the three Bozeman Trail forts—Phil Kearney, C. F. Smith, and Reno. The primary post and Carrington's headquarters was Fort Phil Kearney, which immediately became the focal point of Sioux militancy. As a result, Carrington decided to erect a log palisade, a feature seldom seen in western forts.

Although Red Cloud never attempted a direct assault on the fort, he continually sent war parties against the work crews cutting trees on the slopes of nearby mountains. It was an attack on a train bringing logs to the fort that gave Red Cloud his finest moment and enabled a bold young warrior named Crazy Horse to join the pantheon of American Indian heroes. On a brisk winter day in December 1866, Carrington sent Captain William J. Fetterman and a combined force of some eighty cavalry troopers and infantry to chase away a Sioux war party that had attacked the wood train within sight of the fort. In the war party was Crazy Horse, whose task was to lure the relief column over a nearby hill and into an ambush.

Fetterman was a brash and foolhardy Civil War veteran who ridiculed the fighting abilities of the Plains Indian. Certain that he could overtake the decoy party and Crazy Horse, whose pony appeared to be limping badly, Fetterman dashed over the hill and into the hands of some two thousand Sioux and Cheyenne warriors. Within minutes, only a dog that had followed the troopers remained alive; it, too, was shot when one of the warriors yelled: "Do not let even a dog get away!"

From the condition of the horribly mutilated bodies, it was obvious Red Cloud's warriors intended to make a statement. One corpse, that of a civilian who joined the column to test his new repeating rifle against Indians, had 105 arrows in it. Fetterman and his second in command, terrified at the prospect of being captured alive, evidently committed suicide by shooting each other in the head.

Red Cloud's stunning victory brought immediate and surprising results. Rather than seek revenge, the federal government decided to seek peace by improving the way the nation's Indian affairs were being managed. A peace commission appointed in 1867 toured the Plains and concluded that most instances of Indian violence had been provoked by whites. At the commission's urging, the Army closed the Bozeman Trail and abandoned the offending forts, one of the few occasions the white man retreated. Some scholars, however, now believe the entire episode might have been orchestrated by monied interests who wished to distract Red Cloud and his warriors from the work crews constructing the transcontinental railroad, which was about to make such trails obsolete.

For Red Cloud and the Sioux, it was only a symbolic victory at best, but the Treaty of Fort Laramie, signed in 1868, did negate the earlier agreement approving the trail. It

Red Cloud resisted white encroachment and fought the U.S. Army from 1866 to 1868. Only after the military forts along the Bozeman Trail were dismantled and burned did he finally sign the Fort Laramie Treaty. Later the Oglala chief fought politically for his people while living on the reservation. He did not participate in the Battle of the Little Bighorn. In this 1880 photograph he is wearing a buckskin shirt with hair fringes and beadwork decoration, and a breastplate made of shell beads. Photograph by Charles M. Bell.
National Anthropological Archives

The Oglala delegation to Washington, D.C., 1880. Seated, left to right: Red Dog, Little Wound, Red Cloud, American Horse, and Red Shirt. Behind them is the white interpreter John Bridgeman.
National Anthropological Archives

also established the Great Sioux Reserve west of the Missouri River in Dakota and, by accepting it, the chiefs agreed to settle at agencies and accept reservation life. True to his word, Red Cloud became a reservation Indian, forfeiting the respect of those leaders who had refused to sign.

Another immediate result of the Fetterman fight was President U. S. Grant's "Quaker Policy," so named because it encouraged the appointment of clergymen as Indian agents. Although the religious experiment lasted throughout the Grant administration, it proved to be no panacea. The religious groups squabbled over the division of the reservations; some of the smaller denominations had difficulty finding enough qualified volunteers; and the proselytizing of some sincere but overzealous agents antagonized their tribes. By the time Grant left office, agency administration was pretty much a matter of business as usual, and the worst abuses continued until Civil Service Reform legislation was introduced during Grover Cleveland's presidency.

Grant's peace policy was administered by his friend Ely S. Parker, a Seneca Indian from New York. Parker had been Grant's military secretary during the Civil War. He was one of the best educated and most able persons ever to head the Bureau of Indian Affairs. He was also the first Indian to do so.

Parker was a longtime opponent of the treaty-making system, because he believed it was based on the erroneous assumption that the tribes were sovereign nations. His recommendation that treaty-making be abolished coincided with a drive in the House of Representatives for a more active role in the management of Indian affairs. House participation in Indian matters was seriously curtailed because the ratification of all treaties—with Indian tribes as well as foreign nations—was the Senate's prerogative. In 1871, the practice of negotiating formal treaties with the tribes was terminated. Existing treaties remained in force, but thereafter negotiated "agreements" replaced "treaties." The "agreements" became law only when ratified by both the House and the Senate.

Parker, unfortunately, fell victim to another arm of Grant's peace policy, the Board of Indian Commissioners. Established in 1869 to control the graft and corruption associated with Indian affairs, the board consisted of ten high-minded, unpaid philanthropists whose primary task was to oversee fiscal matters within the Indian bureau. The board had little actual power and proved to be rather ineffective, but it did stir up a hornet's nest for a time as it exposed examples of graft at every level of Indian affairs from the Secretary of the Interior to the lowliest field employee. One of those charged with fraud was Parker. Although eventually exonerated, he resigned.

Especially subject to fiscal abuse were Indian delegations, a key component of Grant's peace policy. Each delegation followed a similar script. During a whirlwind tour of eastern cities, the delegates were showered with presents; guided on tours of

In October 1888, Sitting Bull joined a delegation of tribal leaders from Standing Rock Reservation to Washington, D.C. Although the delegation failed to work out an acceptable land agreement, the group assembled on the steps of the Interior Department for the mandatory photograph. Sitting Bull is slightly to the left of the group, holding his hat in his right hand.
National Anthropological Archives

arsenals, battleships, and forts; and then taken to meet the president, whom they addressed—as a title of respect and not subordination—as the Great Father, never the Great White Father, a phrase from dime novels and the film industry.

No warrior left Washington unimpressed by the vast numbers of white people, the huge cities, and the advanced technology he had seen. Huge shore batteries and rapid-fire Gatling guns were weapons beyond imagining; equally amazing were the tens of thousands of muskets and rifles at the Washington Arsenal—"a forest of guns," muttered one astonished visitor.

Even the most sophisticated Indians had difficulty comprehending all they saw during their eastern visits. An agent accompanying the Red Cloud and Spotted Tail delegation of 1870 overheard several of the Indians discussing the great number of whites they were seeing. The astonished warriors could only reason that they were seeing the same people in each city. The people in Chicago had somehow followed them to Washington, Philadelphia, and then New York. The delegates were convinced that white men, with their superior technology, had developed the means of moving whole cities, much like the Sioux themselves could move their tipi villages from one site to another.

In the 1860s, Sitting Bull drew forty-one pictographs recording his war deeds. His uncle Four Horns made two copies of the drawings. One set, which is now in the Smithsonian Institution, was acquired by an army surgeon at Fort Buford, Dakota Territory. Each drawing is signed with the same glyph, a sitting buffalo bull, which was the chief's signature until a trader he'd befriended while living in Canada taught him to sign his name. In this drawing, Sitting Bull is fighting with a Crow warrior. His shield was a gift from his father.
National Anthropological Archives

A key flaw in the delegation policy was the disbelief of fellow tribesmen of the reports of the returned delegates. Even Sitting Bull, who had not accompanied a delegation before the Battle of the Little Bighorn, discounted the fabulous tales of other Sioux travelers as figments of their imagination induced by the white man's powerful "medicine."

In the end, Quaker Indian agents, delegations, presents, and empty promises could not restrain rising Indian resentments that had been building since 1854, when a foolish young lieutenant at Fort Laramie decided to intimidate a nearby Sioux village for supposedly stealing a stray cow from a passing wagon train. The Grattan Massacre, as this episode is known, was but the first in a series of confrontations between the incomparable light cavalry of the Plains Indians and the U.S. Army: the Fetterman fight, the Wagon Box fight, the Battle of the Rosebud, and the Battle of the Little Bighorn. No corner of the Great Plains escaped the wrath of angry tribesmen who, in the 1870s, lashed out in a final, desperate attempt to keep the white man at bay.

Although Red Cloud had signed the Treaty of Fort Laramie in 1868 and settled on a reservation, many other Lakota and Cheyenne leaders had not. Sitting Bull, Crazy Horse, Gall, Two Moons, and Lame White Man were all at large, living on unceded Indian lands.

Construction of the Northern Pacific Railroad through Dakota and Montana Territories, the heart of Sioux country, triggered the next confrontation. The military decided that a new fort was necessary to guard the railroad, and the ideal site was in the Black Hills, an area in the southwestern portion of the Great Sioux Reservation, which is sacred to the tribe. In 1874, George Armstrong Custer led an expedition into the Black Hills to locate a site for the fort and found gold as well. Soon the Black Hills were overrun with prospectors, and the Army faced a losing battle trying to drive them off. When an attempt to purchase the Black Hills came to naught, the government decided to take action against the Sioux and their allies for failing to meet the terms of the 1868 treaty, a flawed charge at best, because most of the free-roaming bands were on unceded lands.

One of those assigned the task of forcing the nontreaty Indians to move onto the reservation was Custer, the person so instrumental in bringing matters to a head. Although virtually every schoolchild knows what happened when Custer had his rendezvous with Sitting Bull, few people know that Indian allies were in American uniform that day, most of them Crows and Arikaras who were anxious to even old scores. For generations, these small tribes had stood alone against their Sioux and Cheyenne enemies. Constant warfare made them hardy and brave. It also made them embrace the white man as an ally against the Sioux.

Sitting Bull, Hunkpapa chief and spiritual leader of the Lakota people. This 1878 photograph was taken in Canada, where Sitting Bull had fled with many followers a few months after the Battle of the Little Bighorn.
Glen Swanson Collection

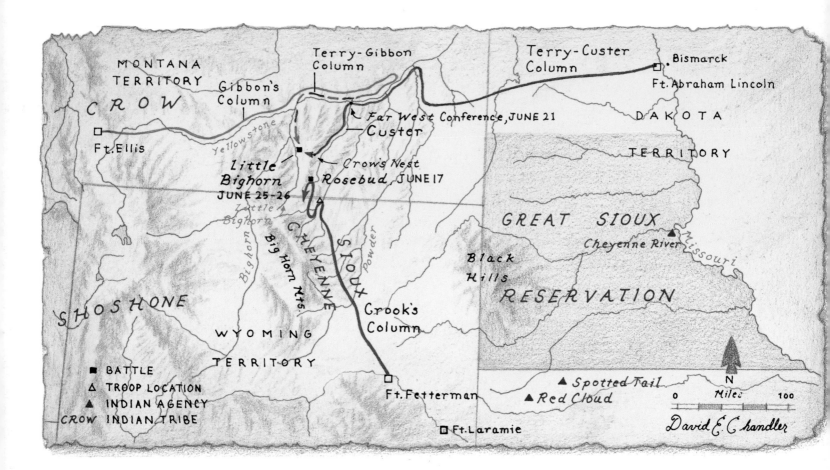

The 1876 campaign of the U.S. Army.
Map by David Chandler

Opposite:
In 1874, Custer blazed the "Thieves' Road" into the Black Hills. Supposedly seeking a site for a fort to superintend the Indians at the Red Cloud and Spotted Tail agencies, Custer included miners and news reporters in his entourage, which suggests other interests as well. The news of gold in the Black Hills preceded Custer's column back to Fort Lincoln, setting off a mining stampede that violated the Fort Laramie Treaty and precipitated the war with Sitting Bull. Custer's wagon train is seen wending its way through the hills.
Glen Swanson Collection

To regard the Crows, Arikaras, and other tribes that helped the U.S. Army as traitors or mercenaries overlooks the legacy of intertribal warfare that long predated the arrival of the first white man on the Plains. As late as the 1860s and 1870s, the Crows and Arikaras still suffered from Sioux aggression, and understandably viewed the Army as a tool in their centuries-old struggle for survival against a determined and more numerous enemy. Unfortunately, these tribes did not realize that, in helping the United States defeat their Sioux enemies, they were dooming themselves to share the same destiny—life on a reservation. Unlike many other tribes, however, the Crow and Arikara reservations at least included part of their traditional homeland.

Authorities forced the conflict in the spring of 1876 in response to reports that young warriors were slipping away from their agencies to join bands of nontreaty Indians in the unceded country east of the Bighorn River. The federal government ordered all Sioux bands, regardless of treaty guarantees giving them the right to hunt on the Northern Plains, to return to the Great Sioux Reservation by February 1 or face the consequences. Sitting Bull, Crazy Horse, and other leaders not only ignored the order but gave every indication they were prepared to fight.

The Army welcomed the challenge and sent three columns of troops to converge upon and trap the defiant Indians, who were known to be somewhere in the Bighorn country. One column, under General George Crook, marched northward from newly built Fort Fetterman on the upper North Platte River. A second column, headed by Colonel John Gibbon, moved eastward from Fort Ellis in Montana. The third column,

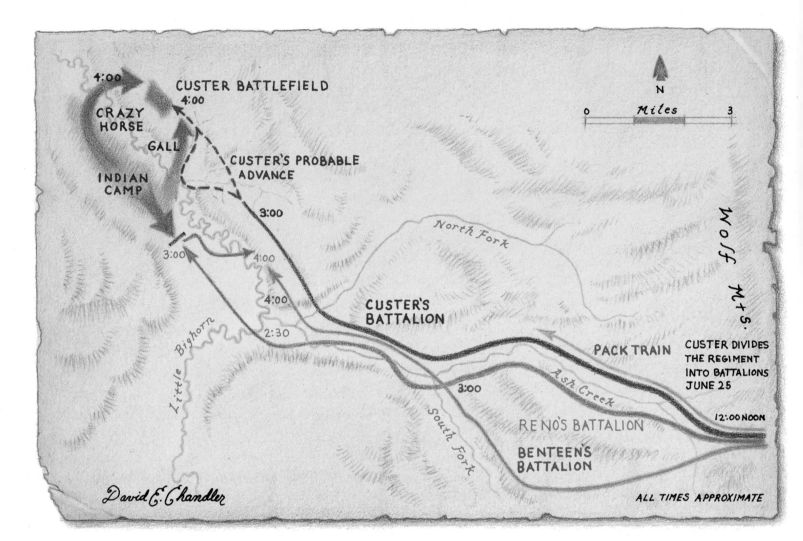

Miles 0 3

N

**Detailed map of the Battle of the Little
Bighorn, June 25, 1876.**
Map by David Chandler

which went west from Fort Lincoln in Dakota Territory, was led by General Alfred H.
Terry. Under his command was Lieutenant Colonel George Armstrong Custer and the
Seventh Cavalry.

By mid-June, Sitting Bull and his followers were camped along the Little Bighorn
River, which they called the Greasy Grass. It was a huge village of some twelve hundred
lodges and six tribal camp circles—Hunkpapa, Oglala, Miniconjou, Sans Arc,
Blackfoot, and Northern Cheyenne—that stretched upwards of three miles along the
banks of the Greasy Grass. No one knows the number of warriors in the camp, but estimates range from fifteen hundred to five thousand men at arms. Contributing to the
confidence of the villagers was knowledge of Sitting Bull's vision. During the annual
Sun Dance a few days earlier he had seen "dead soldiers falling into camp."

Although the Army had enjoyed previous success against Plains Indians with its
"convergence" strategy, this time it failed thanks largely to an unexpected spanking
inflicted on General Crook by Crazy Horse along Rosebud Creek on June 17, 1876. The
six-hour fight caused few casualties to either force, but when the Indians called it a
day, Crook retreated.

Unaware of Crook's defeat, Terry and Gibbon met at the junction of the Rosebud
and Yellowstone rivers without encountering any Indians. Upon receiving word that

scouts had spotted a large fresh trail heading toward the Little Bighorn, Terry sent Custer and the Seventh Cavalry south along the Rosebud in hopes of finding Sitting Bull's camp. Once he found the village, Custer was to block their retreat into the Bighorn Mountains. Terry, meanwhile, planned to march the combined command overland and trap Sitting Bull between both forces.

The plan might have worked had it not been for Custer's eagerness to repeat his Washita triumph. His Crow scouts had no trouble finding Sitting Bull's village, but instead of waiting for the reinforcements with Terry, Custer chose to launch an immediate attack. Just as he did at the Washita, Custer divided his troopers into three columns, leaving a small force to guard his pack train. On the morning of June 25, he sent one column under Major Marcus Reno in a direct assault on Sitting Bull's village. Another column under Captain Frederick Benteen he sent in a sweeping arc to the left to cut off any fleeing Indians. Custer's own column moved along the bluffs to the right of the village. Instead of the small sleeping village like the one he crushed at the Washita, however, Custer found an enormous encampment thronged with angry warriors who quickly surrounded and annihilated his inexperienced and weary force. The troopers with Reno and Benteen avoided a similar fate only because of Terry's timely arrival. The fact that two thirds of the troopers under Custer's command survived the battle has been all but forgotten in the mystique and romance of what is popularly known as Custer's Last Stand.

In truth, it was also the last stand of the Sioux and Cheyenne as well, because their victory over Custer led to their own destruction. Imagine the shock and embarrassment to citizens of the United States enjoying the centennial year of their independence. The U.S. Army went after Sitting Bull and his allies with a vengeance. Within a year, most of them were either on reservations or refugees with Sitting Bull in Canada, where a handful of diehards remained until 1883.

Perhaps the cruelest fate befell the Northern Cheyennes. While in their winter camp, they were attacked by about a thousand cavalrymen who drove them from their village and then destroyed their tipis, clothing, and food supply. That night, eleven Cheyenne babies froze to death. The survivors eventually found shelter with Crazy Horse, but when spring came they surrendered.

Although the Cheyennes expected to be placed on a reservation, they did not anticipate being relocated to Indian Territory in latter-day Oklahoma, many hundreds of miles from their homeland on the Northern Plains. It was their misfortune to become part of a new government program to concentrate as many tribes as possible in a relatively small region. Eventually, some twenty-five tribes were moved to Indian Territory; many of their descendants still live in Oklahoma today.

For the Cheyennes, the policy was a nightmare come true. Of the thousand or so members of the tribe who were shipped to Indian Territory in the summer of 1877, many sickened and died. "In Oklahoma we all got sick with chills and fever," recalled Iron Teeth, an elderly Cheyenne woman who told her story in 1927. "When we were not sick we were hungry."

Rather than die by degrees in Oklahoma, some three hundred Northern Cheyennes under Chiefs Dull Knife and Little Wolf made a desperate dash for Montana. Despite the fact that only one in five was a warrior, that they were poorly armed and mounted,

On September 9, 1876, troops under General George Crook attacked a Lakota village and took several prisoners. In the Indian camp they found the guidon of Troop I and the gauntlets of its captain, Myles Keogh. Here, two officers pose with their prisoners and the recovered guidon.
National Anthropological Archives

and that they were without tents or sufficient food, the fugitives managed to elude the hundreds of troops attempting to intercept them, reaching the Dakota country in early December 1878. They then split into two groups. Some chose to follow Little Wolf, who spent the winter deep in the Wyoming wilderness; the others, thinking themselves finally safe, surrendered with Dull Knife at Fort Robinson, Nebraska, only to be told that they would have to return to Oklahoma. When they refused, they were confined to unheated barracks without food or water. During the night of January 9, the imprisoned Cheyennes made a suicidal break for freedom. Of 149 held in the barracks, 64 were killed. Most of the others, many gravely wounded, were recaptured.

Iron Teeth's experiences were probably typical. Her husband had died in the attack on their village. With her five children, she went to Oklahoma and then participated in the escape. When the group separated, a son and daughter went with Little Wolf. She and the remaining children, including a twenty-two-year-old son named Gathering His Medicine, followed Dull Knife to Fort Robinson. During the breakout, she kept one daughter with her, and they were found hiding in a cave the following day. Her son, who had a pistol, carried the youngest girl on his back into another cave. When soldiers who tracked him through the snow reached the cave, Gathering His Medicine told his sister to stay hidden while he challenged them. "Lots of times," Iron Teeth admitted, "as I sit here alone on the floor with my blanket wrapped about me, I lean forward and close my eyes and think of him . . . fighting the soldiers, knowing that he would be killed, but doing this so his little sister might get away in safety. Don't you think he was a brave young man?"

As the stories collected from descendants of the Indians who fought at Little Bighorn reveal, none of the four tribes involved find any comfort in the events of 1876. All four tribes have suffered to some extent. The Crow and Arikara not only feel betrayed by the government they sought to help, but today they are more often seen as traitors for helping the cavalry hunt down their traditional enemies. The Cheyenne and Sioux, on the other hand, suffered terribly for their victory. In fact, elderly descendants of the Cheyenne and Sioux who were present at Little Bighorn still fear some sort of retribution awaits them if their family connection to Custer's demise is revealed.

Fortunately, some descendants put aside their concerns and contributed their family recollections to this book. Perhaps their example will encourage other Indian families to follow, because there are still questions to be answered and much to be learned about this sad moment in American history.

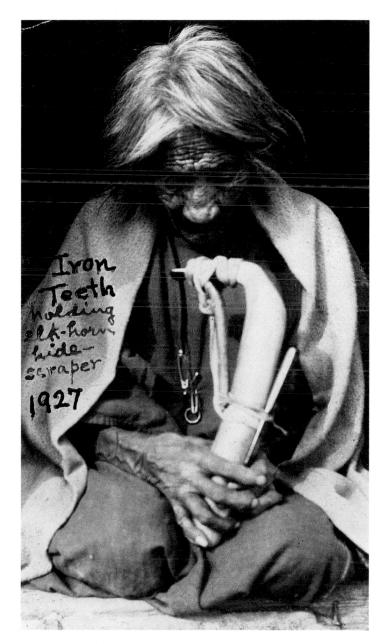

Iron Teeth, age ninety-two. When Thomas B. Marquis took this photograph, Iron Teeth was believed to be the oldest woman among the Northern Cheyenne. After her husband was killed in Colonel Ranald Mackenzie's capture of Dull Knife's village in November 1876, Iron Teeth and her children were taken to Oklahoma, where they joined the Northern Cheyennes under Dull Knife and Little Wolf in their attempt to return to their Montana homeland. Iron Teeth told Marquis that her hide-scraper was made from the horn of an elk her husband killed shortly after their marriage. "The five rows of notches on this one are the age-records of my five children," she said. "Throughout seventy-two years it has always been a part of my most precious pack. I was carrying it in my hands when my husband was killed. It was tied to my saddle while we were in flight from Oklahoma. It has never been lost. When I die, this gift from my husband must be buried with me."
National Anthropological Archives

The Day of Death

HERMAN J. VIOLA

White Man Runs Him, wearing his
warrior face paint. Photograph taken by
Delancy Gill in Washington, D.C., 1910.
National Anthropological Archives

" **I am an old man, and soon my spirit must leave this earth** to join the spirits of my fathers. Therefore, I shall speak only the truth in telling what I know of the fight on the Little Bighorn where General Custer was killed. Curley, who was with us, will tell you I do not lie."

This is how the Crow scout White Man Runs Him once responded when asked to recall his role in the Battle of the Little Bighorn. The longest-lived survivor of the six Crow scouts who led Custer and the Seventh Cavalry into the valley of the Little Bighorn, he became an unwitting figure in the controversies about the battle that continue to fascinate scholars and Custer buffs alike.

How could supposedly ill-armed Indians, no matter how numerous, have so utterly routed one of the most able and popular units of the U.S. Army? Was it the arrogance and reckless leadership of Custer? Was it wholesale drunkenness on the part of his troopers and key lieutenants? Was it widespread panic and even suicide by untested soldiers? Was it the clever generalship of Sitting Bull, who lured the Seventh Cavalry into an elaborate trap? Or was it—as Cheyenne descendants of the warriors who defeated Custer still believe—the Everywhere Spirit fulfilling the prophecy of their chiefs, who had predicted such an outcome if Custer ever violated the truce he had made with the tribe in 1869?

These questions will never be answered to everyone's complete satisfaction. One fact is certain: Lakota and Cheyenne warriors, desperate to protect their families and their traditional way of life, inflicted one of the most stinging defeats ever suffered by the U.S. Cavalry. What made the defeat all the more sensational was that the victims were the colorful and flamboyant Custer brothers leading the Army's showcase cavalry regiment and that the Indian victory took place at the very time U.S. politicians and industrialists were trumpeting the nation's rise to world power at the centennial celebration in Philadelphia.

Although much has been written about this dramatic moment in American history, relatively little of it has been from the perspective of the Indian participants. Students of the battle have paid scant attention to the fact that the Battle of the Little Bighorn can be seen as a concluding chapter in the intertribal wars that had been a fact of life in North America since the first paleo-Indians sorted themselves into discrete bands

Joseph Medicine Crow at the grave of his stepgrandfather, White Man Runs Him, Little Bighorn National Cemetery.
Herman J. Viola Collection

and tribes. Behind the romantic image of guidons, bugles, and cavalry charges was a struggle for survival being fought by Custer's Crow and Arikara allies against their traditional Lakota and Cheyenne enemies. Years earlier, the Crow and Arikara, outnumbered and outgunned by their bitter rivals for hegemony on the Northern Plains, had cast their lot with the *wasichus*—the "white eyes." The events of June 1876 were the natural culmination of that allegiance, as the accounts presented here by Arikara and Crow writers make clear.

Indeed, filmmakers and writers have only recently recognized the fact that six Crow scouts, four friendly Sioux, and approximately thirty-seven Arikaras assisted Custer and the Seventh Cavalry. The week before, at the Battle of the Rosebud, more than two hundred Crow and Shoshone warriors saved General Crook from a defeat that would have been equally embarrassing to the Army as that suffered by Custer. In fact, if any group has been ignored in the Custer story, it is his Arikara recruits; their homeland was hundreds of miles from the battlefield and off the beaten path of the tourists who began making pilgrimages to Custer Hill almost as soon as the last shots had faded away.

This is not to say that historians, soldiers, and journalists failed to question Indian veterans of the battle. Any Indian present that day who was later willing to talk about it had any number of eager interrogators. The primary problem is that the questioners were seeking verification for already formed theories. Then, when the answers were not to their liking, the Indian responses were rejected or distorted to support prevailing explanations, especially the notion that Custer and his men fought to the last man until simply overwhelmed by shrieking hordes of painted fanatics who willingly suffered incredible casualties to defeat their hated white enemies.

Recently, thanks largely to evidence obtained by means of modern technology, students of the battle have grudgingly come to realize that the Indians had told the basic facts of the battle from the outset: that Custer disastrously misjudged the size of the enemy camp, the quality and quantity of firearms in Indian hands, and the willingness of his opponents to stand and fight.

This book presents the Indian perspective of the Battle of the Little Bighorn. It is based primarily on exciting evidence from recent archaeological discoveries including thousands of previously unknown military and Indian artifacts found on the Reno battlefield, little-used drawings by Indian veterans of the battle, and stories passed down through the families of the Arikara, Cheyenne, Crow, and Lakota participants.

The archaeological evidence, as pointed out in "Archaeologists: Detectives on the Battlefield" (pages 165-179), indicates that the troopers with Custer melted away as their units dissolved in the face of superior firepower. The end came so suddenly and quickly that few troopers did much effective fighting. Many panicked and ran toward the center of the large, uneven square that Custer and his officers had attempted to form while waiting for reinforcements that never came. As one of the Sioux veterans later remarked, "It was like hunting buffalo."

This book is the culmination of a career spent studying the history of the Northern Plains and of the friendships that resulted. The friendship I most value is that of Dr. Joseph Medicine Crow, a grandson of Medicine Crow and White Man Runs Him, two Crow warriors who played prominent roles in the events of 1876. Dr. Medicine Crow, the official historian of the Crow tribe, has been a lifelong student of the Battle of the Little Bighorn. He was a personal friend of many of the veterans of the Sioux wars and of the historians who wrote about them, including Thomas B. Marquis, an obscure but dedicated physician who for many years worked with the Cheyenne and Crow people on their Montana reservations. Fascinated by the Custer fight, Dr. Marquis sought out and befriended elderly Lakota, Cheyenne, and Crow veterans of the battle. Most of these aged Indians could not speak English, so he became expert in using sign language. The old Indians liked their kind white friend, who gave them food, money, and medical care. The elderly Indians spoke honestly and freely with him when many of them would have nothing to do with other white people. He also spoke in sign language to Thomas H. Leforge, another scout Dr. Medicine Crow knew as a child. Leforge, an adopted member of the Crow tribe, related his life story to Marquis, who had it published as *Memoirs of a White Crow Indian* (1929).

Marquis and Leforge often rode around the reservation together in the doctor's old Model T Ford. They must have been quite a sight, Marquis sporting a straw boater, a celluloid collar, and bow tie, and Leforge in his buckskins. Once, they were so engrossed in a lively sign-language discussion that Marquis did not watch where he was going and rammed into another car. Leforge had been a white scout for the Army, and had he not broken his collarbone a short time before, he doubtless would have accompanied his friend and fellow scout Mitch Bouyer and Custer down Medicine Tail Coulee, never to return.

At first, when Dr. Marquis lived at Lame Deer on the Cheyenne Reservation, Joseph Medicine Crow recalls, "He would visit our home by driving over the winding dirt roads in his Model T Ford. He camped near the adjacent spring, living in his sheepherder's tent and visiting with us for several days at a time. Later, when he moved to Lodge Grass, we would often visit him. A vegetarian, he would serve my parents hot cocoa and dried bread and then stay up late at night playing checkers with my stepfather, John White Man Runs Him."

Dr. Marquis's books are still considered among the best ever published about the Battle of Little Bighorn. Besides the Leforge biography, he published *Wooden Leg, a Warrior Who Fought Custer* and *Keep the Last Bullet for Yourself: The True Story of Custer's Last Stand*.

I first became acquainted with Dr. Medicine Crow in 1972, when he came to the Smithsonian Institution to research his tribe. At the time, I was director of the National Anthropological Archives, which has custody of unparalleled collections of

photographs, manuscripts, and drawings relating to the Indians of North America. Among these ethnographic treasures is the remarkable set of drawings of the Battle of the Little Bighorn by Red Horse, a Miniconjou veteran of the fight. They are all reproduced in this volume, most of them for the first time in color.

Over the years, the friendship between Joe Medicine Crow and myself deepened, and in 1996 he adopted me as his brother in a ceremony at the Crow Fair held annually along the banks of the Little Bighorn River on the Crow Reservation, little more than a mile from the heart of the battlefield.

Joseph Medicine Crow is a living cultural treasure. He is unique. The first member of the Crow tribe to graduate from college (Bacone) and the first to obtain a master's degree (in anthropology from the University of Southern California), he was working on his doctorate in anthropology at USC when World War II interrupted his studies. Although offered a commission because of his college background, he refused on grounds that a warrior must first prove himself in battle before becoming a leader himself—"the worst mistake I ever made," he jokes, "because the U.S. Army didn't work on the principles of the Crow Tribe, and I never got another chance at a commission."

Lack of rank was no obstacle to a descendant of a long line of famous chiefs and warriors. Private Medicine Crow went on to distinguish himself on the battlefields of Europe, where he counted coup on the enemy (literally, struck, or touched, the enemy; see also page 108) and even captured a German horse in the finest Plains tradition. Yet it is his gift as a storyteller, the carrier of his people's oral history, that makes him so

Planning meeting for *Little Bighorn Remembered*, October 1995. Left to right: Michael Her Many Horses, Joseph Medicine Crow, Dennis Limberhand, Herman J. Viola.
Herman J. Viola Collection

special. His contributions to history were formally recognized in June 1996 by the University of Montana in a ceremony awarding his long-delayed doctoral degree.

While director of the Smithsonian's anthropology archives, I also met and befriended a number of Indian scholars who came to do research in the collections. Several of them were participants in a program I initiated and administered to assist tribes in developing their own historians. Among those interns was David Fanman, a Southern Cheyenne whose grandfather Tall Bull fought at Little Bighorn. The Red Horse drawings fascinated Mr. Fanman. Once, while examining page after page of drawings of dead horses, he recalled his grandfather telling him, "Blood flowed like water that day because so many horses had been wounded and killed during the fighting."

Another participant in the Smithsonian tribal historian's program was Michael Her Many Horses, co-author, with Jeanne Oyawin Eder, of "A Dakota View of the Great Sioux War" (pages 57-81). Michael, an Oglala from Pine Ridge whose family was part of the Crazy Horse band, talked often about the veterans he had known and the information that still remained untapped in Lakota memories.

I gained further insights into the Cheyenne side of the story through Senator Ben Nighthorse Campbell. His Indian ancestry includes Black Horse, a Southern Cheyenne who also fought at Little Bighorn. Through Campbell I befriended his adopted brother Dennis Limberhand, whose ancestor Limber Bones was one of the half dozen Cheyenne warriors killed in the battle. Through Campbell and Limberhand, I became acquainted with a number of elderly Cheyennes on the Lame Deer Reservation whose family histories are also inextricably linked to the events of 1876—Bill Tall Bull, Austin Two Moons, Albert Longjaw, Florence Whiteman, Joseph Walks Along, Alonzo Spang, and others.

The result of these contacts, friendships, and research into the history of the wars on the Northern Plains was the desire to document stories that remain in Indian families while it is still possible to obtain them. It was a near thing. Several key storytellers—among them Austin Two Moons, Bill Tall Bull, and Albert Longjaw—died before the research was completed. Albert Longjaw, confined to a wheelchair and a resident in the home for the elderly on the Cheyenne Reservation, lived long enough to share with us a Cheyenne victory song composed after Custer's defeat.

Among the hurdles faced—in addition to the extremely advanced age of most of the individuals whose family stories we hoped to record—was the effort to get onetime tribal enemies to work together to make the project as comprehensive as possible. The Crows and Arikaras had no trouble with this, but the Sioux and Cheyennes were less than enthusiastic. The Cheyennes were particularly reluctant to cooperate.

Their feelings are easy to understand. Of all the tribes involved, they fought the hardest to maintain their traditional way of life and suffered the most as a result. There is a popular saying in Indian country about the Custer fight that reflects the feelings that still exist among the participating tribes: "The Sioux got the glory, the Crows got the land, but the Cheyennes did the fighting."

It is no exaggeration to say that the Cheyennes were all but destroyed by a vindictive army and government. Their cultural heritage was shattered before the handful of survivors were dumped onto a barren reservation in southeastern Montana. Their

harsh treatment at white hands left the Cheyennes a bitter, impoverished, and suspicious people. Even today, Cheyennes are reluctant to talk about the events of 1876. Considerable Custer memorabilia is rumored to remain in the hands of Cheyenne families, but their owners would prefer to see it burned or buried rather than make it public and give the government the evidence needed to inflict still more punishment on them, whose only crime in 1876 was to defend themselves and their families from surprise attack.

Nevertheless, the dozen or so elderly Cheyennes interviewed for this book shared a number of Custer stories that have been handed down orally from one generation to the next. Remarkably, these tales do not focus much on the details of the actual fighting on the banks of the Little Bighorn. Who was where, when, and why are of secondary interest to these storytellers. Their concern is the meaning of the outcome, and much of the concern seems to arise from Cheyenne spirituality.

Still, their accounts include some suggestive military details. Custer was too hasty, says Ernest American Horse. Custer failed to connect with General Terry, says Phillip Risingsun, and then he dismissed the estimates of his Crow scouts when they said he was outnumbered. But both these storytellers follow the spiritual thread in the tale. Custer foolishly ignored the warning of the ill omens, says Risingsun. The Cheyennes paid close attention to their religious traditions, says American Horse; therefore the elders had foreknowledge of the event.

The cosmic meaning of the Indian victory at Little Bighorn is clearest in the often-repeated story of Custer's broken vows. Wittingly or unwittingly, Custer made a sacred promise never again to fight the Cheyennes. Consciously or unconsciously, he broke

Austin Two Moons, grandson of Chief Two Moons; Barbara Satir, former superintendent of the Little Bighorn Battlefield; and Senator Ben Nighthorse Campbell, whose great-grandfather Black Horse, a Southern Cheyenne, fought at Little Bighorn.
John Warner

that sacred promise. The inevitable outcome—Custer's personal annihilation and all the consequences—was proof of the working of great spiritual power.

Viewing the Battle of the Little Bighorn as an event of spiritual importance casts another light on Cheyenne reluctance to talk about it. Fear is less the motivation than respect. Stories that connect teller and listener with powerful cosmic forces should never be told lightly. Talk about these events should not be treated as casual conversation.

As can be seen in Alberta Fisher's account (page 38) of recording the Risingsun stories, the spiritual component of the Custer story has not diminished among contemporary Cheyennes. It is especially evident in the remarks by William Walks Along that conclude this book's Cheyenne account (page 50). This eloquent address was given at the battlefield on the 121st anniversary of the Battle of the Little Bighorn by the then chairman of the Northern Cheyenne tribe. The audience that day was moved, as readers now can be, by the sustaining power of the story.

One of the more remarkable accounts to come from Indian witnesses to the events of June 25, 1876, was collected by Edward S. Curtis, the photographer who devoted his life to documenting the traditional world of America's native people. Curtis, fascinated by the Battle of the Little Bighorn, persuaded the Crow scouts White Man Runs Him, Goes Ahead, and Hairy Moccasin to retrace for him their route with Custer. Their

William Tall Bull teaching Cheyenne students about the medical benefits of plants found on the Northern Cheyenne Reservation. The historian of the Northern Cheyennes, he was an authority on the tribe's oral history, tradition, and ceremonies and taught classes on these subjects at the Dull Knife Memorial College in Lame Deer, Montana. When he died in 1996, the tribe lost one of its most important links with its cultural past.
Herman Viola Collection

David Fanman (left), grandson of the Southern Cheyenne chief Tall Bull, at the Cheyenne cemetery at Old Cantonment, Oklahoma, showing his grandfather's grave to Joseph Viola, son of the author, 1974.
Herman J. Viola Collection

explanation of what happened after Custer separated from Reno so shocked and disturbed Curtis that he never published it. A half century later, his son gave his father's notes and documents to the Smithsonian Institution. James Hutchins, curator emeritus of military history at the Smithsonian Institution, presents those findings here for the first time. According to the Crow scouts, Custer watched the Sioux maul Reno's troops, thereby fatally delaying his own attack on the Sioux village. When Curtis's findings were shown to Dr. Medicine Crow, he said it must be true, even though he had never heard that particular account before, because his grandfather liked and trusted Curtis and could have told the photographer things he told no other white man.

Here, then, is the Indian side of Little Bighorn. It brings no discredit to those who fought and died there. Its purpose is to provide a glimpse of a little-known aspect of one of the most popularized and romanticized moments in American Indian history.

Opposite:
James King, grandson of Mexican Cheyenne, was the unofficial Cheyenne tribal historian, archivist, and curator. For many years he operated a museum at Lame Deer in which could be found numerous mementos of the Battle of the Little Bighorn, memorabilia of the Cheyennes who became U.S. Army scouts after the Indian wars, and a large collection of photographs and manuscripts related to Cheyenne history. "Jimmy," who was also a key member of the Cheyenne VFW post, died in 1998.
John Warner

Cheyenne Memories of Little Bighorn

Contributed by
**Alonzo Spang, Joseph Walks Along,
and Alberta American Horse Fisher**

James Blackwolf, Sr., for many years keeper of the sacred medicine hat of the Northern Cheyennes. The medicine hat, which has been passed along for generations to specially chosen hat keepers, is entrusted only to a person of strong spiritual values. The welfare of the Northern Cheyennes is intimately associated with the welfare of the medicine hat. When Red Horse made his pictograph history of the Battle of the Little Bighorn, he included the hat keeper's distinctive yellow and black tipi in one of his drawings of the Indian encampment. Presumably, each of the five drawings of tipis represented a tribal camp circle. This one (the background for this image) was the Northern Cheyenne camp circle. Blackwolf, the spiritual leader of the Northern Cheyenne tribe, died in 1998.
John Warner

The Battle of the Little Bighorn was fought well over one hundred years ago. Yet the reality of this battle, where the Northern Cheyennes and Sioux totally destroyed Lieutenant Colonel George Custer and much of the Seventh Cavalry, is still very much with us. Day in and day out, there are reminders that our once great and proud nation utterly defeated the U.S. military.

A question often asked by non-Indians is, "Why don't the Cheyennes tell all they know about the Battle of the Little Bighorn?" It is a simple question, yet the answer is rooted in complex feelings. I can recall listening to my grandparents talk about our history and cautioning us to be very careful with whom we shared the information. My Grandpa Limberhand was an infant at Little Bighorn. His first cousin, a young warrior about fourteen years old, was killed in the battle. Grandpa would regularly observe that "you cannot trust the white man to keep his promises—he may be speaking fine words, but there is no honor in the person who speaks them." Grandpa and Grandma always impressed upon us that the reason the Northern Cheyennes should not share their knowledge of the Battle of the Little Bighorn is fear of retribution by the U.S. government.

Custer himself certainly fulfilled that widely shared evaluation of white men. As so many of the Cheyennes who contributed stories to this book have repeated, Custer had smoked the pipe of peace with our people and vowed that he would not fight us anymore. His legacy, such as it is, is proof that the Northern Cheyenne people have made a proper and valid assessment of the integrity of the white man. Until the white man demonstrates his honor in upholding his word, this fear will be steadfastly held. Every Northern Cheyenne will be reluctant to come forth to share what knowledge about the battle he or she may possess. The fear of some type of retribution is still very much with us.

The double tragedy of this position is that as time elapses, we are losing the older Cheyennes who have knowledge of those interesting times, and much valuable information will be forever lost. On the other hand, maybe that is what Maheo, the Great Spirit, intended.

—Alonzo Spang

Stories of William Yellow Robe

Told by Joseph Walks Along

I was born on the Northern Cheyenne Reservation in 1931. I was very fortunate to know my grandpa William Yellow Robe, who was a young boy of about twelve years of age at the time of the Battle of the Little Bighorn. My grandfather described his age like this: "I was not man enough to be a warrior. I was a young boy at the age when I could still cry. Cheyenne warriors do not cry nor are they fearful of going into battle." He loved living on the Northern Cheyenne Reservation because our people went through bitter times to return here. Grandpa lived to a grand age of eighty-six years.

As I grew older, Grandpa enjoyed telling me about how he grew up, how he was raised and taught by his family and elders. The first time I recall him telling about the pre-reservation days was when I was about nine years old. He sat me down by him and said, "My grandson, I am going to tell you how we used to raise our young boys to become men. My uncle and other men would lecture us that we were very special persons, that we had to protect our camp—protect our elders, women, and children—even at the cost of giving our life. This was told to us in many different ways and in many different settings. Soon, it became a way of life for us."

The Reverend Joseph Walks Along, grandson of William Yellow Robe, holding a rusted Winchester rifle found buried under the old man's cabin years after his death. Walks Along, a Mennonite minister, is currently president of the Northern Cheyenne Tribe.
John Warner

Grandfather never forgot the Battle of the Little Bighorn. He was reluctant to talk about it, but when he felt the need to share, I would try to listen. I believe my grandfather would not be offended and would like me to share two or three of the stories of the battle he told me.

Back when Grandpa was alive, we did not have tape recorders to tape our storytellers. We had pencil and paper, but he would never let us write down what he shared. When he began to tell a story, he would say, "Now, this is for your ears only. You remember what I say so that you can tell your grandchildren one day of what great Cheyenne warriors did to Yellow Hair. You must never write this down—you must remember it and pass it on through word of mouth."

He said there was a huge encampment of Indian people along the embankment of the Little Bighorn River. "All of a sudden," Grandpa said, "the village crier announced that soldiers were coming, and they were not carrying a white flag along with the American flag. This meant the soldiers were not coming in peace, so all our warriors were told to prepare for a fight. The crier told the rest of us to go to our designated areas for cover. At first, there was a great commotion as mothers rushed around looking for their children, and this confused some of the people. Things quickly straightened out, and we made our way to the crest of a hill on the west side of the river." Grandpa told us that prior to the battle, at a different place, Custer had told the Cheyennes that as long as the cavalry carried a white flag and the American flag they would be coming in peace. On that day, Colonel Custer did not come in peace. One very important thing Grandpa always stressed when he talked about the battle was that we did not break our promise to Custer not to fight him again. Custer and his soldiers attacked us first.

"The battle seemed to take a long time," Grandpa recalled, "but it did not last all day. It was a terrible, horrible, and unmerciful event. All the Cheyenne and Sioux warriors were ready and well prepared to fight."

One of his vivid memories of the battle was the great volume of dust that the fighters and horses of both sides created that day. "Dust seemed to just rise up everywhere," he would say. "I could not imagine how our warriors kept from hitting each other instead of the enemy."

Another memory my grandfather shared with me involved the movement of the tribe after the battle. He said, "Right after the fighting ended, we broke camp. We headed for the big mountains to the west and south of the battlefield [these would be the Bighorn Mountains]. We went this way because our scouts told us that soldiers were in the mountains south of the battlefield [the Wolf Mountains]. Also, our scouts knew that there was another group of soldiers to the north of the battlefield along the Elk River, or the *mo ch he yohe* to the Cheyennes [the Yellowstone River country]. Because we knew this, there was only one way to go—west, then south. This was very rugged country. We camped there for a few days." Grandpa never really identified the spot nor was he very specific about many details. Like the other elderly Cheyennes who lived through those terrible times, he was afraid to tell everything.

He said, "After we made camp, some of the scouts and young warriors returned to the battlefield. These scouts told us that the bodies were still laying there and that it was a terrible thing to see. They told us that because the temperature was so hot during the battle, the bodies of the soldiers and horses had gotten very bloated. They brought back some of the military stuff that they could use, like rifles and ammunition and other combat material. Some also came back with paper that the white men used for money."

My grandfather never spoke of how the Cheyennes came out of the mountains or what route they took. He would not talk about those things because he feared possible retaliation by the U.S. government.

My last recollection is the story Grandpa Yellow Robe told about what the Cheyennes did with the paper money, weapons, and other military gear that was taken from the dead soldiers. He said, "Members of our tribe were afraid to keep any of the things taken after the battle. Our leaders were concerned that soldiers would shoot us if they found us with any of it. After much discussion and having carried the materials with us for much of the time while we were trying to evade the soldiers after the battle, they decided it would be best to bury it all in a prominent place that the Cheyennes loved the most." As we sat in the shade next to our house, Grandpa was looking east when he said, "Our leaders chose a group of our finest men to take these things and bury them where the soldiers would never find it and where no one could ever trace it back to us. It will always be there." Hiding those things brought an end to a matter of great concern to our people.

Grandpa Yellow Robe later became a scout for the U.S. Cavalry. He took great pride in his experiences riding with General Nelson Miles. Grandpa was involved in the surrender of Chief Joseph and was part of a protective unit at the Battle of Wounded Knee. I believe my life and the lives of my children have been enhanced and blessed because I was able to know my grandfather, a grandfather who shared his memories of one of the greatest Indian war victories in the history of this nation.

Thomas B. Marquis, M.D., interviewing Wooden Leg, a Northern Cheyenne Little Bighorn veteran. Marquis, who died in 1935 at age sixty-six, became fascinated by the Custer fight and spent nearly a half century befriending the aged veterans. The life story of Wooden Leg, Marquis's favorite informant, was published in 1931 as *A Warrior Who Fought Custer*. Marquis learned Indian sign talk to such a degree that he rarely needed an interpreter. "I held out continual invitations for Custer-battle veteran warriors to visit my home, partake of my food, and smoke my tobacco. After a long siege, they began to come. Later, they began to talk, but only a little. Still later, after they had found out that this ingratiating white man was not scheming to entrap them into fatal admissions, they told the whole story. Not only did they answer all questions, but they added spontaneous information concerning every detail of the battle and of the entire hostile Indian movements during that eventful summer of 1876" (from the preface to *A Warrior Who Fought Custer*).
National Anthropological Archives

Wooden Leg 1927 Dr. T.B.M

Ledger art by Wooden Leg depicting his battle deeds at Little Bighorn. Top to bottom: Wooden Leg seizing a soldier's carbine during Major Marcus Reno's retreat; Wooden Leg and a dead soldier at the Reno retreat crossing; and Wooden Leg "counting coup" on an Arikara, June 25, 1876.
Little Bighorn Battlefield National Monument

Northern Cheyenne Little Bighorn veteran John Issues with his Seventh Cavalry carbine. Photograph by Thomas B. Marquis.
National Anthropological Archives

Stories of Ernest American Horse

Told by Alberta American Horse Fisher

The late Ernest American Horse was my father. Although there was a Chief American Horse in the Custer battle, they were not related. My father would sit down with his children and tell us stories about the Cheyennes, our traditions and culture. He told us both the sad and the happy memories of our history. One of the sad memories was the Custer battle.

Custer followed the Cheyennes until he met his death. He followed them from the Elk River [the Yellowstone River] to where he was killed. Moving along the Rosebud Creek, the Cheyennes camped at the place where the big sand rock [Deer Rock] stands, what is now known as Jimtown. From there they moved on to the region now known as Busby. Then the Cheyennes moved camp toward Reno Creek and the place now known as Crow Agency. The Cheyennes had to keep moving to avoid meeting the cavalry.

While fleeing from the soldiers, the Cheyennes never failed to ask for help and guidance through their spiritual leaders. Their strong faith in their religious ceremonies blessed and protected the Cheyennes. Whatever the spirits revealed to the Cheyenne people, they did very faithfully. The Cheyennes knew beforehand that an incident was going to take place, and they were warned not to stray from their ceremonies and spirits. After the Custer battle, one of the elderly ceremonial chiefs told everyone that this was the incident that they had been warned about.

The Cheyenne elders always stressed that the tribe should never rush into doing anything. If you are hasty, there are bad consequences. In this case, Custer rushed into doing something, and he paid for it with his life.

During the battle, the women, children, and elderly fled in the opposite direction away from the fighting. They could see the cavalry and warriors rushing back and forth. Bullets were flying everywhere. Horses were running in every direction. They saw men running to the river and thought it was the Crow scouts with Custer fleeing to the river and hiding in the grass.

It was common for the children and women to scavenge the battle sites after each encounter with the white man or with other tribes.

Stories of Laura American Horse Rockroads

Recorded by Alberta American Horse Fisher and Dennis Limberhand

My great-grandfather was Chief Iron Shirt, who took part in the Custer battle. My mother, Margaret Risingsun Two Moons, also knew a lot about Cheyenne history and the Custer battle. Her stories were sad memories of children, women, and the elderly being slaughtered, tortured, and starved because of the soldiers. At times, young women were the sexual victims of cavalrymen. The mission of Custer and the white man was to do away with anyone with brown skin, meaning the Indians, any Indian tribe.

Northern Cheyenne Little Bighorn veteran Two Feathers with his Seventh Cavalry carbine. Photograph by Thomas B. Marquis.
National Anthropological Archives

Afterwards, no one dared speak of the Custer battle for fear of what the white man might do to Indians for punishment. No one dared use the names of those who took part in the battle.

It was early in the day when the cavalry attacked the village. Suddenly everyone started running, crying, looking for a place to hide. The cavalrymen were shooting their guns. White men and Indians were hiding all over the hillsides. Clouds of dust filled the air. Horses were screaming and running everywhere.

After the battle, when everyone had calmed down, the women and children scavenged the battle site. One of the old ladies saw some of the white men laying there. Although they were all bloody, some of the soldiers were still very much alive. Once again she fled the battle site. As she was fleeing the area she saw two cavalrymen down in a gully. They saw some horses coming down from the hill towards them. One cavalryman took his pistol and shot the other one and then shot himself, but there was no one riding on the horses. In other words, murder and suicide among themselves killed some of Custer's men.

Much later many different tribesmen tried to take the credit for killing Custer, but it was actually two old ladies who killed him.

Stories of Phillip Risingsun

Told by his grandson Eugene Russell and his great-grandson Matthew Two Moons, Sr.
Recorded by Alberta American Horse Fisher

Phillip Risingsun, the son of Chief Iron Shirt, died in 1952 in his mid-nineties. He faithfully and respectfully followed the ritual of smoking his pipe every night for good life for himself, for his family, and for the Cheyenne people. Often at these times, Risingsun would tell his grandsons to sit down, offer to smoke his pipe with them, and proceed to tell them different stories about his younger days.

Risingsun related his experience in the Custer battle. General Miles was known as Bear Coat in Cheyenne, and Custer was known as Long Haired Man. The two were to meet northeast of what is now Forsyth, Montana, at the mouth of Rosebud Creek on the Yellowstone River (also known as Elk River to the Cheyennes). Miles and Custer did not meet as planned. Custer continued southeast to what is now known as Busby, Montana. There were four tribes camped where the Gabriel Parker ranch is now located. They were Cheyennes, Sioux, Suhtio, and another tribe we have forgotten because Risingsun named them in the Cheyenne language. The Cheyennes moved first toward the place now known as Crow Agency, Montana, near the actual battle site. The other tribes followed. Custer followed them there.

Risingsun said that Custer had two pieces of cloth—one black and one white in color. Each time he would move his troops he would toss the cloths up in the air. The black cloth would come back down landing smoothly on the ground, and the white cloth would come back down crumpled. This was not, Risingsun said, a good sign for Custer.

Custer ordered his Crow scouts to station one man to each tipi, but his Crow scouts warned him that it was not a good plan as there were more tipis than his men. Custer did not listen, nor would he heed the warnings from the black and white cloths. He proceeded to do what he said he had planned to do, and that was to kill and get rid of all the Indians.

The Cheyennes resorted to having sweat ceremonies as often as time permitted because they were always on guard for any altercations with other tribes. It was through the sweat ceremonies that they received their visions from the spirits and guidance as to what to do next. Upon arriving from the east, where the battle site is, there were Cheyennes and Sioux camped to the west. The Arapaho camp far to the south was plagued by some now unknown disease that kept them from fully participating in the fighting.

Risingsun was a young man at the time of the battle. He said two groups of Cheyenne warriors went into battle. He was riding with the first group, but as he was leaving the Cheyenne camp he saw a little girl staggering along alone. She had been left behind and was separated from the children, elderly, and women who were already in hiding. He picked up the little girl and took her to where the rest were hiding. The little girl passed away in the late 1940s. Her name was Greasy Dog. She had one daughter, Fannie Greasy Dog, a deaf-mute who died in the mid-1960s. After retrieving the little girl and carrying her to a safe place, Risingsun joined the second group of Cheyennes riding to the battle.

4 generations in male line

Iron shirt 96   Rising Sun 68   Wolf 40   Medicine Bull 6

1927

Four generations of Northern Cheyennes. Left to right: Iron Shirt, Little Bighorn veteran Phillip Risingsun, Wolf, and Medicine Bull. Photograph by Thomas B. Marquis. *National Anthropological Archives*

Risingsun said Indians and troopers were everywhere, and clouds of dust made it difficult to tell friends from enemies, but the battle was over in a short time. Risingsun said that immediately after the battle, people came out to look over the battlefield. He remembered two elderly ladies in particular. One of the old ladies recognized Custer. She had seen him before. Custer was still alive when she found him. Apparently after the battle, Custer played dead. When the old lady recognized him, she took her awl and pounded it into his ear and killed him.

Risingsun also related that Custer had smoked the peace pipe with the Cheyenne chiefs. He had taken an oath and promised that he was never to bother the Cheyennes again. An oath taken with a pipe is highly respected by the Cheyennes and is never broken. The Cheyennes knew what the consequences would be, so they never broke an oath taken with a pipe. Custer did not keep his promise, and he paid a high price. He paid with his life.

When Risingsun told of his experiences or of others who fought in the Custer battle, he would never reveal any Indian names. Nor did he say anything about anyone who did actual killing. In fact, no one who fought there dared say anything. They were always so afraid of being sent to prison, tortured, or even killed. They were afraid the entire tribe would be slaughtered.

Risingsun said no Crows were directly involved in the battle. What few Crows were there as scouts for Custer fled for their lives. They sought refuge in the Little Bighorn River and stayed under water using reeds as breathing tubes.

The Story of Alberta American Horse Fisher

I have done a lot of work regarding Cheyenne history in the past twenty to thirty years, and I have never had such an experience as I did with this book project. With my knowledge about and respect for traditional ways among people out in the community and off-reservation, this project was a very rewarding yet eye-opening experience.

The interviews with Phillip Risingsun's descendants were scheduled one week ahead of time, but for reasons unknown they didn't happen—canceled. Again I rescheduled, for Sunday, October 27, 1996. Inviting the two gentlemen to my home, I prepared a traditional meal, the works. I gave a food offering. After the meal, one of the men spoke and said, "Due to the severity of this particular event, we must pray, speak, and coerce the spirits to help us to relate the truth of what our grandfather and great-grandfather Risingsun related to us, since this is going to be the first time this is going to be reviewed by anyone."

The ceremony began with talking and addressing the spirits of the Risingsun and Greasy Dog family, and lasted approximately twenty minutes. I got the cassette player ready and we started recording. The men told the story in Cheyenne. I sat with a pen and paper writing down highlights of the events. I would translate and type it up later. We finished after about one hour and nineteen minutes and rewound the tape. Yet when we played it, from beginning to end of the tape there was absolutely no sound of any kind. I was very puzzled. The cassette player was new; the tape was fresh; et cetera. What went wrong? My husband took the tape out, reexamined it, tried another tape, turned on the cassette, and it worked well on "testing 1-2-3" several times.

I was sitting there reliving the Custer battle, and then the cassette player didn't record. What now? Eugene Russell said, "Well, there's a reason for this. You listened to all that was said." So with that, they did not repeat the story. I was dumbfounded, not really knowing what to say. We sat and visited for another couple of hours. I thought to myself that I should just ask them to repeat the story once more, but I didn't dare ask. After they left, I wondered what I should do. Then I remembered we had prayed, talked, and addressed the spirits of the Risingsun and Greasy Dog family. So I prayed and asked for guidance to remember. After several days, I started to write what was related to me and this is the exact story I was told. The two I interviewed read and can attest to the story as it was related to them by Risingsun.

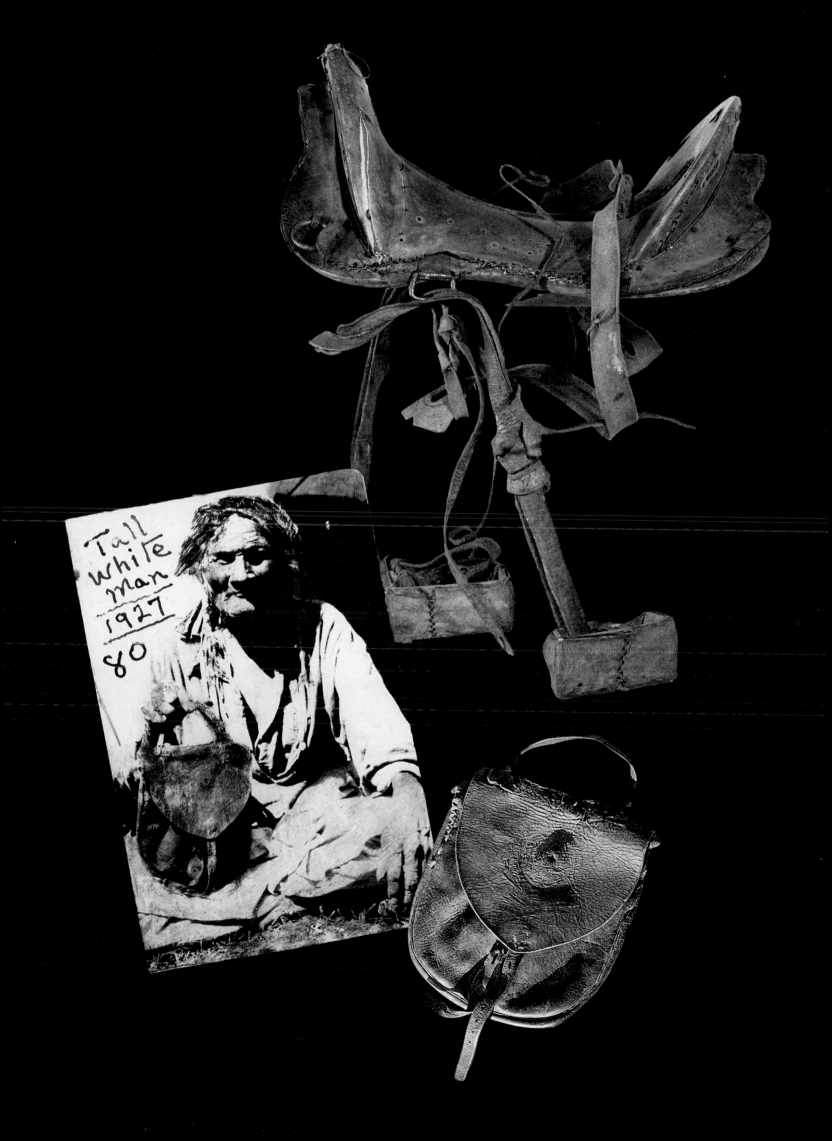

The Story of Mia-ahoche and Nishe wadonschei

Told by Burton Fisher, Sr.
Recorded by Burton Fisher, Sr.

My wife's grandfather Mia-ahoche ("Beard," or "Mustache") and his friend Nishe wadonschei ("Two Feathers") took part in the Custer battle. Mia-ahoche related that it was during the season when the cottonwoods shed cotton from the tree buds. As for the time, he stated, the sun had not risen too far from dawn. At the camp site there were approximately seven circles of tipis. The white man had aroused a few people, and like a chain reaction the Cheyennes notified the rest of the camp that there were cavalry arriving. Women, children, and the elderly started running, fleeing for a place to hide.

Mia-ahoche and Nishe wadonschei took part in the battle. They were on foot, running, jumping along the hillside, shooting at the cavalry. In the course of the battle, two unknown Cheyenne warriors took off after a cavalryman who was riding a large black horse toward the Benteen and Reno part of the battlefield. The warriors chasing him were riding Indian ponies, or mustangs. These ponies were known for their great endurance. They could travel a long way. The warriors noticed the cavalryman's horse was getting tired. When the warriors came up to the top of a hill, they saw the cavalryman had come to a stop down in the ravine below and had gotten his pistol out. The warriors thought he was going to shoot at them, but to their surprise the cavalryman shot himself in the head and fell to the ground.

When the battle was over, Mia-ahoche and Nishe wadonschei scavenged the battle site. They saw Custer lying there nude and dead. They remember a small gust of wind came up and there were pieces of paper with pictures scattered around and blowing in the wind. Mia-ahoche gathered some of the pictured paper, took it to the camp, and gave it to the children. The pictures amazed the children. This pictured paper was probably money. Maybe some of it belonged to Custer.

Mia-ahoche also told about the time Custer smoked the pipe with the Cheyennes and took an oath that he was never to bother the Cheyennes again. The chiefs emptied the ashes from the pipe bowl on the heel of Custer's boot. Custer was supposed to meet the other cavalry prior to the battle, but he wouldn't wait. That's when he met his fate. He got killed and also his men.

The Story of Charles Limpy

Told by Albert Longjaw
Translated by Alberta American Horse Fisher

All the old men are gone who fought in the Custer battle. For instance, my grandfather Charles Limpy fought in the battle. When they circled and surrounded Custer and his troops, Limpy got shot in the leg. That is how he acquired the name "Limping Man." The bullet went through his leg and also into his horse. Limpy died at the age of

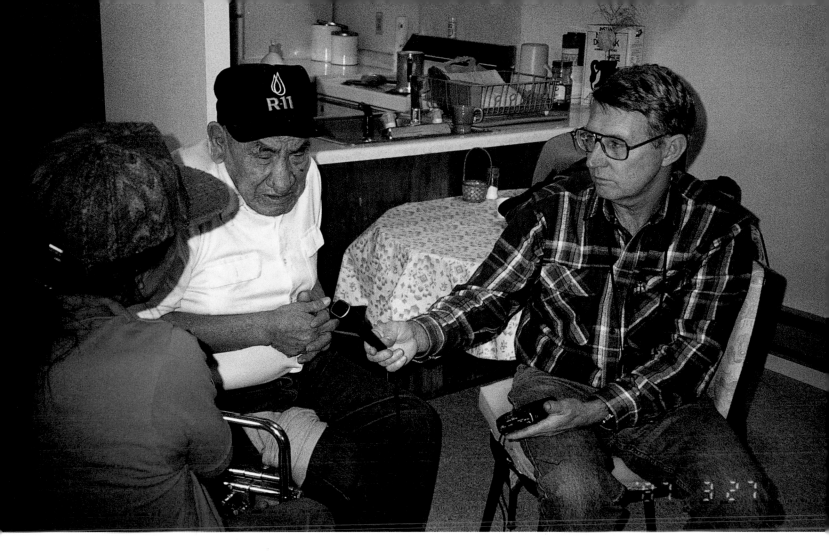

Albert Longjaw being interviewed for *Little Bighorn Remembered*, Lame Deer, Montana. Left to right: Eddy White Dirt, Albert Longjaw, Felix Lowe.

ninety-eight. I knew him very well. Another man named Big Crow from Ashland was in the battle. So was Chief Iron Shirt, who lived along the Rosebud Creek, and old man Yellow Robe, who used to live a little way east from Busby. They are all gone.

Charles Limpy told how Custer fought and defeated the Cheyenne people in Oklahoma. In Oklahoma the Cheyennes made a peace pipe offering to Custer. Custer said he would never fight the Cheyennes again. They smoked the pipe with Custer and the old man emptied his pipe ashes on the right side of Custer's boot, then on the left side, touching him. The Arrow Man made him take an oath.

But Custer wanted to fight with the Cheyennes and came north, tracking the Cheyennes up here and resting where Lame Deer is now. ["Lame Deer" is a mixed translation; correctly it should be in English "Lame Antelope."] The Cheyennes were moving along the Rosebud Creek toward Busby, camping at the flats now known as Busby Village. Custer was still behind them, tracking the travois marks in the ground.

On the morning of the battle, at about 9:00 A.M., Custer told his troops to move and attack the Cheyennes and Sioux. A Cheyenne scout saw Custer and his troops coming. He rode down to the camp and told the Cheyennes, "There's a lot of dust out there!" He said that the soldiers had caught up with them. Sioux chief and camp crier Yellow Horse announced the coming of the troops, "Get ready, prepare for battle!" Another camp crier, a chief also, said to wait. The Cheyennes and Sioux were all in line, and the Sioux chief camp crier told them to wait until the soldiers shot first. Custer and his troops were all in line, he hollered, cocked his gun and shot first. The Sioux and

Cheyennes began hollering, yelling out their war cries. They charged, facing Custer and attacking his troops.

As I have heard from my grandfather Limpy, Chief Big Crow, and Yellow Horse, the soldiers were near the coulee. They chased them back up the hill. After chasing them back up the hill they went east of the battlefield, and there they shot the troops down. They surrounded Custer and his troops; they shot Custer and his men. Charles Walks Last is the one who first shot Custer. They disrobed them all and took their belongings. Custer was in the midst of his dead men. Custer played dead. When he opened his eyes, Chief Big Crow shot him and said, "He's still alive." He went toward him. Custer was lying on his back, his head downhill. An old lady, whose Indian name meant Deaf Woman, scalped Custer. Custer and all his men were lying there naked.

That night at the camp the Cheyennes had a victory dance, a bonfire. They danced and waved Custer's scalp tied to a stick. I know the Cheyenne victory song they sang that night. These are the words: "Long Haired Man came to the Bighorn River and we bloodied him." [No word in the English language exactly translates the Cheyenne word given here as "bloodied."]

The Story of Louis Dog

Told by Florence Whiteman

Recorded by Herman J. Viola

My name is Florence Whiteman. My first husband was named Waters. When I was about three years old, my mother took me to my grandmother and gave me to her to raise. That's the Cheyenne tradition. The firstborn is raised by the grandparents. I thought when I was five years old that my mother didn't love me, that my mother threw me away to my grandmother. But she had a reason to do what she did.

My grandfather Louis Dog was one hundred years old when he died. His Cheyenne name was Ho-ta Me-he, "dog" in Cheyenne. After the Custer battle, he joined the Army as a scout at Fort Keogh. Later on, the government built him a house on his land near Busby because he was a veteran. When he died, the people came to get him in a hearse. They brought him a coffin. They brought him an American flag and they embalmed him. They took care of him. They gave him the flag and they put him in uniform, and then they put him in the coffin. I thought that was something good, you know, that they were doing this for him, these white people. I thought he must have earned it some way.

I grew up with my grandfather, and he taught me things about Cheyenne culture. He wouldn't even go anywhere. He was an old man. I didn't realize at the time how old he was. Early in the morning he would get me up and I would go with him. We would go get his horses. He had two horses. As soon as they saw him the horses would come running to him because they knew he was out there to greet them. And he would stand there and talk to them, in Cheyenne.

I learned Cheyenne pretty well from both my grandparents. But my grandmother had lost her hearing by then. She said it was because she had performed some cere-

Florence Whiteman lives near Lame Deer on the Northern Cheyenne Reservation. Raised by her grandparents, at age twelve she was initiated into the Elk Warriors Society, and she is the last woman warrior among the Northern Cheyennes. She also has the distinction of being the last Cheyenne woman given to her husband for a bride-price of four horses. The traditional marriage, which took place in 1943, when Florence was fifteen years old, was arranged because of her special status as an Elk Society warrior. After her first husband died, she married her present husband, Philip Whiteman. "I picked him myself," she laughs. "I told my Society brothers that one arranged marriage was enough." She is the mother of two sons and seven daughters.
John Warner

mony and did not live up to the rules. She said the medicine man warned her that would happen if she didn't follow the rules. She slowly lost her hearing. She couldn't hear, so I had to communicate with her in sign language. I got to know pretty good sign language from her and from my grandfather. That was the only way we could communicate with each other.

My grandfather told me that Custer had met the Cheyennes before. He had talked with them in Oklahoma. They had a meeting with Custer to make peace. At the meeting they smoked the pipe. All of them, the chiefs and Custer, they smoked the pipe. The chiefs told him that they were going to become friends, because they were smoking a pipe. They explained this to Custer. After Custer got all through smoking this pipe, there was nothing left in it but ashes. The chiefs then told him to stand up. He had his boots on. They told him to take that pipe and tap it on his boots, so the ashes could come out of the pipe and fall on the ground. Then they told him to take the sole of his boot and rub the ashes into the ground, so that's what he did. The chiefs then said, "Now, if you ever double-cross the Cheyenne, that's how you're going to end up. That's the purpose of smoking the pipe and rubbing those ashes into the ground. There's going to be nothing left of you, if you ever double-cross the Cheyenne." And that's what happened to him at Little Bighorn. That happened because he probably didn't believe us. That's the way it was back then. Whatever the medicine men said at the time after they did ceremonies, it always, always came true. That's one of the stories my grandfather told me.

Louis Dog, grandfather of Florence Whiteman. Like many other Cheyenne warriors, he became a scout for the U.S. Army at Fort Keogh, Montana. Photograph taken in 1941 at a Sun Dance on a South Dakota reservation.
Don Tenoso Collection

My grandfather thought Custer was the greatest—the way he looked, the way he acted. He thought Custer could have been one of the best warriors. I guess he was.

My grandfather said he could always tell who was going to become the best warrior. He told me about a little boy the Cheyennes captured once when they attacked a Ute camp. There was this little boy standing around crying. You know how it is. One of the Cheyennes picked up the little boy and took him home on his horse. When the chiefs saw what happened, they said to the warrior, "Go give this little boy to an old lady to raise, a grandmother. We'll raise him as a Cheyenne. We won't tell him that he's from another tribe. We'll raise him as a Cheyenne and see what happens." Well, this little boy was raised by the grandmother. He was raised like a Cheyenne. Everybody watched him grow up because they knew he was not a Cheyenne. But he turned out to be the best of them.

My grandfather said on the day Custer came to attack their village, the Cheyennes had runners watching in the hills. This boy was one of the runners. He came running down to warn the village that soldiers were coming. He told them how far away Custer was and what part of the day he was going to be there. He could tell by the sun. When the sun gets to here, that's when the soldiers are going to come riding.

These runners—there were two of them—used this root that grows out here. It glows blue at night. They use that. They put it on their ears, on their arms. It makes them strong. It's Indian medicine. They used it when they had ceremonies like the Contrary Ceremony. They would use it, too, to represent animals. The medicine men

48

put that root on these two runners. When they put their ears to the ground, the runners could hear those hooves coming. They could analyze how far away Custer was. And they could see from that point those flashing buttons on their coats. One of the boys ran down to the village and one stayed up there. The runner told them, "This is how far away they are."

Some of the warriors were down by the river in sweat lodges. They were sweating. Someone sent the Crazy Dogs to go down and tell them to get out of there and to get ready. The Crazy Dogs also took the Sacred Hat Keeper, some of the girls and boys, and some families up into the hills where they would be safe, where they wouldn't be hurt in case the warriors all got killed. The Cheyennes knew that's what Custer was determined to do, to kill all the Cheyennes. So they left. The old people and the children, they went out of the village, but the warriors came running.

As the warriors were running around getting ready, a man got up and took his drum and began singing. He was singing the Suicide Song. And all these warriors who were getting ready, they were putting on their best moccasins, so that they could die in their best. They were getting their horses ready too. They came running to this man who was playing the Suicide Song. They began dancing to the song. If you dance to that Suicide Song, it means you must stay out there to the very end, because you have made a vow to win or die. That's the purpose of the Suicide Song.

Today if anyone sings that Suicide Song, we would probably all head for the hills because we're different now, you know! But at that time, those young men came running over and began dancing. Some young girls, when they saw their brother dancing, why they said, "I'm going to go join my brother. I'll die with my brother today." Some of the first ones did that, not that many. Most of the young women took care of the old ladies, the elderlies, and the children. That was their job.

My grandfather said that Ute boy was the first one over there dancing to the Suicide Song. Then he got on his horse and he was leading the charge to meet Custer. This shows that he was raised to be one of the best warriors that they could ever have as a Cheyenne, but he wasn't a Cheyenne at all, he was a Ute. He was the first one out there ready to meet the soldiers. He made everyone proud. He showed everyone that old lady did a good job raising him.

My grandfather said that when the fighting stopped some women ran up there to see who was still alive, to see who died, to see who needed help. Some of the dead were facing down, and they were turning them over. I read in a book somewhere that Indian women went through the pockets of the dead soldiers, robbing these men. My grandfather never said anything like that. He said they were worried, because someone might still be alive that needed help, that might be just wounded. That's what they were doing when they were out there. And he also said, "I really felt bad that all those young people died, including white kids. From what I seen of them, they were just young boys, like kids. They had to die because of Custer." My grandfather felt sorry for them, because they were forced to do what they did. He said that day shouldn't have happened at all, that many people should not have died. He said, "It still hurts me inside when I think about it." He said he couldn't sleep for a long, long time after that. What happened that day was saddest thing that could ever happen.

Address by William Walks Along,

President of the Northern Cheyenne Tribe,
Little Bighorn Battlefield,
June 25, 1997

Greetings to all our friends and allies, the Great Sioux Nation and Arapaho Nation who have come here to this battlefield to honor our valiant and undaunted warriors who went forth with faith and stamina to set a courageous example for others to follow. In my short journey here on Mother Earth, I have observed that it is very important never to mistake education for knowledge; those persons who have had the privilege of education must combine experience with knowledge and then balance all that with humility. In this way we become humble leaders with a modest sense of our own significance in God's Universe.

I have always shared with many non-Indians that my heroes fought to protect our families and were truly peaceful people, not soulless barbarians who worshipped no God. The reverse was true: My heroes always called upon the Great Spirit for guidance and gave thanks for being granted the gift of life another day. Our warriors who fought on this battleground passed their leadership abilities on to others, especially their conviction to preserve the future generation and the will to carry on. They actively mentored their children and grandchildren with great loving kindness in a terrible era of our tribal history, leaving a powerful legacy. Our Northern Cheyenne and allied leaders had the courage to stand for something, not against something. They stood for our families and for the freedom to live our own way.

How many times have our people been rejected, criticized, or ridiculed? How many times has our courage been tested? How many times have our people been faced with seemingly insurmountable odds? To ask oneself penetrating questions about one's own capacity for courage is truly to test one's mettle. The Northern Cheyenne who live today are evidence of the determination and sacrifice of our legendary heroes. They passed on the commitment to trust in the Great Spirit; to be loyal to our families and to the Northern Cheyenne Nation.

I believe it is important to know the pain our ancestors experienced during the period of history in which the U.S. government Indian policy was genocidal in nature. Also, it is important to know our own pain, because I believe it destroys our self-pride, our arrogance, and our indifference toward others. It makes us aware of how much we must depend upon the Holy Creator of the Universe. Very slowly, we begin to understand the pain and suffering inflicted upon our Indian nations by the U.S. government and others. Even today, our journey through the twentieth century has taken many of us to points of no return. This is why it is very important to have anchors—events or happenings that allow us to appreciate the gift of life. This gathering is a celebration of life. We know this in our hearts as Indian people. Our people were filled with the fire of inspiration to protect the lives of their families—people filled with this kind of inspiration have no fear of anyone, whether wild beast or man.

The continuing story, the dilemma, of American Indians is, in a sense, a window onto the American soul; through its cloudy and often confusing lens, we may see our-

The warrior tradition continues among the Cheyenne people. Shown here is the conclusion of a warrior honor ceremony performed on the Northern Cheyenne Reservation for Private Ron Big Back in May 1991, upon his return from Operation Desert Storm. Confirming the revival and continuation of centuries-old traditions in which war heroes received the praise and plaudits of friends and relatives, Private Big Back underwent a purification with the incense of sage to cleanse him of any evil spirits that lingered around him after his combat experience; then he received a new name, Charging Eagle, in recognition of his bravery in the face of a Scud missile attack while on sentry duty. According to his commanding officer, who informed Ron's family of his heroism and whose letter was read during the ceremony, Private Big Back had alerted his sleeping comrades with the Cheyenne war cry, thereby awakening the camp as he rushed forward to put out the ensuing fire. The goods piled in front of Charging Eagle were given away by his family to the hundred or so tribal members who witnessed the ceremony.
Herman J. Viola Collection

selves at both our worst and our best. Treatment of our people has sometimes been cruel and inhumane and filled with an intense moral attitude. We Indian people have a determination to make the United States live up to its highest ideals. Mr. Felix Cohen, an interpreter of Indian law, wrote, "Like the miner's canary, the Indian marks the shift from fresh air to poison gas in our political atmosphere, and our treatment of Indians, even more than our treatment of other minorities, marks the rise and fall of our democratic faith."

Today, the Indian Nations who participated in the battle in 1876 acknowledge the intangible eternal values our ancestors defended. Today, we have the self-worth and courage to stand and be counted. The awesome power of serving others and the wisdom of self-sacrifice have enhanced the self-worth of those of us here today.

Personally, I realize how much my own outer and inner life is built upon the commitment and actions of my fellow men, both living and dead, and how earnestly I must exert myself in order to give in return as much as I have received. We all have received abundantly from our ancestors, who made a difference on this ground 121 years ago. Let us practice faithfulness and persistence, and take action to protect our families. The eternal values—faith, trust, hope, life, justice, mercy, honesty, service, sacrifice, humility, and charity—will assist us in giving back to our communities and allow us to focus on issues and problems that have been ignored for too long. Thank you for inviting me to speak here today. It is a great honor and privilege to be here. Travel safely to your homes, and God bless you. *Ha-ho.*

Custer's Cheyenne Connections

HERMAN J. VIOLA

Little Bighorn was not Custer's first assault on a Cheyenne village. A decade earlier, on November 27, 1868, he had led the Seventh Cavalry in a surprise winter attack against the village of Chief Black Kettle, which was camped along the Washita River near the panhandle of Texas. The "victory" over the sleeping village launched Custer on his career as Indian fighter and doubtless encouraged his impetuous surprise attack at Little Bighorn. In the moments before his attack on Black Kettle's village, when it was suggested there might be too many Indians for his troops to handle, Custer is said to have retorted: "All I am afraid of is we won't find half enough. There are not Indians enough in the country to whip the Seventh Cavalry."

Custer prevailed at the Washita, and a few months later he capped that triumph by exacting a promise of peace from the demoralized Southern Cheyennes. Custer's success, however, led to his later demise, according to present-day Cheyennes, who support their claim with two widely known stories.

One story, told by the elderly Cheyennes interviewed for this book, concerns Custer's violation of a promise made when he persuaded the tribe to make peace. In March 1869, a few months after the Battle of the Washita, Custer, accompanied by only one other officer, had boldly entered a Cheyenne camp and smoked the pipe during a ceremony in the lodge of Chief Medicine Arrows. Custer doubtless did not realize he was sitting beneath the sacred arrows of the Cheyenne tribe, nor could he have known that the holy man conducting the pipe ceremony was the arrow keeper. Speaking in Cheyenne, the arrow keeper warned Custer of disaster if he ever betrayed the sacred pact of friendship he had just made with the Cheyenne people. The holy man then ended the ceremony in dramatic fashion by tapping the pipe bowl on the toe of Custer's boot and spilling the ashes on the ground.

This event, known to young and old alike, is central to Cheyenne oral history of the Battle of the Little Bighorn. It is not likely that the story was acquired through reading historical accounts of the episode. Indeed, for our interview with Albert Longjaw, who also repeated the story, we needed a Cheyenne-English interpreter.

In the second story, less widely told, the Cheyennes say Custer fathered a son by a Cheyenne woman taken after the Battle of the Washita. I first heard this story from David Fanman while at the National Archives with him one day, seeking proof that his grandfather had served as a scout for the Army after the war days. The Veterans Administration, Fanman insisted, would provide a military tombstone for his grandfather if we could find proof of his enlistment. (We did, and the tombstone now marks Tall Bull's grave in the Cheyenne cemetery at Old Cantonment, Oklahoma.)

As we were scanning a roster of the U.S. Army Indian scouts, Fanman suddenly exclaimed, "Well, I'll be darned! Even Custer's son became an Indian scout."

"What are you talking about?" I replied. "Custer never had any children."

"Maybe not by his white wife." Fanman laughed. "But the Southern Cheyennes all know he had an Indian boy."

The opportunity for such an indiscretion resulted from the Battle of the Washita, where the Seventh Cavalry captured about one hundred Cheyenne women and children and returned with them to Fort Hays. Captain Myles Keogh, for one, evidently enjoyed the spoils of war, as this comment in a letter written from Fort Hays indicates: "We have here about ninety squaws—from our last fight [at the Washita]—some of them are very pretty. I have one that is quite intelligent. It is usual for officers to have two or three lounging around." Captain Benteen, admittedly no fan of Custer's, later charged him with keeping a woman named Monahsetah as his mistress. Custer, in his book, *My Life on the Plains*, described her as a woman of rare beauty.

Monahsetah did, in fact, remain with the Seventh Cavalry for several months, serving as an intermediary between the Army and her people. She was the daughter of Chief Little Rock and seven months pregnant when captured. As Robert Utley points out in his prizewinning biography of Custer, *Cavalier in Buckskin*, Monahsetah remained with the dashing and handsome officer for three months after the birth of her baby, and Cheyenne oral tradition tells of the birth of another child later that year.

Another version of the story was recorded in 1927 by Thomas Marquis, the physician who befriended the Cheyenne and Crow veterans of the Indian wars. This version is particularly interesting, because the personal story of Monahsetah is specifically connected to the more familiar story of Custer's broken pact of peace with the Cheyennes. Marquis's informant for this tale of parallel betrayals was Kate Big Head, a Northern Cheyenne witness to the Battle of the Little Bighorn, who spent her early life with the Southern Cheyennes. She had been one of the refugees from the Washita attack, she told Marquis, when Custer again found the Cheyennes in spring 1869. "We were far westward, on a branch of the river the whites call Red River, I think. This time there was no fighting. Custer smoked the peace pipe with the Cheyenne chiefs. He

promised never again to fight the Cheyenne, so all of us Cheyennes followed him to the soldier fort—Fort Sill. Our people gave him the name Mi-es-tzie, meaning 'Long Hair.'"

Kate Big Head recalled that the Cheyenne women, herself included, considered Custer very handsome, but her cousin Me-o-tzi (Monahsetah) already had his eye. "She often went with him to help find the trails of the Indians. . . . All of the Cheyennes liked her, and they were glad she had a place so important in life. After Long Hair went away," Big Head continued, "different ones of the Cheyenne young men wanted to marry her, but she would not have any of them. She said that Long Hair was her husband and had promised to come back to her and that she would wait for him. She waited for seven years and then he was killed."

After the battle, according to Kate Big Head, two Southern Cheyenne women in the camp on the Little Bighorn came across Custer's body and recognized him.

While they were there looking at him, some Sioux men came up and were about to cut up the body. The Cheyenne women, thinking of Me-o-tzi, signed to them, "He is a relative of ours." The men cut off his little finger but otherwise did not mutilate the body. The women then pushed the point of an awl through his ears. "This was done," they said, "to improve his hearing in the afterlife, as it seemed he had not heard what our chiefs had said when they smoked the pipe of peace with him. They told him then that if he ever again broke his word and fought the Cheyennes, the Everywhere Spirit would surely cause him to be killed."

Several of the Cheyennes at Lame Deer tell versions of the story of a woman pushing an awl into Custer's ears. This might be dismissed as fanciful fabrication but for the condition of Custer's body when found. It was relatively unmarked except for two bullet wounds—one to the chest and one to the side of the head—and an arrow that had been shoved up his penis. The officers who examined his body speculated that the blood from his ears had been caused either by the obvious gunshot to the head or by a less obvious bullet that had gone through his head entering and exiting his ears. Perhaps. But the arrow shoved up his penis (rarely mentioned out of concern for Libbie Custer) and the blood from his ears could also have been the work of two angry Southern Cheyenne women who remembered a jilted lover and unkept promises.

Opposite: Custer for the ages, in a photograph taken by Matthew Brady in Washington, D.C., May 23, 1865, the day of the Grand Review of the Union Army along Pennsylvania Avenue. This was Custer's favorite portrait of himself.
Armed Forces History Division, National Museum of American History

Sitting Bull

HERMAN J. VIOLA

At the Battle of the Little Bighorn, Sitting Bull was at the peak of his power. No other Lakota chief approached his achievements as a spiritual and political leader.

Approximately forty-five years old, he was strong and nimble despite a limp caused by a Flathead bullet when a teenager. In 1876, the Hunkpapa's influence extended across the Northern Plains. Fiercely resistant to reservation life, he rebuffed every U.S. government overture. "All agency Indians I have seen are worthless," he once sneered. "They are neither red warriors nor white farmers. They are neither wolf nor dog. If the Great Spirit had desired me to be a white man, he would have made me so in the first place. It is not necessary for eagles to be crows. Now we are poor but we are free."

Sitting Bull had probably never met or even seen George Armstrong Custer, but the events of June 25, 1876, have forever

In 1882, while a prisoner of the Army at Fort Randall, Dakota Territory, Sitting Bull drew at least three autobiographies. Unlike his earlier drawings copied by Four Horns (page 14), these were obviously intended for white audiences, because none show him killing white people. Not only had he been influenced by the work of white artists, as shown in the realistic depiction of his horse in this series of drawings, but he signed each one with his signature instead of a glyph, as he'd been taught by the trader he'd befriended while exiled in Canada.
National Anthropological Archives

united them. When fighting began, Sitting Bull later recalled, he was resting in his tipi when some young men shouted that soldiers were charging the camp. "I jumped up and stepped out of my lodge. The old men, the women, and the children were hurried away. There was great confusion. The women were like flying birds; the bullets were like humming bees." To the men he yelled, "Warriors, we have everything to fight for, and if we are defeated we shall have nothing to live for; therefore, let us fight like brave men."

Although caught by surprise, the young men rushed to the defense of their families. Giving them added confidence was the vision Sitting Bull had received while undergoing the Sun Dance ten days earlier. As a Sun Dance pledge, Sitting Bull had promised the Great Spirit to cut one hundred pieces of flesh from his body. "I fulfilled my vow," Sitting Bull declared. "My brother Jumping Bull cut tiny pieces of skin—fifty from each arm—using an awl and a sharp knife. I danced two days and two nights. God sent me a vision. I saw white soldiers and enemy Indians on horseback falling into the Sioux camp. They were coming down like grasshoppers, headfirst, with their hats falling off. Just then I heard a voice from above, saying, 'I give you these because they have no ears!'"

According to some Indian accounts, the stunning success could have been even greater had Sitting Bull the following morning not called off the attack on the troops with Reno and Benteen. "Let them go," he told the young men. "Let them live. They have come against us, and we have killed a few. If we kill them all, they will send a bigger army against us."

It had indeed been a great victory. Altogether the Indians killed 263 men, including 3 Arikara scouts—212 were with Custer and 51 were with Reno. The Indians suffered far fewer casualties. Perhaps as few as 30 were killed, though a number of wounded later died. Several women and children also died in the initial attack on the village. Some of the Indians who died were "suicide" warriors who had vowed beforehand to be killed in battle.

For the Lakota and their Cheyenne allies, however, the victory over Custer was their undoing. The U.S. Army wanted its revenge. Even in the dead of winter, when the Plains Indians normally went into camp and waited patiently for spring, they got no rest. In May 1877 Crazy Horse led his band into Red Cloud Agency in South Dakota and surrendered. Four months later, he was stabbed to death while supposedly resisting arrest.

As the Army continued its relentless search for the Indian bands that had participated in the Custer fight, Sitting Bull,

Gall, and several hundred followers crossed the border into Canada, where they remained safe from pursuit. But life was lonely and hard in Canada. In small groups, the refugees quietly began returning to their friends and relatives until the remaining diehards, fewer than fifty families loyal to Sitting Bull, surrendered with him in 1881.

Although a virtual prisoner of the U.S. government, Sitting Bull enjoyed great notoriety for his role in defeating Custer. One of those to capitalize on his popularity was William F. Cody, better known as "Buffalo Bill," who operated a successful "Wild West Show" that toured cities in the United States and abroad; Cody got permission from the Bureau of Indian Affairs to let Sitting Bull tour with him for one season in 1885.

Although now an old man, Sitting Bull was still feared and mistrusted by U.S. government officials. Their worst suspicions appeared to materialize when he became an advocate of the Ghost Dance religion in the late 1880s.

Defeated, dispirited, and trapped between two worlds, many western Indians sought escape through a new religion preached by Wovoka, an Indian prophet who urged his followers to return to Indian lifeways. The Ghost Dancers were convinced that all whites would disappear, all dead Indians would return to life, and the buffalo would return to the Plains in vast numbers.

The Lakota became fervent believers. Within a remarkably short time, large numbers of tribesmen on the reservations in North and South Dakota embraced the new religion, which their white neighbors viewed as anti-white and militaristic. When Sitting Bull, now in retirement on the Standing Rock Reservation in North Dakota, threatened to join the dancers, he was ordered arrested. A fierce gun battle ensued on December 15, 1890, in which the old chief, seven of his followers, and six Indian policemen died.

The Ghost Dance phenomenon ended two weeks later, on December 28, 1890, when the Seventh Cavalry tried to disarm a Miniconjou band of Ghost Dancers led by Chief Big Foot. The result was little more than a massacre of the frightened, freezing Indians. As many as three hundred men, women, and children died in that needless tragedy, known as the Battle of Wounded Knee. More a massacre than a battle, Wounded Knee is often said to mark the end of the Indian wars on the Northern Plains, but in reality the wars had ended within months of Sitting Bull's stunning victory on the banks of the Greasy Grass.

A photograph of Sitting Bull taken in Bismarck, Dakota Territory, about the time the chief signed on with Buffalo Bill's Wild West Show in 1885. Photograph by David F. Barry. *National Anthropological Archives*

A Dakota View of the Great Sioux War

JEANNE OYAWIN EDER,
with Stories Collected by Michael Her Many Horses

Gall, a Hunkpapa chief and adopted brother of Sitting Bull, successfully led the defense against Reno's charge toward the village and then played a major role in the fight against Custer. Gall's two wives and three children were killed during the initial assault. "It made my heart bad," he later declared. "After that I killed all my enemies with the hatchet. I killed a great many." After the battle, he joined Sitting Bull in Canada. Born about 1840, he died in 1895. In his later years, he won praise as a model agency chief. The photographer is unknown, possibly David F. Barry. *National Anthropological Archives*

I am an enrolled member of the Dakota Sioux tribe. My great-grandfathers and great-grandmothers were there on the battlefield of the Little Bighorn that day in June. And like other Sioux of my generation, I have been told the story of the Sioux people's struggle to maintain their identity, to defend their ancestral lands, and to stand up for their rights.

A century ago, the Sioux people made up a great nation. They were the people of the woodlands, the prairies, the hills, and the mountains. Their homeland was composed of Minnesota, South Dakota, North Dakota, and portions of Montana, Nebraska, and Wyoming. The name that they had for themselves was very different from "Sioux," which means "snakes" or "enemies." Ella Deloria, Sioux linguist and anthropologist, has said: "Peace is implied by the very name of the people, Odakota, a state or condition of peace. . . . We Dakotas love peace within our borders. Peacemaking is our heritage. Even as children we settled our little fights through kinship that we might live in Odakota."

Throughout the 1700s, the Sioux moved westward from their eastern homelands. This westward movement resulted partly from the territorial expansion of their traditional enemies, the Ojibwa, who had by that time acquired the gun. By the mid-1700s the Sioux were also owners of the horse and gun and were rapidly becoming a dynamic people of the Plains.

The *wasichus*, the white man, came without the Sioux inviting him. He came like a flood that nothing could stop. All in a day, it seemed, the invasion by the white man spoiled the peacefulness of the Sioux, confused their minds, and gave them one choice—conform or die.

Tremendous changes took place in the lives of the Sioux and all Plains Indian peoples from 1800 to the present. After the War of 1812, U.S. officials began signing treaties whose ultimate purpose was to acquire and exploit lands that belonged to the native peoples of the Far West.

57

The first treaties with the Sioux, in 1825, were to procure friendship rather than land. However, by 1851 the government was interested in acquiring a right-of-way through Indian country for white settlers en route to Oregon and California. The Fort Laramie Treaty was designed to permit the U.S. government to establish roads and military posts within Sioux territory to safeguard the route for white travelers. Despite the fact that white travelers were already utilizing Sioux hunting grounds and depleting the buffalo herds, the Sioux granted them peaceful right-of-way. The treaty in no way implied surrender of sovereignty or lands.

Within a few years, numerous events led to the Red Cloud War with the United States and, ultimately, the Battle of the Little Bighorn. The killing of a cow belonging to a Mormon in August 1854 led to the death of Conquering Bear of the Brule Sioux and the slaughter of Lieutenant Grattan and a handful of soldiers. The following year, William Harney, intent on disciplining the Sioux and securing the Platte road, attacked Little Thunder's camp at Ash Hollow in present-day Nebraska. Little Thunder had not been involved in the Grattan affair, yet eighty-six of his men, women, and children paid the price. Another event that played an important role was the Minnesota Sioux uprising of 1862. Frustrated after decades of broken promises, the Sioux terrorized the Minnesota lands and killed as many as 760 invading settlers. Thirty-eight Sioux were hanged for this event. It was the largest mass hanging in United States history and inspired hatred in both Indian and white communities.

The Red Cloud War came about when the Sioux were faced with new assaults from the Northern Pacific Railroad and western mining interests. Congress at this time gave away Indian-owned lands as "grants." Troops were ordered to drive the Sioux off their lands. When the Army began to build forts along the Bozeman Trail, the Sioux, under the leadership of Red Cloud, resisted. The U.S. Army was defeated and in the Fort Laramie Treaty of 1868 agreed to abandon all the military forts along the Bozeman Trail and leave the Sioux in peace. The 1868 treaty also stipulated that no future treaties would be ratified unless three fourths of all adult Sioux males signed the agreement. This treaty, too, was broken by the United States.

In the agreement of 1876, the Black Hills would be ceded by the Sioux, but the agreement was not fully signed by three fourths of all adult Sioux males. The failure of the United States to comply with the 1868 treaty led to the long-standing suit brought to the Supreme Court by the Sioux against the government for illegal taking of the Black Hills. According to Robert Utley:

> In none of the treaty councils were the chiefs fully informed of the contents of the documents they were asked to sign. Treaty commissioners made much of the rations and other gifts that were promised but said little if anything about the land and freedom that Indians would be expected to surrender. . . . Repeatedly victimized, it is not surprising that the Sioux brought to all subsequent councils a profound distrust of the white men.

But what the Sioux perhaps did not understand fully at first was that from the middle of the nineteenth century, the United States undertook to colonize the Great American Desert and integrate it into the vast and rapidly increasing United States of America.

A lithograph by John C. Wise showing the execution of thirty-eight Santee Sioux Indians at Mankato, Minnesota, on December 26, 1862.
Herman J. Viola Collection

Yet did this war of 1876-77 come about purely because of the lust for gold, or was it because of colonial objectives by an imperialist power? One need only look at early government geological explorations of the region to answer that question. In his *Second Annual Report of the United States Geological Survey of the Territories Embracing Wyoming* (1869), F. V. Hayden, U.S. geologist, recalled a report made to Lieutenant G. K. Warren in 1856. "The Black Hills, which appear in the distance, and derive their name from their dark and gloomy appearance, contain an inexhaustible quantity of the finest timber, mostly pine, which will doubtless remain undisturbed for many years to come. I will, however, propose a plan for obtaining this timber, and rendering it useful to future settlers." It is clear that as early as 1856, the U.S. Army knew about the value of the natural resources of the Black Hills. This is still twenty years before that fateful day at the Little Bighorn.

In a later report of 1872 Hayden spoke about the Great American Desert: "Must this vast area remain forever unproductive and useless, without a vigorous effort being made to redeem it and make it valuable? If but one fifth of it could be brought under culture and made productive, this alone, when fully improved, would add $400,000,000 to the aggregate value of the lands of the nation."

Elsewhere in the report Hayden stated: "I also believe that the chief impetus that can be given to bring about the settlement and development of these Territories will be by judicious land grants to colonies and railroad companies." These lands would need to be connected by roads, which, Hayden said,

wherever they pass through Indian countries, would not only greatly lessen the expense of military transportation, but would also have a tendency to check their depredations. Therefore it is not wise for the Government so to bind itself by treaties that the right of way for railroads cannot be given through reservations. In fact, it is my opinion that the policy of making treaties with them, as quasinationalists, is detrimental to the agricultural development and best interest of the West.

The Brown and Anderson debate centers around the issue of the Black Hills and the discovery of gold as a key factor in the causes of war. Paul Hedren has said:

Several vital elements underlie the seeming inevitability of this remarkable conflict. By the 1850s the Teton or Western Sioux Indians dominated the prairies of Nebraska, Dakota, Wyoming, and Montana. Numbering some thirty-five thousand people—far more than any other plains tribe . . . the Sioux were angered . . . when an 1874 exploring expedition led by Lieutenant Colonel George Armstrong Custer, Seventh Cavalry, penetrated the Black Hills. Custer's official mission was to site a new military post; unofficially, but equally clear was his intention to report on the presence of gold. Confirmation of gold in the Black Hills . . . brought a rush of miners . . . and ultimately triggered the Great Sioux War.

World opinion of the time acknowledged that the United States broke the treaty of 1868. In his book *I Am Looking to the North for My Life*, Joseph Manzione pointed out that Canada and Great Britain had an interest in the Sioux War. Manzione said:

In the spring of 1876, Edward Thornton, the British Minister in Washington, passed along relevant information to the Foreign Minister in London . . . a copy of the Fort Laramie Treaty of 1868 along with several covering letters explaining how the present war was simply the latest example of American capriciousness in their relations with the Indians. He seemed to be making a point about the reliability of negotiations and agreements with the United States.

Manzione said further that when news of the Battle of the Little Bighorn came to the attention of Great Britain: "Standing in the House of Commons in mid July 1876, Sir William Watkins questioned the Undersecretary of the Colonial Department, James Lowther, about the situation in Montana. After noting that the war began with an American breach of a treaty, Watkins claimed that many of the Sioux were British subjects by virtue of their affiliation with Canada . . . and asked if the British government would intercede on behalf of the Sioux." Parliament declined to take action.

The issues that faced Sioux people were not just issues of gold. The issues had been building ever since Lewis and Clark's first exploration. The bigger issues were the invasion of their homeland and the violation of their treaty rights. The discovery of gold was a catalyst that started the invasion. But that gold discovery sealed the fate of the sacred lands of the Sioux. From the Sioux perspective, the Great Sioux War was a war to remain independent and to guarantee the rights of the Sioux people to their homeland. It was a war to guarantee their treaty rights. It was a war to guarantee their hunt-

American Horse

Flying By

He Dog

#51 "HUMP & FAVORITE WIVES"

HUFFMAN'S Indian Portraits. STUDIO, MILES CITY, M. T.
Northern Pacific Views. Badland and Big Horn Scenery.

Little Big Man

Lakota veterans of Little Bighorn.
Top: American Horse and wives, Crow King, Flying By, Long Bull, Low Dog, No Flesh.
Bottom: He Dog, Hump and wives, Little Big Man, Rain in the Face, Spotted Eagle, Louie Sitting Bull.
Glen Swanson Collection

Loong Bull

No Flesh

Rain in the Face
Killed Tom Custer

#3 SPOTTED EAGLE.

HUFFMAN'S Indian Portraits. STUDIO, MILES CITY, M.T.
Northern Pacific Views. Badland and Big-Horn Scenery.

ing rights. Theirs was a sacred fight for freedom. It was born of the Sioux people and fought for the Sioux people. This was a people's war.

A people's war means long-term resistance. The military resistance of the Sioux people began in the early 1800s and would not stop until 1890. That is long-term resistance.

A people's war means that there is a need to maintain and increase forces. It means that the form of fighting must take on the tactics of guerrillas: When the enemy is strong, avoid him, and when he is weak, attack. This kind of war can be waged with mediocre weapons and even allow the people to eventually equip themselves at the expense of the enemy. The rules of a people's army are simple. Warriors serve the people's interests and devote themselves to the nation.

"The Sioux were a proud, arrogant, warlike people," Mark H. Brown said, "and when emigrants began to travel the Oregon Trail in great numbers these Indians were not long in discovering that this was a fertile field for scalps and plunder." Perhaps Brown forgot that the emigrant trains were an invasion of another people's homeland. And where did these Indians learn about the business of scalping? According to Edward Lazarus in *Black Hills, White Justice,* Sioux scalps sold for two hundred dollars in the capital of Dakota Territory.

I had the opportunity to compile the oral histories of descendants of Indian survivors of the Wounded Knee massacre of 1890. Claudia Iron Hawk Sully is a descendant of a survivor. Her father's mother was Comes Crawling, one of the women who got away. In her interview, Claudia recalled her grandmother's fears: "My father told me . . . every little noise she hears, banging noise, she'll jump. And she has fear in her all the time. Like when some white people come to take stories or talk to my grandpa about the Little Bighorn. They said she used to hide. She didn't want to be around. She had fear of white people for a long time."

When I was a teenager, my grandfather Mark Eder, Sr., stood with me on a hot day in June on the battlefield at the Little Bighorn National Park. As we stood together looking west toward the river bottom he said: "Custer did not die on this hill! Custer died down by the river." I was stunned by this blunt statement. Then he told me that his mother was six years old and she had been at the battle, although he said that the Sioux called it the Battle of the Greasy Grass. Her brothers, who were his uncles, were also at that battle. He said that individuals were sworn not to talk about it for fear that the children and grandchildren would be punished. Several white tourists started to gather around us. One pointed a microphone toward my grandfather and asked him to say something in "Indian." He said: *"Chesadee-ta-tanka-ota."* Then he bent over and whispered in my ear the meaning of his words. We laughed because the literal translation of what he said was "droppings of the big buffalo bull."

One of the perspectives that Dakota people have is a fear of reprisals for elaborating on their oral traditions as they relate to specific events such as the Battle of the Little Bighorn. In the interviews with descendants of survivors of Wounded Knee it is apparent that there is some reluctance to expand on details. Jessie Kills Close to the Lodge said: "There are things that books tell that are not true. I guess Indian people were scared to tell."

No Two Horns, one of Sitting Bull's clos-
est companions, accompanied him to
Canada. During the Battle of the Little
Bighorn, his war pony was shot seven
times. He commemorated the valiant
animal by carving this dance stick (top),
which features the seven bullet wounds;
hair from the slain horse is used for the
dance stick's mane and tail. This drawing (right) by No Two Horns, a prolific
artist, shows the horse with its wounds
and the scalp lock amulet that hangs
from its bridle.
*War shield, dance stick, drawing, and
photograph of No Two Horns from the
Glen Swanson Collection*

At the present, we live with the advantages of peace, but we are still aware of the
challenges to our sovereign rights. Our wars and guerrilla tactics have changed. We
now fight in the courtrooms. We did not win the Great Sioux War because we fought
alone without the support from progressive peoples worldwide. Today our battles have
the support of oppressed people everywhere. Tomorrow we will not be alone!

Johnson Holy Rock

When I was a small boy all I could do was sit and listen, because in Indian culture children are to be seen and not heard. It's a male-oriented culture. So when people get together the women are over here, and the children are kept or swept out of the way so they don't interfere in men's affairs.

I was born late in the life of my parents. Most of my life was among older people, because my mother and father were along in years when I was born. I didn't have much time or chance to mingle with children of my age, and there weren't very many of them anyway. We lived way out northwest of Manderson, South Dakota, way out in the boonies along the Grass Creek. There weren't too many children along that creek. What children lived there were busy with their own lives, and they came from larger families so they had opportunities for recreation and so forth. I pretty much had to find my own recreation. I had a lot of time to see things and be a part of nature. I rode a lot. I was taught early to ride a horse, and I rode and spent a lot of time in the open range.

When my father would talk about his experiences along the Little Bighorn he would tell my mother. So I caught it secondhand. Later when I got older he began to talk directly to me. He told me he was born along the Tongue River. He didn't know exactly when his birthday was, but said it was in the season of the blossoming wild rosebushes. That would be probably around June, July, or thereabouts.

We had our own *tiospaye* or "extended family," which was identified as the Badger Band. My grandfather Holy Bull, or Holy Buffalo, and his brother were twins. The one

Johnson Holy Rock, a former Oglala Sioux tribal president, is now co-chair of the Gray Eagle Society, an organization of Lakota tribal elders who advise tribal councils on treaty rights and other issues. His father, Holy Rock (inset), was ten years old when he confronted Reno's troops in the opening moments of the battle, and lived to become a tribal and family leader of the Badger Clan. Johnson Holy Rock is shown here with the chief's blanket, featuring a beaded band and colored plumes, that belonged to his father, who wore it for special occasions and ceremonies. "My father represented all who were wild and free and willing to die to preserve a way of life," Johnson Holy Rock says. "When I think of him and what he lived for, it makes me downright proud."
Eric Haase

that was born first got the honor of being the chief. My father's father came into the world second. His older twin brother was a chief of the Badger Band. My father told how the band migrated from one place to another following the food supply. They depended on wild game like the buffalo, elk, deer. Of course the streams were real clean, the water was pure. It is not like it is today. So they had their choice of camping areas, usually sites where there was plenty of wood, shelter, plenty of grass for their ponies. As they moved around in that area, of course, they identified rivers and water-ways by different names from what they are today. The Tongue River name is still the same today, but other waterways had different identities. But they roamed pretty much in that area. They were known as the Northern People or Northern Band. They were identified by the United States as hostile because they didn't want to make any deals with the United States. This was their land and their country and they weren't going to negotiate away any part of it for anything. Of course, history has indicated that the government divided the bands. The military catered to certain prominent leaders or to leaders they appointed so they could make deals with them. But my grandfathers were hard-nosed about any deals. They stayed up there. Sitting Bull and his Hunkpapas roamed around the same area. Crazy Horse was there too. They didn't want to make deals about the Black Hills or any part of the area west of the Missouri. This was their land. But it was divided. The southern groups were the bands of Red Cloud, Young Man Afraid of His Horses, and other prominent chiefs at that time. Subchiefs. Spotted Tail, the Brules, Rosebud, they hung out pretty close together. That's probably why our reservations are adjacent to each other.

What finally culminated in the incident along the Little Bighorn was that the Secretary of the Interior wanted the military to drive the bands up north back over here within the Great Sioux Reservation that was set aside by the treaty of 1868. They were no longer to roam in that area. But that area had always been known as Indian Country. Everything from the Missouri to the Little Bighorn was within the boundaries of the 1851 treaty. The 1851 treaty, as you are probably aware, was just a guarantee of a right-of-way or road across Indian Country while the settlers, the emigrants, headed west. A right-of-way. Nothing more, nothing less. So as far as the Lakota, the Indians, were concerned that territory was still theirs, and they felt free to roam out there. But when Spotted Tail and Red Cloud made an agreement at Fort Laramie it left our bands exposed. They insisted they didn't sign the treaty of 1868. They were bound and deter-mined they weren't going to negotiate away one square foot of their land to anyone. Legally they were still within their territory, because the 1851 treaty was incorporated as part of the later one, the 1868 treaty, and it gives the right of hunting and fishing outside of the Great Sioux Reservation. So, to me, they were right and the government was wrong. But the government did it for expediency, to make room for the Anglo people. They wanted elbow room, and they kept sending messages out there, and we weren't paying attention, so they finally called for military intervention. So they were supposed to drive us back like a bunch of cattle.

Surprisingly, the older people that came back here after the Little Bighorn said that the chiefs and headmen had held a council and determined for the best interest of their people that they would come back to the Great Sioux Reservation peacefully if they were requested. Of course there was no such request, just the military assault that took place along the Little Bighorn. They were forced to fight. They didn't start the battle. It was George Armstrong Custer who decided that, and he disobeyed orders. General Terry told Custer to scout and he was on a scouting expedition. While he was scouting the area General Crook was supposed to come from the south, Fort Laramie, while Terry and Gibbon came from the northwest and northeast and converge along the Little Bighorn and drive the Indians into a trap. But Crazy Horse—and I don't know whether he knew of the presence of General Crook to the south or not, it's pretty hard to say how that happened—but he took a war party and went south and then engaged General Crook along the Rosebud and whipped him. He caused so many casualties and so much damage to his military force that Crook had to return to Fort Laramie. Of course, that stopped the trap from closing. Generals Terry and Gibbon had a lot of foot soldiers and so they were slow moving. But the Crow scouts with General Custer saw the camp. They told him and warned him that the valley was crawling with Indians. I suppose, being a Civil War veteran, Custer figured that my grandfathers were nothing but ants that he could squash.

At the time of the battle my father was about ten or eleven years old. The camp he was in was the furthest to the south upstream. The others were more to the north and that was the area that Major Reno was assigned to attack. He was told to ride through the camps and shoot up everything and anything he saw moving to create confusion. Captain Benteen was supposed to swing to the west and catch any Indians trying to escape the trap, while Custer attacked from the east.

The sun was pretty well up when the attack began. The first thing that my father heard was a camp crier riding inside the camp area and warning them that soldiers were coming. They didn't know at that time that Reno was right at their backs. Custer had it figured out pretty sharp, and if it had been executed properly history might have taken a different turn. Anyway, the family was just sitting down to breakfast and my grandmother was sitting there getting ready to ladle out the soup bowls when the messenger rode around the camp and told able-bodied warriors to get their horses and prepare themselves for battle. Soldiers were in the area.

My father was at that age where he was curious. All of a sudden his hunger disappeared and he was seized with excitement. He ran out of the tipi and saw a line of horsemen along the ridge. In that first sight he saw one of them was carrying something and there was something waving in the breeze. His mother had come out by then and saw what he saw. She told him, "Son, go get the mare that's ground-staked. Bring it towards the river."

So my father ran toward the west of the camp. Most of their horses were grazing there west and south of the camp. My father's family had this one mare with a little bell, probably a sheep bell, or something around her neck. She was ground-staked so she could go out only so far, and all the other family horses stayed around her. So he ran after and pulled the rawhide thong loose and threw a couple of loops around her nose and one over her ears. But she was a tall horse, he said, what we would call in Lakota *tasunke*. It was a white man's horse and built like a white man's horse. It was a tall mare. My dad had a hard time trying to get up on her. By that time firing began.

Here's the sound of rifle fire and there's horses running all over disturbed by the sound of the guns, and my father couldn't find anything on which to get up high enough so he could get on the mare's back. He tried climbing her leg like a monkey, but she wouldn't stand still. She began to move around because she was getting upset, too. About that time a bunch of the horses stampeded. As they raced by, the mare jerked the line out of his hand and went with them.

There wasn't anything more he could do, so he turned and ran back towards camp. When he ran into the camp circle everybody was gone. He ran to his parents' tipi, but nobody was there. He remembered his mother's advice to go towards the river so he started to run across the camp circle towards the river.

He heard something so he turned, and there was a line of men—some were kneeling and some were standing and they were pointing guns right at him. But he didn't stop. He kept running. As he ran, he could hear the bullets going by like a bunch of angry bees or bees traveling in a swarm. He got close to a clump of small brush, so he threw himself headlong into the brush. Above him it sounded like a hailstorm. They must have all been trying to bring him down. That's the first thing that hit me here and got me mad as a boy. Why did they have to do that? He wasn't a soldier! He wasn't a warrior! That began to establish my feelings in connection with what he went through. It was just a spontaneous reaction of sympathy, anger, whatever. I began to develop an adverse feeling towards the white man. For warriors it was a different thing. They were the protectors, so it's understandable when they go out to do battle that they are prepared to die if necessary. But for a turn in battle to fall upon children, upon those who aren't old enough to fight or women or even babies. Even in the heat of battle where there is a lot of excitement, even soldiers should be humane. If they see a woman running they shouldn't fire. But I suppose they had their orders. General Sheridan would remind the raw recruits signing up for Indian fighting, "Always remember that nits grow into lice," as though we were something detestable to be rid of. It's another thing that brought an adverse feeling in my breast; I have never forgiven Philip Sheridan for those words. But the Army was on a campaign of extermination, and our grandfathers were too active or too able at defending themselves and they were costing the government a lot of money. They were determined to take this land one way or the other. I suppose they figured my father was going to grow into lice, so they tried their best to bring him down. But it just wasn't his day to die. Hundreds of bullets flying and one of them should have had his name on it, but it didn't. He survived.

So the battle was engaged. Strangely, Reno dismounted his cavalry so those soldiers that were kneeling and standing and firing at my father were cavalry. They were horse soldiers, yet they were attacking on foot. At the time that I heard this story I wondered why should a horse soldier dismount? What were they doing on foot? This was a question that rose in my mind and it was strange. There were not supposed to be any foot soldiers. Terry had all of the foot soldiers and the Gatling gun. Here Major Reno dismounted his cavalry and attacked on foot and that was a mistake he made. It provided time for the warriors to get their horses and prepare themselves for battle. A battle that came to them and not because they desired or anticipated it but a forced military engagement. They responded to it as true warriors and defenders of the people.

By the time my father hit the river, a lot of the old people were already there. Also women with babies. Little babies had to be quiet even in moments of sudden stress and noise. They were taught to be silent. They were taught that in order for the Lakota people to survive. There were roaming bands of enemy tribes and military forces and other groups that sometimes attacked Indian camps for no reason at all. Little babies wrapped up learned to make no noise. They might whimper a little, but then their mothers would shush them. All they would have to say is "shh" or "*lece, ah, ah,*" and the little baby would stop crying immediately and lay there and listen. Children were taught from the ground up to have a sense of survival.

My father found his mother and they stayed with the children and the women and the old men and the infirm huddled down in the brush. They could hear the horses, the sounds of bullets, hoofs striking the ground, the rattle of gunfire, and the shouts of men. They knew the battle was engaged, but they didn't actually see much of it because they were all rounded up and taken to a place of safety. My father was down there with the women and the old men when all of a sudden a warrior rode up and here it was an uncle of his. He never told me his uncle's name. My father yelled to him, "*Lekse wawan, naopin honiwe, nawana wocuglasotape.*" "Uncle," he yelled, "they are killing us. We are running out of people." His uncle heard him and rode over to him and said, "*Hala hu tunska anpetu gi le winicasa kte le.*" "Nephew, you will be a man today." The uncle then grabbed him by the arm and jerked him up and put him on the back of his horse. My father was going to ride to the battle site with his uncle, but his mother hung on to his leg and wouldn't let him go. She had given birth to two children, him and a sister, but his sister died early. Now he was the only one, and his mother didn't want to let him go. She cried and wept, saying he was too young, so his uncle put him down. He used to wonder what would have happened if his mother had not intervened. He might have been killed. His uncle told him that there was a group of soldiers surrounded on the hill, and they were going to make the final run at it. He wanted him to become a man that day at ten or eleven years old. But unfortunately my grandmother intervened and he never got the chance to experience combat.

When the battle was over, some historians say that there was a great celebration and dancing. My father said there was no such thing. Many warriors had died, and there were many wounded. Some women and children were killed during Reno's attack.

Incidentally, according to my father, when the warriors got mounted they came like a great whirlwind and just enveloped Reno's troops. They ran them through the trees. The cavalry horses and horse handlers were back in the trees, but the warriors' assault was so sudden and swift that a lot of them missed their horses or the horses stampeded. So a lot of the soldiers were on foot. Some of the ones that got mounted had no time to do anything. They were all trying to save themselves because the battle took a turn in favor of the warriors.

His uncle told my father that a lot of the soldiers were shouting for their buddies to help them. Some had dropped their guns and now had no weapons. They were hollering at their fellow soldiers, but they were trying to save themselves too. So the warriors rode among them and just clubbed them down. They didn't want to waste bullets, and

Opposite, above:
Marvin Stoldt's Lakota name is Waunkiza Duweya Chikala, which means "Little Warrior." He is the grandson of Little Scout, also known as Little Warrior, a veteran of the Fetterman fight and the Battle of Slim Buttes as well as Little Bighorn. At age fifteen, Marvin walked several hundred miles over the Black Hills with his dogs, hunting and fishing along the way. An expert shot, he has been a professional hunting guide in Montana. He is a fluent Lakota speaker and knowledgeable about the dietary and medicinal plants his people have used since time immemorial. Marvin especially enjoys teaching this wisdom to his grandson John Cameron Stoldt. "I'm just as familiar with this country as my home," Marvin says. "I know this as well as every room in my house. I know where there is water to drink, the plants to eat, and the plants with medicinal value in the event I get sick or hurt. I'm more comfortable here than I am in the city, where telephones and other things are available to me."
Eric Haase

Opposite, center and below:
Randy Plume is the great-grandson of Little Bighorn veteran Iron Plume, who was so fascinated with the watches carried by the soldiers that he gathered fourteen from the dead bodies. Over the years, the family sold most of the watches; only these two remain. In 1997, Randy brought his sons to see the battlefield; here he is showing them the watches for the first time (Matthew, age seven, is at left; Michael, ten, is at right). These photographs were taken near Randy's mother's home in Wakan Community, just north of Manderson, South Dakota, on the Pine Ridge Reservation. Shirley Plume was the first woman to serve as a Bureau of Indian Affairs (BIA) superintendent; Randy has served as the director of education for the Oglala Sioux tribe. Holding the watches is Randy's sister Emma Clifford, who is a member of the tribal council. "Elgin National Watch Co." is engraved on both watches.
Eric Haase

some didn't have any guns anyway. They managed to corner the rest of the cavalry against the river so they jumped the horses down into the water. He said the banks were high, and as the horses jumped down there some got stuck in the mud and threw their riders. Some were able to get across the river, but the banks were high on the other side and some had to dismount to crawl up the banks. So when Reno's attack was blundered and the whole force fell on Custer, there was no way he could have survived. When he retreated up towards the ridge and was trying to keep his force intact, Crazy Horse had swung around to the north and made a crossing somewhere along the river and came up from behind. That's what history tells me. The final assault just engulfed them.

My grandfather's brother, the older twin, died on the way trying to escape into Canada. So they buried him in the mountains. They didn't say what mountains, whether it was the Rocky Mountains or some other mountains. But of course, those to the west of the Little Bighorn they called them the Wolf Mountains. Just short of the Rocky Mountains. My father didn't identify the place, but I figure it had to be *hesta oglate,* below the mountains, but he didn't say what mountains. But their escape route went through the Wolf Mountains. They buried him and they went on into Canada. They stayed up there with Sitting Bull, the remnants of the Badger Band that survived the battle. Of course, there were other bands that were there: the Hunkpapas, Oglalas, Miniconjou, the *Idasheep cola,* a few of the Two Kettle Band. There was just a conglomeration of Cheyennes, a lot of Cheyennes, Blackfeet Sioux; they weren't part of the Blackfeet as we know them over there further west. The Blackfeet Sioux was a band of the seven campfires but part of the Miniconjou. They were a subband.

So the military began the waiting game, harassing the Indians, keeping them on the move so they didn't have time to rest and gather supplies. They wanted to starve them into submission. They tried to surround Crazy Horse, and they had a lot of informers running around the country trying to locate him. They wanted to whip him in a decisive battle, but they couldn't do it. He had an uncanny sense of survival and many times managed to escape their traps. But they knew, the military knew, that so long as he lived they would always have to be looking over their shoulders to see where he was at. So they had to get rid of him. That was their whole intent.

Spotted Tail was related to Crazy Horse, and, this is the worst part, he was the one that gave him pipe and tobacco and gifts to bring Crazy Horse back and make peace and said we are going to send him to Washington. But Sheridan had given orders, and he comes in and put him in chains. The intent behind bringing Crazy Horse back was ulterior, and the United States is completely to blame for his death. But it was our own people that went up there to bring him back and entice him in so they could get their hands on him. He thought he was coming back on his own terms, but when he arrived at Fort Robinson they took all his horses, took all his weapons, and left him afoot. His horses were divided among the southern bands. I just can't find peace within myself with these people that hung south that they would do that to their own people. But, of course, that is a personal viewpoint.

It's at this time that Holy Bull and the remnant of the Badger Band started back. They were following the Crazy Horse Band, but they stopped off in the mountains

Four generations of descendants of battle veteran Little Warrior, a Lakota medicine man. They appreciate the sacrifice of those who died at Little Bighorn, because they know that many Lakota people would not be alive today had the attacking soldiers succeeded in destroying the village. Left to right: Rhonda Two Eagles, the personnel director at Oglala Lakota College and an instructor of Lakota history and language; her mother, Evelyn Big Owl; her daughter Monet Two Eagle–Phillips; and her newborn grandson Shane Theodore Phillips.
Eric Haase

below the Rocky Mountains. They used to say *hesta oglate,* meaning "the general area," not a particular identified place.

Holy Bull wanted to visit the grave of his twin brother. So they stopped and camped there. So he went up in the mountains, and he insisted on going alone and he didn't come down for three or four days. They finally went up and brought him back, and he was just deathly sick. They couldn't move or travel with him because he was very ill. Of course, they tried to doctor him, but he died. So they took him back in there and buried him next to his twin brother. I don't know who replaced them from there on back to Fort Robinson.

I guess most of my relatives of the Badger Band must have gotten killed because my grandmother never did say who they were. One reason was that they didn't want to be identified as hostiles for fear of retaliation or retribution. So the relatives on that side I don't know today. But every now and then I will run into someone or someone will come visiting and tell me we are related. I had a visit from a fellow from Cheyenne River one time when they used to have a Sun Dance across the creek from town, and he said, "You and I are related close." I said I didn't know. My parents never told me everybody I'm related to, so I didn't know. But he said we are. He identified himself as Red Horse, Charlie Red Horse. Later Molly Red Horse married High Hawk in Porcupine, Jim High Hawk. Molly Red Horse and Charlie were brother and sister.

Somewhere there are relatives around, but I don't know them all. I was born late to my parents and nobody deemed me important enough to tell me those things that I should really have known. So a lot of what I know I had to glean from others. Except that my father was right in the heat of the battle along the Little Bighorn. And all of that didn't come to light until after I came back from military service in 1946. I used to say if I had known all these things as a fact in 1943 when I went in, they would have paid hell getting me to pack a rifle. I would have sat in the stockade for the length of the war. It was mistreatment pure and simple. The government ought to face up to the treaties and valid agreements. That's why I keep myself involved even as old as I am. I have promised myself that before I go on a long journey that some understanding is going to be reached. Then I will be ready to go on a long journey.

They celebrate Little Bighorn today, although of our people those who go up there in commemoration of that event most of them are southern people or southern bands. Very few are the northern bands. In that I'm a little selfish in my viewpoint, because the descendants of the northern people should participate. Even now most of the celebration is done by the Crows and Arikaras. I don't know what they are celebrating, probably their defeat. I've taken a dim view of it. Bonnie (my daughter) went up there, but I said I'm not going to go because it's not being done properly and the people who should have recognition are not being identified. I do agree that most of the survivors of those turbulent years chose to be silent, just like the survivors of Wounded Knee. Even today sometimes I find it surprising when certain people are identified as descendants of Wounded Knee survivors. Because of the desire to keep quiet, to keep silent, a lot of information is lost.

My father-in-law used to tell me that from about Oglala straight across around Manderson from there north all the descendants of the northern band are living up in there. I don't know how true it is, but he's probably right.

They don't talk much about it, except that those who know each other and know that no one from the group is going to go and present himself as the only one with knowledge about it. They make sure that what they tell others among themselves stays there. So you don't hear many stories. The writers that write books, a lot of it is guesswork. Much of it comes through the Crow scouts, the Arikaras, and the white scouts that they had. Some of them saw the battle from a vantage point like Reno Hill. They tried to go and help Custer but there were just too many Indians.

The songs they sang were *"Ceyapi kola tokya, kola tokyela." "Ceyapi ah heka akicita maka mani napa winya napa pa enyacapi."* These are the songs. At those rare moments when pride hits, it sounds real good.

The Story Told by Manuel Iron Cloud

Pine Ridge

The story comes from Red Necklace, sister of my great-grandfather Eagle Bear, who was sixteen at the time of the battle. Eagle Bear said that during the fighting he came across a wounded Arikara lying on the battlefield. "Brother," the wounded scout said, "do not kill me. I have a wife and children at home waiting for me."

"If that's true," Eagle Bear answered, "then why are you here trying to harm our wives and children?" He then put his gun to the Arikara's head and killed him.

Stories Told by Oliver Red Cloud to Gerard Baker

In the last moments of the battle on Custer Hill, one of the troopers started running away. Instead of shooting him, the warriors nearby yelled, "Let him go. Let him tell what happened here. Then the soldiers will know this will be their fate, if they return." The soldier got some distance away when he had the bad luck to meet a Sioux hunter returning to the camp with a dead deer on his horse. This man had missed the battle because he was one of the men sent out to get food for the large camp. Although the Indians on the hill signaled to him to let the soldier get away, the hunter did not see their signals. As the soldier ran past him he shot and killed him with his rifle. There is a marker all by itself to the east of the battlefield and near the boundary fence. It marks the spot where this runaway soldier was killed.

Later, as the Indians returned to the Reno part of the battlefield after killing all the soldiers with Custer, some of them heard loud moaning coming from a clump of juniper bushes. Upon investigating they saw it was an Arikara scout still on his horse but impaled on a broken juniper branch that had gone through his torso at the upper part of his thigh. He was tangled up with his horse and could not free himself. When he saw the Sioux approach him, he signaled them in sign language to kill him quickly. The Sioux instead made him suffer more. They pulled his horse out from under him, and as he dangled there on the branch they shot him with arrows until he died.

Interview of Chris Eagle Hawk by Michael Her Many Horses

Michael Her Many Horses: How important is it to carry out those traditions of songs that celebrate the past military experiences of our young men?

Chris Eagle Hawk: They are slowly coming back. The ceremonies, like the one for the making of a warrior, are slowly coming back. A lot of our young men and women are going out to military service, and they have been given that ceremony. I've participated in a couple of them. There was one song that kind of like came to my mind. I was asked to sing, so I just sang that song. A lot of the older people said, "Where did you get that song?" Well, that song was always sung in Manderson way back. I had almost forgotten it. But at that ceremony, because of what was going on, it just came right back. I just brought it back, so I sang that song.

The *tokala* ("warrior") societies are important, and within my job here at Public Safety the *akicita* society has been formed. We are going to be bringing a lot of the songs back. This is for the protection of our people. The warrior has strength to accomplish those things that need to be done. There's a lot more to it than going

Chris Eagle Hawk is the lead singer for the Crazy Horse Singers drum group. The Crazy Horse Singers typically perform traditional Lakota songs at powwows, Sun Dances, and other community gatherings. In Lakota philosophy the drum is considered the heartbeat of the nation.
Eric Haase

through basic training and all that stuff. You are not just a robot, you are more of a human soldier.

Her Many Horses: What are the words to that song?

Eagle Hawk: The words to that song are *"Unci cesne ye, meish me wicasa, unci ceyesni miyesh miya winacasa. Epa ni akicita."* In English those words mean, "Grandmother, don't cry for me. Sing me a song. I am a man so this is me [names himself]. I give myself to be a warrior." The words in the song and the tone or tune of this song just fit right together to express honor, plus all these other good feelings that come with it. It just brings out a lot of feelings and not just one or two. Recently the parents of a young man going into military service asked me to sing this song for him. I could just tell from his eyes what commitment was there. He is going to be responsible and strong for what he is going to do. The willingness to sacrifice is there and the recognition that the family is always very important. He has written letters back and he is doing well, and he thanked his parents for the ceremony.

The *tokala* societies have been having their dances lately, so the old songs are coming back. This is going to take a while. These young singers are just now enjoying themselves, like we listened to rock and roll when we were young, and they are going through that phase. Maybe when they get a little older they'll pick up the old songs and go from there. In the meantime we, and people like Chub Thunder Hawk and that group, they are really preserving their songs. They are still singing them. I notice some of the younger guys are starting to record. Not the real young ones or the late teens and early twenties, but the ones that are getting into their late twenties and early thirties. They are starting to record those songs. I know that they have some knowledge, but there ought to be a teacher there to explain to them about what those words actually mean and not just the bare, straight-out translations. What happened? What is the story behind the song? That's the interpretation, that's what those songs mean. How do you share that song with your heart?

Her Many Horses: Tradition tells us that after Little Bighorn the people had to disperse because they knew that other military forces were going to be sent against them. A lot of our people went north up into Canada and others went west up into the mountains to wait and see what was going to happen, what type of retaliation there would be on the part of the soldiers after our people wiped Custer out. I know there are some songs attributed to that event or period that are sung today at practically every gathering that we have. Maybe you could explain the words and tell a little bit about what it means for us today to connect to that event.

Eagle Hawk: One of the songs that they always sing at a gathering is *kola tokiye.* The singers are asking, "My friend, where are you?" The answer is, "He hides up north." The singers then are asking him, "Where are you? We need your help." Today, when you hear that song, you look around and you are starting to see people stand up for that song. Before, nobody really knew what the song was about until the announcers started talking. When I am the announcer and I hear that song I tell the people to stand because it is the Little Bighorn song.

There are a lot of victory songs that connect to that time. I am still learning the history and the words to some of those songs. As soon as I learn them I will teach my son so that he can have them too. But for a long while there were no feelings for those kinds of songs. Everything went under then, songs, objects, even religion. Everything went underground and people just didn't want to bring them out. Even people that were at the Battle of the Little Bighorn, if they had a rifle they hid it. They wouldn't even sing the victory songs until the 1920s or 1930s. They were afraid of retaliation, of what might happen to them. You know a lot of our people were sent out to the prisons and different places like Oklahoma to be punished. Others were economically punished. They put them way out on reservations. That song, *kola tokiye*, that song really sticks out in my mind when you say "Little Bighorn." I can envision what was going on from the stories that I heard from my aunt who raised me. She was born in 1900, and she heard the stories firsthand. So she told me and my sister, Bernice White Hawk. Bernice knows some stories too. We heard stories that could make you feel like you are right there, like you are watching and seeing what is happening. The truth is a lot different than what we read in the books or see in movies. When our people sing that song, I really get the sense of being there and watching. Sometimes in my mind I feel like I am participating. You know, it is a special song to me and I really have this in my heart.

Steve Emery, a member of the Crazy Horse Singers drum group, was the last person to collect stories and songs from Little Bighorn survivors. In addition to being a traditional dancer, musician, and songwriter, he is the attorney general for the Cheyenne River Sioux tribe.
Eric Haase

Interview of Ben Black Bear, Jr., by Michael Her Many Horses

Michael Her Many Horses: We are talking about the Little Bighorn and what stories have been passed down in your family that is active here in the tribe.

Ben Black Bear, Jr.: I guess as I was growing up I wasn't really aware of these things. Not until much later on and especially after my grandmother passed away, that's when a lot of this came out. My mother said she kept a lot of articles, items that her parents had picked up at the Battle of the Little Bighorn. It was mostly just soldier items, you know, like buttons from coats or actual coats themselves or sabers or just items that they picked up on the battlefield. Bullets, whatever. Saddles, spurs, things like that. My mother said that my grandmother, her mother, had those items for the longest time, you know. They never brought them out to show to anybody or talked about them. They pretty much kept them "underground," kind of kept them covered up and in the

Following pages:
Nine survivors of the Battle of the Little Bighorn at a reunion held at the State Game Lodge, Custer State Park, South Dakota, September 2, 1948. Left to right: Little Warrior, Pemmican, Little Soldier, Iron Hail (Dewey Beard), John Sitting Bull, High Eagle, Iron Hawk, Comes Again. Inset: Nicholas Black Elk.
Bill Groethe, First Photo, Rapid City, South Dakota

Tom Conroy, Jr.'s, great-grandfather was Wasicula, later named John Conroy. After the Indian wars, John Conroy served as a scout for the U.S. Army under "Black Jack" Pershing in the Pancho Villa campaign. Tom Conroy, who is shown here holding a section of a cavalry saber that belonged to Wasicula, is a councilman for the Wakpamani district on Pine Ridge and a former director of land operations for the BIA.
Eric Haase

attic. They just never talked about them. And this was pretty much a very common practice that they didn't talk about those kinds of things. Because there was still some tension that existed, you know, even up to the present day regarding the hostilities that took place back in those times—the 1870s to 1890 and Wounded Knee (which also my great-grandfather was involved in, my grandmother's father).

She had those items for the longest time and over a period of time they started disappearing. She didn't realize that, and every once in a while she would check and something would be gone, you know. I guess that a lot of my uncles had drinking problems and they lived with her. So apparently what she had there my uncles would take and sell to a museum or someplace out there to get some money. So things kind of started vanishing a little bit at a time. She ended up with just some buttons and really small items that were left over, I think. When she passed away the relatives probably took them.

Her Many Horses: What were the names of family members who were at Little Bighorn?

Black Bear: That would be High Hawk. His name was High Hawk, and his father's name was Brown Hat or "Wapostan," who was the winter count keeper of the Brule. I don't know if Brown Hat himself was at these places, but apparently High Hawk must have been. His family and his children and relatives were associated with Crazy Horse. Crazy Horse, Two Strike, and He Dog, those people. So they all settled over here in Rosebud at the western end there at He Dog Community, Upper Cutmeat Community, Iron Shell, Hollow Horn Bear Creek, and those places.

The Story Told by Albert White Hat, Sr., to Herman J. Viola

My mother's name was Emily Hollow Horn Bear. She was born in 1893, the youngest daughter of Chief Hollow Horn Bear. Hollow Horn Bear was not in the battle. He was out scouting somewheres. However, he told my mother about it. He said in those days everybody was running. The people were scared. They were being killed. They never knew where or when it was safe. They were always fearful. Cavalry and infantry attacked our villages day or night. The people had never before known this kind of warfare.

One morning, while camped along the Little Bighorn River, scouts rode into camp yelling, "They're coming. Soldiers are coming and are going to attack." Our warriors got ready, and when the soldiers came to that river, Crazy Horse and some of his men got on their horses and pushed them back. The cavalry went back up the ridge and dug in. Before they got away, our men had captured a soldier as a witness. Two of the warriors took this witness to another hill so that he could see everything. Crazy Horse got his men ready. He told them, "Wait until I give the signal." He jumped off his horse and ran over to a molehill and grabbed a handful of loose dirt and rubbed it on himself and his horse. He got back on his horse and told the men, "Watch! Watch where the soldiers shoot!" He then rode towards the soldiers until he got in rifle range and then across in front of them. The soldiers opened fire, but no bullets hit him. When Crazy Horse got to the end of the line of soldiers, he came back. Same thing. He said to his men, "I will go one more time and when I come back, then you charge." He went again. They shot at him, but they couldn't hit him and he came back. But by then the men knew where the soldiers were shooting from. After crossing in front of the soldiers four times, Crazy Horse turned around and said, *"Hokahey!"* This is the equivalent of "Let's go!" The warriors all attacked at the same time. It didn't take very long. They went through the soldiers very fast. When the battle was over, the warriors holding the witness told him, "You have seen everything here. You go back and you tell your people what happened here and be honest about what you've seen." Then they let him loose. He never looked back. He just took off, back to wherever he came from.

About fifteen years ago, Lionel Bordeaux, the president of our college, said to me, "I just heard a story I never heard or read before." He's an older cousin who grew up in another part of the reservation. He said his grandfather told the story of the battle and he started telling me about Crazy Horse and what he did. And the story was just identical to what my mother had told me. I asked, "Was there a witness?" He said, "Yes. That was what he said."

Michael Her Many Horses is the great-grandson of Blunt Horn, who fought at Little Bighorn. Michael likes to say that Blunt Horn was a "blue-collar warrior" in the fight, meaning that he rode to the defense of the village but left his family no stories or war deeds to extol, which was probably typical of most of the young men who fought that day. Blunt Horn, who died during the great influenza epidemic of 1918, was a noted historian of Lakota history. His legacy has been continued by Michael Her Many Horses, who has taught Lakota studies at Oglala Lakota College and is also a photohistorian. Michael has been executive director of the Pine Ridge Reservation and is currently a member of the tribal council.
Eric Haase

In 1881, Red Horse, a Miniconjou chief, drew the following forty-one pictographs of the Battle of the Little Bighorn for an Army surgeon at the Cheyenne River Agency in Dakota Territory. This photograph of Red Horse was taken by David F. Barry.
National Anthropological Archives

One of the Smithsonian Institution's treasures is a set of pictograph drawings of the Battle of the Little Bighorn by a Miniconjou Lakota chief named Red Horse. Housed in the National Anthropological Archives, these remarkable drawings combine a journalist's sense of story with an artist's eye for detail. The entire set is reproduced here in full color for the first time.

Red Horse gave the forty-one drawings to assistant army surgeon Charles E. McChesney, who interviewed the warrior-artist at Cheyenne River Indian Agency in 1881. Done with colored pencils and ink on 24″ x 26″ sheets of brown manila paper, the pictographs are a Native American Bayeux Tapestry, chronicling the events of June 25, 1876. In this instance it was the invaders who were conquered, but for the free-spirited followers of Sitting Bull, the ultimate outcome was the same as for the Saxons of England.

Red Horse's powerful depictions have an epic quality. Unlike the typical ledger art of warrior-artists found in notebooks and sketchbooks, these drawings are conceived on a grander scale, providing panoramic views of the Indian encampment on the banks of the Little Bighorn, the approach of Custer's troopers, the spirited counterattack by angry Lakota and Cheyenne warriors determined to protect their homes and loved ones, and then sheet after sheet graphically portraying the excitement, the glory, and the carnage of combat. Shown here in vivid detail is the hand-to-hand struggle recalled by many of the survivors. Left to the imagination is the suffocating dust and the sounds of combat—the gunshots, the shouts, the screams of pain voiced by wounded and dying horses and humans.

Even as fighting continues, proud warriors are seen leaving the battlefield with captured cavalry horses complete with

Red Horse and the Battle Drawings

HERMAN J. VIOLA

saddles and riding gear. The horses were greatly prized, as were the saddle bags crammed with ammunition and personal belongings. Less desired were the heavy, cumbersome McClellan saddles, which the new owners immediately stripped to the bare essentials. Indeed, buckles and other pieces of metal ripped from the saddles must have littered the Indian village, because Jason Pitsch found hundreds of saddle parts during his archaeological reconnaissance of the Hunkpapa campsite. Further confirmation is provided by a Seventh Cavalry McClellan saddle later retaken from its Lakota owner by the Army. Now in the Armed Forces Collection of the Smithsonian's National Museum of American History, the McClellan saddle was transformed into a modified pad saddle with rudimentary stirrups hanging from leather thongs (see page 43).

Not all of the Custer horses became prizes of war. Many were killed, some by troopers who used them as barricades; others fell in the general melee. When non-Indians reflect on the Battle of the Little Bighorn, not much thought is given to the horses. However, for a people to whom the horse was at the core of their culture and way of life, the slain animals were an especially tragic loss. The number of horses that died at Little Bighorn is unknown, but based on the quantity of bleaching bones that littered the battlefield for years afterward, it must have been considerable. Red Horse devoted five sheets to the images of dead horses.

Red Horse also gave considerable attention to the slain soldiers and Indians. The total number of dead Indians in his drawings is 61, although he told Surgeon McChesney that 136 Indians were killed and 160 wounded. Nonetheless, his tally does not agree with those of other Indian informants. Crow King believed only 30 to 50 Indians died at Little Bighorn.

Gall claimed the death count was 43. The Cheyenne say that no more than a dozen of their warriors were killed, one of them Chief Lame White Man, who died leading a charge against the remnants of the troops with Custer.

Red Horse's depictions of the dead soldiers are confirmed by the testimony of officers and troopers who had the unpleasant task of attempting to identify the bodies. Many of the bodies were horribly mutilated, and almost all were stripped of clothing and boots.

According to Red Horse, the young men wore the clothes in their renewed attack on the troops huddled with Reno and Benteen on the bluffs across the Little Bighorn River. One of those young warriors was the Cheyenne Wooden Leg, eighteen years old at the time of the battle, who had killed a soldier early in the fighting and then wore his coat and trousers the rest of the day. Upon returning to the Cheyenne village, he later recalled, "The first person I met who took special interest in me was my mother's mother." First, Wooden Leg told her of his exploits during the fighting, then they discussed his soldier clothing. "Neither the coat nor the breeches fit me well. The arms and legs were too short for me. But she said I looked good dressed that way. I had thought so, too."

The filching of the clothing was understandable to the soldiers who came upon their slain fellows after the Indians departed, but the mutilations horrified them. Few realized that much of the mutilation was of a ritual nature, documenting for those who discovered the bodies the tribal affiliations of the killers. To non-Indians, the mutilations were the work of savages who must have delighted in torturing their victims before dispatching them, and were further evidence of the wisdom of the frontier adage "Keep the last bullet for yourself." In fact, several Lakota and Cheyenne battle veterans reported instances of soldiers killing themselves. Dr. Thomas B. Marquis, a leading authority on the battle, eventually concluded that widespread suicide among the troopers with Custer caused the destruction of his entire battalion. Marquis's theory was so controversial that no one would touch his book when he completed it in 1938. Decades passed before *Keep the Last Bullet for Yourself* (Reference Publications, 1976) found a publisher.

In addition to the drawings, McChesney recorded Red Horse's oral description of the battle, obtained through a combination of sign language and the interpretive skills of Lieutenant William Philo Clark of the Second Cavalry.

"I was a Sioux chief in the council lodge," Red Horse told the surgeon. *"My lodge was pitched in the center of the camp. The day of the attack, I and four women were a short distance from the camp, digging wild turnips. Suddenly one of the women attracted my attention to a cloud of dust rising a short distance from the camp. I soon saw that the soldiers were charging the camp. To the camp I and the women ran.*

"When I arrived, a person told me to hurry to the council lodge. The soldiers charged so quickly we could not talk. We came out of the council lodge and talked in all directions. Young men—mount horses, take guns, and go fight the soldiers. Women and children—mount horses and go.

"The day was hot. In a short time the soldiers charged the camp. The soldiers came on a trail made by the Sioux camp in moving, and crossed the Little Bighorn River above where the Sioux crossed, and attacked the lodges of the Hunkpapas farthest up the river. The women and children ran down the Little Bighorn River a short distance into the ravine. The soldiers set fire to the lodges. All the Sioux now charged the soldiers and drove them in confusion across the Little Bighorn River, which was very rapid, and several soldiers drowned in it. On a hill, the soldiers stopped, and the Sioux surrounded them.

"Among the soldiers was an officer who rode a horse with four white feet [later identified as Captain. Thomas H. French]. The Sioux have for a long time fought many brave men of different peoples, but the Sioux say this officer was the bravest man they ever fought. I don't know whether this was General Custer or not. Many of the Sioux men that I hear talking tell me it was. I saw this officer fight many times, but did not see his body. It has been told me that he was killed by a Santee Indian, who took his horse. This officer wore a large brimmed hat and deerskin coat. This officer saved the lives of many soldiers by turning his horse and covering the retreat.

"A Sioux man came and said that a different party of soldiers had all the women and children prisoners. Like a whirlwind the word went around, and the Sioux all heard it and left

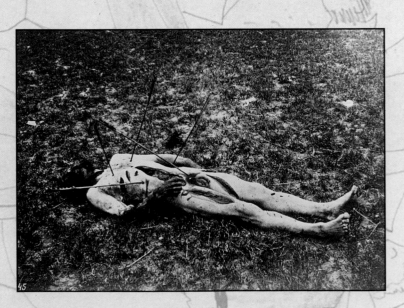

An immigrant from England, Sergeant Frederick Wyllyams, Troop G, Seventh U.S. Cavalry, was one of seven soldiers killed during a skirmish with a mixed war party of Lakota, Cheyenne, and Arapaho warriors near Fort Wallace, Kansas, on June 26, 1867. A friend who had been visiting Wyllyams at the fort took this photograph the next day, and then forwarded it to President Andrew Johnson. Although the lack of blood indicates that the ritual slashing was done after death, sights like this hardened the hearts of the frontier soldiers, who sought revenge on innocent as well as guilty Indians.
National Anthropological Archives

the soldiers on the hill and went quickly to save the women and children.

"The soldiers charged the Sioux camp about noon. The soldiers were divided, one party charging right into the camp. After driving these soldiers across the river, the Sioux charged the different soldiers below and drove them in confusion. These soldiers became foolish, many throwing away their guns and raising their hands saying, 'Sioux pity us: take us prisoners.' The Sioux did not take a single soldier prisoner, but killed all of them. None were left alive for even a few minutes. These different soldiers discharged their guns but little. I took a gun and two belts off two dead soldiers. Out of one belt, two cartridges were gone; out of the other, five.

"The Sioux took the guns and cartridges off the dead soldiers and went to the hill on which the soldiers were surrounded and fought them with the guns and cartridges of the dead soldiers. Had the soldiers not divided, I think they would have killed many Sioux.

"The different soldiers [meaning those with Custer] that the Sioux killed made five brave stands. Once the Sioux charged right in the midst of the different soldiers and scattered them all, fighting among the different soldiers hand to hand.

"One band of soldiers was in rear of the Sioux. When the band of soldiers charged, the Sioux fell back, and the Sioux and the soldiers stood facing each other. Then all the Sioux became brave and charged the soldiers. The Sioux went but a short distance before they separated and surrounded the soldiers. I could see officers riding in front of the soldiers and hear them shouting. Now the Sioux had many killed. The soldiers killed 136 and wounded 160 Sioux. The Sioux killed all these different soldiers in the ravine.

"While the different soldiers and Sioux were fighting together, the Sioux chiefs said, 'Sioux men, go watch the soldiers on the hill and prevent their joining the different soldiers.' The Sioux men took the clothing off the dead and dressed themselves in it. Among the solders were white men who were not soldiers. The Sioux dressed in the soldiers' and white men's clothing [then] fought the soldiers on the hill.

"The banks of the Little Bighorn River were high, and the Sioux killed many of the soldiers while crossing. The soldiers on the hill dug up the ground, and the soldiers and Sioux fought at long range, sometimes the Sioux charging close-up.

"The fight continued at long range until the walking soldiers came. The coming of the walking soldiers was the saving of the soldiers on the hill. Sioux cannot fight the walking soldiers, being afraid of them, so the Sioux hurriedly left.

"There are many little incidents connected with this fight, but I don't recollect them now. I don't like to talk about the fight. If I ever hear any of my people talking about it, I always walk away."

This 1877 photograph shows some of the horse bones that littered the Little Bighorn battlefield. To a people whose survival depended on mobility, the loss of Indian and cavalry horses was a major tragedy.
National Anthropological Archives

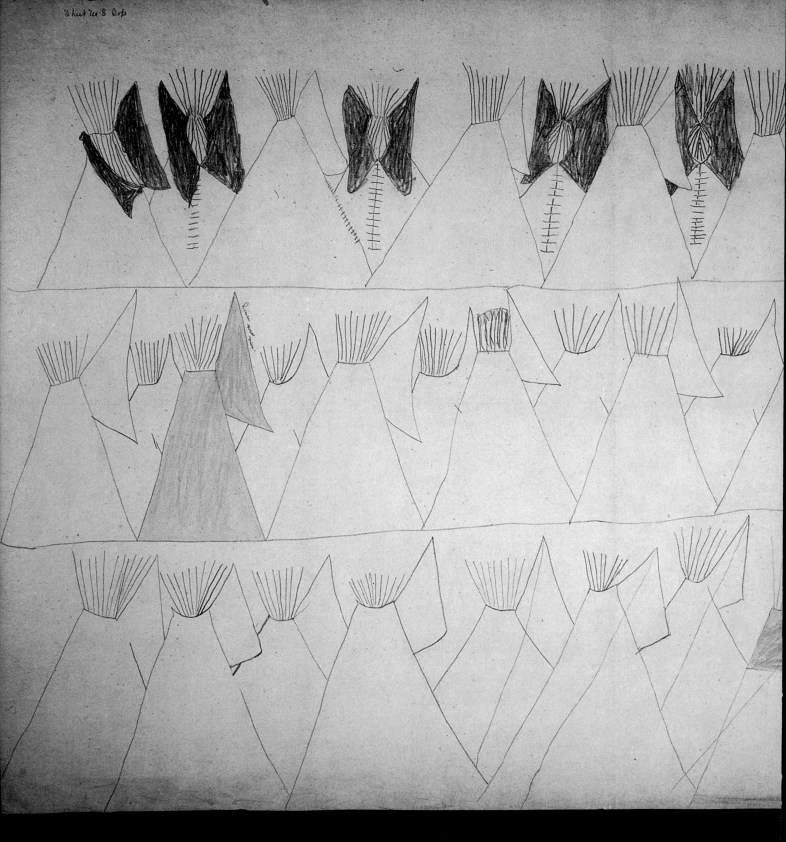

"Every one of the six separate camp circles had its open and unoccupied side toward the east. Every lodge in each of these camps was set up so that the entrance opening was at its east side. . . . Our tribal medicine tipi, containing our sacred Buffalo Head and other revered objects, was in its place at the western part of the open space enclosed by our camp circle. . . . Ours was the only tribal medicine lodge in the whole camp."

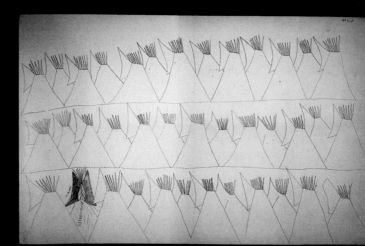

"As we came nearer, [we] could distinguish mounted men riding in every direction, some in circles, others passing back and forth. They were gathering up their ponies and also making signals. We were then at a fast walk. Soon the command was given to 'trot.' Then as little puffs of smoke were seen and the 'ping' of bullets spoke out plainly, we were ordered to charge. Some of the men began to cheer in reply to the Indians' war whoops when Major Reno shouted out, 'Stop that noise,' and once more there came the command, 'Charge!'"

—Private William O. Taylor, Seventh Cavalry

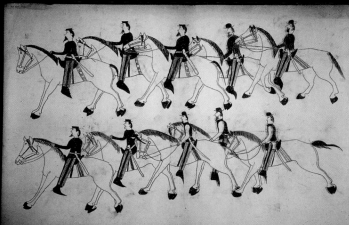

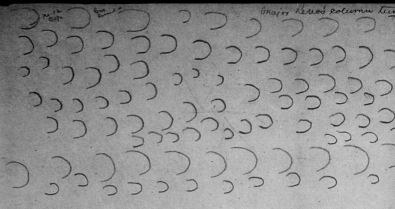

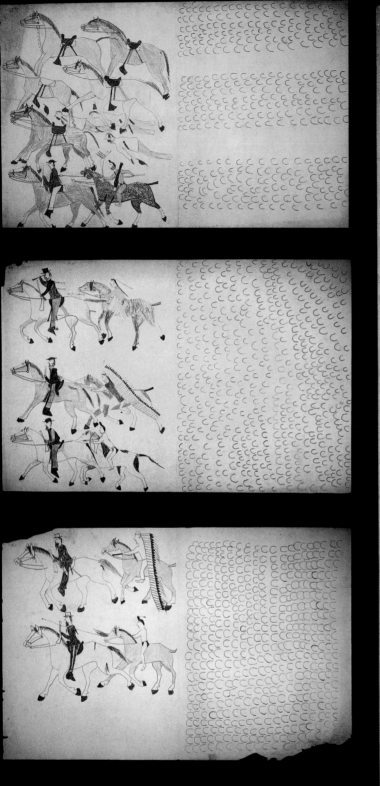

"They came on us like a thunderbolt. . . . We retreated until our men got all together, and then we charged upon them. I called to my men, 'This is a good day to die: follow me.' We massed our men, and that no man should fall back, every man whipped another man's horse and we rushed right upon them."

—Low Dog, Oglala

"Everywhere our warriors began yelling: 'Hoka Hey! Hurry! Hurry!' Then we all went up, and it got dark with dust and smoke. I could see warriors flying all around me like shadows, and the noise of all those hoofs and guns and cries was so loud it seemed quiet in there and the voices seemed to be on top of the cloud. It was like a bad dream."

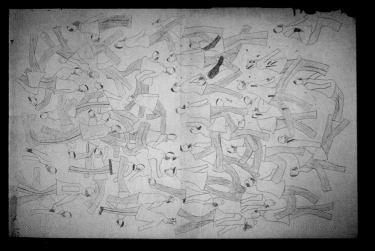

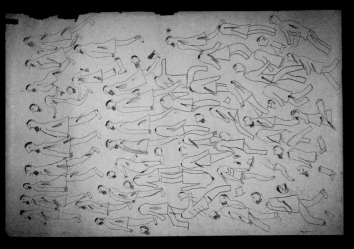

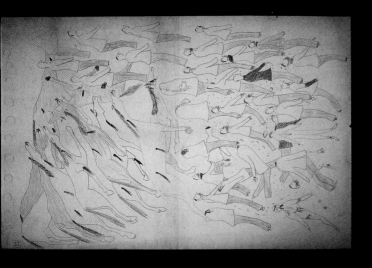

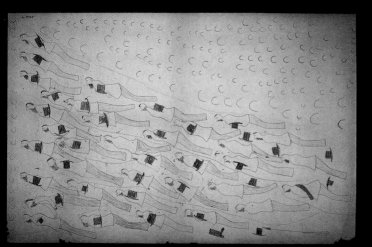

"It was a horrible sight. There the bodies lay, mostly naked, and scattered over a field maybe a half mile square. We went among them to see how many we could recognize."

—Private Charles Windolph, Seventh Cavalry

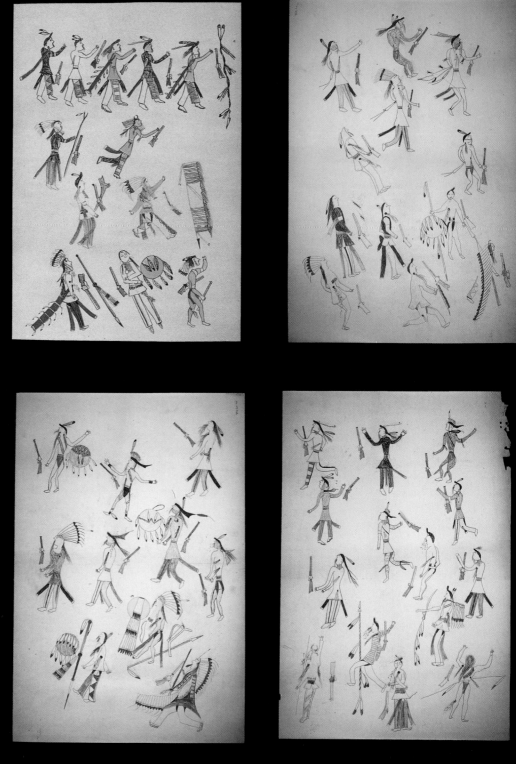

"Each warrior lost was disposed of by his women relatives and his young men friends. . . .
I accompanied the relatives of Limber Bones, one of our young men who had been killed.
We took him far back up a long coulee. We found there a small hillside cliff. Four of us young
men helped the women to clear out a sheltered cove. In there we placed the dead body, wrapped
in blankets and a buffalo robe. We piled a wall of flat stones across the front of the grave. His
mother and another woman sat down on the ground beside it to mourn for him. The rest of us

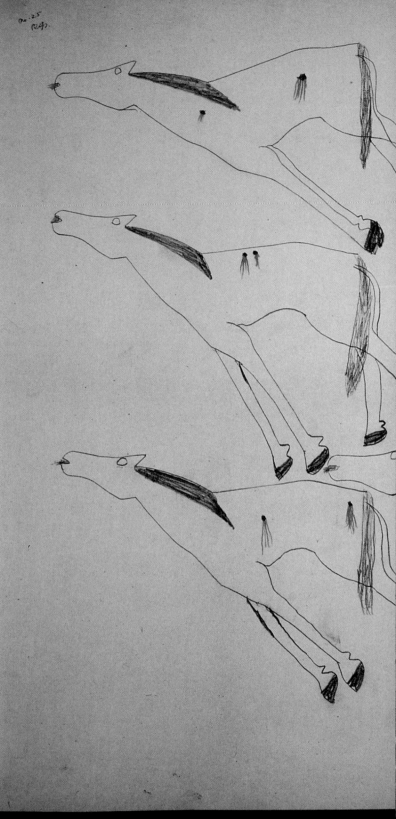

"I warned my people not to touch the spoils of the battlefield, not to take the guns and horses from the dead soldiers. Many did not heed, and it will prove a curse to this nation. Indians who set their hearts upon the goods of the white man will be at his mercy and will starve at his hands."

—Sitting Bull, Hunkpapa

Custer and His Crow Scouts

JOSEPH MEDICINE CROW

Four of Custer's Crow scouts pose among markers on the Little Bighorn battlefield, 1908. This picture and the one on page 108 were taken for Rodman Wanamaker, son of the Philadelphia department-store magnate John Wanamaker, who sponsored photographic expeditions to Indian country to document tribal life before the old ways were completely gone. The first expedition ended on the Crow Reservation, where these pictures were taken, and climaxed with the filming of a motion picture about Hiawatha. A second expedition, in 1909, involved a motion-picture reenactment of the Battle of the Little Bighorn. Shown here, left to right, are White Man Runs Him, Curley, Hairy Moccasin, and Goes Ahead. Photographer unknown.
National Anthropological Archives

My tribal enrollment name is Joseph Medicine Crow. My enrollment number is 3378. The first white people who met my people called us the Crows, but our tribal name is Absarokee, which means "Children of the Large Beaked Bird." My Crow Indian name is High Bird. I am eighty-five years old. In March 1948 I was appointed Crow tribal historian by the Crow tribal council, and I have held the position since.

My association with the Battle of the Little Bighorn and its participants is unique. In fact, I am perhaps the one living person who has had the longest period of direct association with the battlefield itself, the scholars and researchers, the journalists and filmmakers, the National Park Service personnel, the Custerphile organizations, the Crow and Cheyenne and Lakota veterans of the fight, and all the others who have come and gone over the decades and said their pieces.

My interest in the battle began as a youngster listening to the stories of White Man Runs Him, the brother of my grandmother. He had been one of the six Crow scouts with Custer at the Little Bighorn. In the Indian way, he was my grandfather. He was the longest-lived of the Crow scouts and died in my parents' home in 1927. Thanks to him, I met and befriended all but one of the Crow scouts who were at the battle. As a boy, I greatly enjoyed listening to White Man Runs Him and the others talk about their scouting for Son-of-the-Morning-Star, the Crow name for George Armstrong Custer.

White Man Runs Him—or, more accurately, Chased by a White Man—received the name from a clan uncle who had once been chased in jest by a white trader, much to the amusement of some Crow men who had witnessed the incident. In accordance with the Crow nicknaming custom, they named the man's clan nephew Chased by a White Man. He was said to be Custer's favorite of the Crow scouts. He was six feet, six inches tall, handsome, and a likable young man. After the battle he was interviewed by

more writers than the other scouts put together. He was eventually regarded as the most reliable informant about the battle.

The former scout was also known to be a person of great power. My favorite demonstration of this power occurred in June 1927 when a movie company was filming a silent western in Lodge Grass, not far from the battlefield. The movie was called *Red Raiders,* and starred Ken Maynard, a top "cowboy" celluloid hero of the time. About midday a thunderstorm suddenly came towards the set, with lightning flashing and a gale-force wind blowing. The director became very upset because the sudden storm would ruin the set and the cameras.

Henry Pretty-on-Top, the Crow man in charge of the Indian cast, saw how upset the director was becoming. He went to him and said that the tall Indian playing the head chief was a medicine man who could make the storm go the other way.

With an offer of a bonus if he could save the set, White Man Runs Him walked towards the coming storm. Then he stopped, raised his right arm high, and sang his power song. As he waved his arm to the north we could see the storm, which was now approaching with increasing velocity, suddenly swerve to our right and roar away. As a youth, White Man Runs Him had fasted and sought vision power by fasting and praying. He received the power to perform difficult feats. No doubt his "medicine" protected him during the Custer fight and it was still with him fifty-one years later.

The first written account of the Battle of the Little Bighorn was published on July 6, 1876, when the *Bismarck Tribune*'s EXTRA came off the presses with a bold headline: MASSACRED GEN. CUSTER AND 261 MEN, THE VICTIMS! That triggered a journal-

The Crow delegation to Washington, D.C., 1880. Delegates, from left to right: Old Crow, Medicine Crow (Joseph Medicine Crow's grandfather), Two Belly (standing), Long Elk, Plenty Coups, and Pretty Eagle. The three white men are, left to right, interpreter A. M. Quivly, Crow agent Augustus R. Keller, and interpreter Tom Stewart. Photograph by Charles M. Bell. *National Anthropological Archives*

istic and historical avalanche which has been blowing up a continuous storm of controversy ever since.

There is no sign of a let-up. It will go on and on. Now it is my turn. At age eighty-five I have decided to get into the Custer arena and say my piece.

First, there were visions. Many generations before the coming of Europeans, Crow prophets saw their arrival in our country. The first white man is reported to have reached the Northern Plains around 1775, but after the Lewis and Clark expedition of 1803–1804 others arrived. They came as lone adventurers or in groups as trappers and traders.

It was about that time that a Crow chief said to his people: "These men with light eyes and hairy faces are here now. . . . We can kill them off, but more will come. They are like ants. Trample them, and more will come out. My advice is that we, the Absarokee treat these 'light eyes' kindly and give them protection from other tribes. Some day they will reciprocate and be our friends. Give your daughters to them as wives. In time their children will have their blood and ours; and they will be strong and wise and grow up to be our future leaders."

From that time to this day, the prophecy and advice have been accepted and maintained. Crow chiefs kept the legacy alive as a tool of diplomacy in their dealings with white men in general and with the Great Father, the president, in particular.

In 1825, Major Benjamin O'Fallon's treaty commission came up the Missouri River. A band of Crows was in the village of the Hidatsa when the commission arrived. Chief Long Hair signed a treaty of friendship with the United States. The pledge was solemnized with both Major O'Fallon and Long Hair touching the point of a knife to their tongues. This was a sacred oath that will be kept forever!

The Crow Tribe, particularly the Many Lodges Band, took it upon themselves to provide protection and safe refuge to white trappers and traders coming into the Crow country. The white eyes often fled into Crow camps when threatened and attacked by the Blackfeet, the Lakota, and other tribes that hated them.

By the middle of the nineteenth century, Lakota intrusion into Crow territory had become more and more threatening. About 1860, the Lakota made the first serious attempt to conquer our tribe and take our homeland. The Crows were then camped on Pryor Creek and the battle is remembered as "Where the entire camp was surrounded." The sole purpose of the Lakota, Cheyenne, and Arapaho invaders was the annihilation of the Crow people. The Lakota chief in charge of the enormous war party said: "Let us kill the men but save the boys to be trained as Lakota warriors. We will marry their women and girls to raise future Lakota warriors. This we must do to become strong and able to stop the white man in his relentless pursuit of us."

The Crows prevailed in this battle and those that followed, but we paid a dreadful price in lost warriors with each victory. The Crow head chief, Sits-in-the-Middle-of-the-Land, known as Blackfoot by the whites, and his council of chieftains met often to consider the future of the tribe. They pondered what policies to pursue. When the white soldier chiefs came to ask for help against the Lakota and Cheyenne, the decision was made to join forces. Crow survival was at stake. The Crows believed then—

and still believe—that they honorably used the white men as allies in their continuing intertribal struggle with their worthy traditional enemies.

In 1876 Crow survival as a people was no longer threatened—but the Crow way of life was. As the final campaign of the U.S. Army to conquer Indian tribes still resisting reservation life came to a climax, intertribal warfare on the western plains diminished rapidly. The Lakota and the Cheyenne were now too busy fighting the *wasichus*, the white men, and could no longer provide Crow warriors with competition in the dangerous, yet sporting and essential game of Plains Indian warfare.

Unlike *wasichu* warfare, Indian warfare rarely had the object of exterminating the enemy and then controlling his territory and his society. Even winning the battle was not the overriding objective. Success was marked by "counting coup," a French word that to Plains Indian warriors meant, literally, "to touch the enemy." Simply put, it was the action of a single warrior proving his bravery against an enemy warrior. To "count coup," the warrior might kill an enemy, injure him, struggle with him, or merely touch him. Each such feat of bravery allowed the warrior to count coup. Without the chance to count coup, young Crow men could not become famous warriors or renowned chiefs.

By 1876 young Crow men were dispirited from the lack of opportunity to prove themselves in battle. That is one reason they welcomed the opportunity to go again on

The four Crow scouts in 1908 standing among the tombstones on the battlefield. Left to right: **White Man Runs Him, Hairy Moccasin, Curley, and Goes Ahead.**
National Anthropological Archives

the warpath, this time in pursuit of "hostiles," the Lakota and Cheyenne bands that refused to settle on reservations. The invitation came from General George Crook, who had marched his troops from Nebraska and established a base camp at the confluence of two small streams called Goose Creek (now Sheridan, Wyoming). In about the first week of June 1876, General Crook dispatched emissaries to Crow Agency on Mission Creek (now Livingston, Montana). Chief Blackfoot assembled his council of advisory chiefs to consider the request for Crow warriors made by Three Stars, as they called Crook. Without much hesitation, the council authorized a force of 176 warriors under the joint command of war chiefs Medicine Crow, one of my grandfathers, and Plenty Coups to join General Crook as allies, not merely as noncombatant scouts.

So on June 17, 1876, the Crow warriors rode with General Crook's forces along Rosebud Creek, where they engaged a large body of Lakota and Cheyennes who, a week later, confronted Custer at the Little Bighorn River. The Battle of the Rosebud was fought intensely but ended with few casualties. From the military tactical point of view, the result was a draw. Afterwards, however, General Crook had to move south to regroup and resupply. That meant he was out of position to be of any help to General Custer on June 25.

For Indians, the Rosebud fight had other importance. To the Lakota and the Cheyenne, it was a battle between them and the combined forces of the Crow and Shoshone warriors. (The Shoshone, like the Crow warriors, had agreed to help Crook so that they could once again count coup on their enemies and earn war honors.) To the Indian combatants, the white soldiers were just there, and they were sometimes in the way.

That day many acts of bravery were noted. Two Crow women fought as warriors and counted coup. Medicine Crow, my grandfather, had a hand-to-hand struggle with a Lakota and fatally subdued him. A transvestite named Finds-Them-and-Kills-Them counted coup. Even those who failed to count coup took pride in fighting the mighty Lakota and Cheyenne once more.

But the incident that eventually made the greatest impact on me concerned a Crow chief by the name of Bull Doesn't Fall Down. At Rosebud, he had singled out a Lakota who was wearing a flowing war chief's bonnet of eagle feathers. This man's horse had been shot, and he was on foot. Here was a worthy enemy, thought Bull Doesn't Fall Down, and he must count coup on him. The Lakota warrior in the bonnet did not stand and fight, however. Instead, he turned and ran. He did not even pause to take off his dead horse's bridle as a brave warrior was expected to do. Bull Doesn't Fall Down quickly caught up with the fleeing Lakota, but instead of killing him, he flogged him severely with a riding quirt and then let him go. This was a humiliation worse than death.

According to Lakota accounts, this embarrassing incident was especially bitter because the man was Jack Red Cloud, the young son of the great chief Red Cloud, and he had worn a war chief's bonnet that he had no right to wear. This impertinence had dismayed the Lakota warriors, especially the proven older chiefs.

Fifty years later, I was a teenage boy when Indian veterans of the Custer campaign gathered at the Little Bighorn for a reunion and celebration, and I witnessed the sequel

The fiftieth anniversary of the Battle of the Little Bighorn in 1926 brought together former friends and foes and attracted considerable media attention, including a story in the *National Geographic* magazine. This photograph, taken during the commemoration activities, shows (standing, left to right) Colonel J.M.T. Partello, White Man Runs Him, General Edward S. Godfrey, and Max Big Man. Godfrey, then a lieutenant, commanded Reno's Company K at Little Bighorn. Of Max Big Man, Joseph Medicine Crow says, "He was a clan brother of mine and was always ready to help me as a tribal historian. He was very knowledgeable about Crow history and culture. Max was tall, handsome, and always dressed in traditional Crow style. Every summer he would set up an Indian camp near the main entrance to the battlefield and stage a program of Crow Indian dances and give talks to the tourists. He was a good storyteller."
National Geographic Society

to the incident at Rosebud. By then an old man, Bull Doesn't Fall Down arose from the Crow side of the camp circle and walked briskly to the Lakota men. Suddenly, he pulled out a quirt and lightly flogged a dignified but startled Lakota man. Bull Doesn't Fall Down explained to the shocked onlookers that he was repeating what he had done to this same man at Rosebud fifty years before. During all this, Jack Red Cloud sat still and proud, displaying no sign of insult, for he was a recognized and respected Lakota chief.

After Bull Doesn't Fall Down finished his explanation, I watched him summon a man, probably a relative, who drove into the circle a team of horses in new harness and hitched to a new buggy. The buggy was loaded with fine gifts. Bull Doesn't Fall Down called upon Jack Red Cloud to come forward and receive his gifts. Jack Red Cloud shook hands with Bull Doesn't Fall Down and then said: *"Aho! Aho!"* (Thank you! Thank you!), to the warm approval of his fellow Lakotas. The Crows also regarded this as a magnificent gesture of friendship between two former enemies.

About the time of the Rosebud battle, Colonel John Gibbon, heading the U.S. Army's Montana column, was making his way eastward down the Yellowstone River to join General Alfred Terry's Dakota column then marching westward upriver. Colonel Gibbon stopped at the Crow Agency on Mission Creek and authorized Lieutenant James Bradley to enlist Crows as scouts. This time there was great reluctance. Chief Blackfoot told Lieutenant Bradley he could not afford to spare more warriors, as that would jeopardize the safety of women, children, and old people in camp nearby. He added that he had already sent 176 of his best warriors to assist General Crook.

When Lieutenant Bradley raised the promises made in the 1825 treaty, Chief Blackfoot relented somewhat and said that some warriors might go, but only as volunteers. Lieutenant Bradley signed up twenty-nine men for the combined forces of General Terry and Colonel Gibbon, along with two white men married to Crow women, Barney Bravo and Thomas Leforge. A man named Mitch Bouyer, half Lakota and half French, who was then living with his Crow wife, signed up as chief interpreter to help Bravo and Leforge. Six Crow men, ages sixteen to twenty-five, were assigned to General Custer's regiment, which marched with General Terry's command.

The six scouts who rode with Custer were: Goes Ahead, Hairy Moccasin, Curley, Half Yellow Face, White Swan, and White Man Runs Him. As a boy, I knew all those men except White Swan, who died about 1904. I often listened to my grandfather White Man Runs Him and some of the others talk about their scouting for Son-of-the-Morning-Star. They often expressed admiration for Son-of-the-Morning-Star, especially his courage. In their minds only a person of great personal courage would have attacked that huge camp filled with the dreaded enemies of the Crow and Arikara people.

Custer, in turn, was equally impressed by the Crow young men assigned to him as scouts. In his last letter to his wife, Libbie, written on June 21 just four days before his death at Little Bighorn, he noted,

> I now have some Crow scouts with me, as they are familiar with the country. They are magnificent-looking men, so much handsomer and more Indian-like than any we have ever seen, and so jolly and sportive; nothing of the gloomy, silent redman about them. They have formally given themselves to me, after the usual talk. In their speech they said they had heard that I never abandon a trail; that when my food gave out I ate mule. That was the kind of a man they wanted to fight under; they were willing to eat mule too.

The events of June 25, 1876, have produced many questions and fueled many controversies, some of then unanswerable. One of the most persistent is: Did Custer and his soldiers drink whiskey before the battle? I think there is little doubt that some officers and troopers with Custer did some drinking. Fresh evidence is provided by Lieutenant William Van Wyck Reily, who died with Custer that day (see pages 182–85). In a recently found letter to his mother written while en route to the rendezvous at Little Bighorn, he boasted of his newly learned ability to ride and declared that there was a "standing rule in the seventh that any officer thrown from his horse had to open a bucket of champagne."

Further testimony is found in a recently published account of the campaign by Private William O. Taylor of A Troop, *With Custer on the Little Bighorn*. In recalling Reno's charge, Taylor wrote:

> The Major and Lieutenant Hodgson were riding side by side a short distance in the rear of my company. As I looked back Major Reno was just taking a bottle from his

CURLEY
General Custer's Scout and only survivor of that
Horrible Massacre of 1876.

lips. He then passed it to Lieutenant Hodgson. It appeared to be a quart flask, and about half or two thirds full of an amber colored liquid. There was nothing strange about this, and yet the circumstances remained indelibly fixed in my memory. I turned my head to the front as there were other things to claim my attention. What that flask contained, and [the] effect its contents had, is not for me to say, but I have ever since had a very decided belief.

This newly found testimony supports the stories told by White Man Runs Him and Curley. It also supports similar stories told to Dr. Marquis by Cheyenne veterans of the Custer fight who reported finding canteens and bottles partially filled with whiskey after the battle. Dr. Marquis, whom I knew quite well, gave Custer the benefit of the doubt. He claimed that Custer himself did not drink and that he would not allow drinking by either his officers or his troops. Marquis admitted, however, that there was evidence of considerable drinking at Custer's last camp on the Rosebud, the evening of June 24. In fact, Black Horse and other Cheyennes traveling with Little Wolf on their way to Sitting Bull's camp found a tin cup with whiskey at the Custer campsite.

From what I have heard from the Crow scouts and their families, the troopers drank whiskey on the day of the battle. Since the scouts were all loyal to Custer and held him in high regard, they had no reason or ulterior motive to discredit him.

The late Robert Yellow Tail, once a son-in-law of White Man Runs Him, knew the old scout quite well and told me that White Man Runs Him swore up and down that the soldiers had firewater that day, contrary to the writers who claimed that Custer never drank. White Man Runs Him said that when they were coming down Dense Ashwood Creek, now called Reno Creek, they stopped to water their horses. Everyone then got some crackers and cold bacon. While they were resting, a pack train of six or eight mules came along. Each mule carried a keg on each side. These kegs were quickly unplugged, and soldiers lined up with their tin cups to receive their share. The scouts were told to go and get some for themselves.

White Man Runs Him said: "I took my canteen and almost filled it up. It tasted terrible. It was the first time I'd ever tasted firewater. They said drink it up, so I finally drank most of it. Before I got to the bottom, I was all warm, and my lips and fingertips felt numb. I felt like singing. All of the scouts drank. The soldiers were drinking, all of them. Pretty soon they started whooping it up and getting drunk."

White Man Runs Him said that the scouts then asked Mitch Bouyer: "How come they're drinking, going crazy, at a time like this?"

"Oh," Bouyer laughed, "Custer wants to make them brave."

"He sure didn't make them brave," White Man Runs Him said. "It made them crazy."

I also heard about whiskey drinking from George Curley, a grandson of Curley. I interviewed him in 1974 as part of my research to assist in the compilation of material for *Keep the Last Bullet for Yourself,* Dr. Marquis's analysis of the Custer fight; its controversial thesis was that Custer's troops panicked and many of them committed suicide.

"I recall my grandfather often telling this story," George Curley told me. "During the march up the Rosebud, my grandfather was dispatched with a message to the rear of the column. As he approached the main mule train he noticed a smaller outfit some distance back, so he went there instead. The soldiers were drinking something, and they offered him some. He thought it was coffee, but it was whiskey."

George Curley told me that his grandfather saw them again when the column stopped at Dense Ashwood Creek. "These same mules," his grandfather said, "were brought up and the kegs were opened and whiskey poured into the cups of the soldiers. We scouts joined the line and drank the 'bad water.'"

About fifty years ago, I also obtained independent verification of whiskey in the Army camp from a half-blood Crow Indian named Richard Pickett. His father, Joe Pickett, had been a trader in 1875 at Fort Benton in northern Montana. Joe Pickett was ordered to take several wagon loads of whiskey kegs to the Army camp. He loaded two eight-mule wagons with nothing but whiskey. Pickett reported that from Fort Benton he traveled all the way to the soldiers' base camp at the confluence of the Tongue and Yellowstone rivers.

As far as the Crow scouts were concerned, the evidence was overwhelming that the troopers with Custer had whiskey that day. The failure of white interviewers to accept the word of the scouts in this matter made them increasingly reluctant to talk about the battle as they grew older. Several times I saw White Man Runs Him become irritated or disgusted with interviewers when he recounted the drinking incident.

On one occasion, when I acted as his interpreter, he told me: "Tell this man I don't like him. He asks leading questions. I am tired. I am insulted. When I tell the truth, he won't listen."

Controversy also surrounds the activities of the Crow scouts before and during the battle. When the Seventh Cavalry approached the battleground on June 25, 1876, the Crow scouts were right at the front with their interpreter, Mitch Bouyer, and Custer. At some point before the attack, Custer noticed that several of the scouts had dismounted and were in the process of removing the pieces of military clothes they were wearing and putting on their traditional Crow battle regalia.

"What are they doing?" Custer asked Mitch Bouyer. When Bouyer repeated the question to the scouts, Goes Ahead got up, pointed his finger at Custer, and said in Crow to Bouyer:

"Tell this man he's crazy! He's no good. Tell him that in a very short time we are all going to be killed. I intend to go to 'the other side of the camp' dressed as a Crow warrior and not as a white man."

When Custer heard this explanation, he got very upset. He probably told Bouyer something like: "Tell those superstitious Indians to get the hell out of here! I don't want that defeatist attitude around my soldiers. We'll do the fighting, if they are afraid of the Lakota."

Evidently Mitch Bouyer softened Custer's remarks somewhat, because White Man Runs Him said that Bouyer addressed them in the Crow language to this effect: "You are fortunate! He [Custer] says you can go now. You have completed your work. Go now! Hurry! Don't stop! As for me, I cannot go. When you get home, tell my friend Leforge to take care of my wife Magpie Outside and my children." (Leforge later married Bouyer's widow and adopted his children.)

The account of the Crow scouts changing clothes was told to me in 1932 or 1933 by Frank Shively, a half-blood, then an old man in the hospital at Crow Agency. Shively said he got the story from both Goes Ahead and White Swan. I think, although White Man Runs Him never mentioned it specifically to me, that all the Crow scouts were preparing themselves for battle by changing into their Indian regalia. In fact, one of the Arikara scouts in his old age told Professor Orin Libby of North Dakota that he and other Arikara scouts had switched into their Indian regalia before going into battle, which later made it difficult for the troopers to tell friend from foe.

Just when the Crow scouts did this is unclear, but it must have been sometime before Custer divided his force into three units (see map, page 18), because Half Yellow Face and White Swan got caught up in Major Marcus Reno's attack on the Indian village. White Man Runs Him, Curley, Goes Ahead, and Hairy Moccasin rode on with Custer. By the time they reached the head of Medicine Tail Coulee, however, Curley also was also gone. (See pages 164-79 for an account of archaeological evidence regarding

The Crow warrior tradition continues to this day. At the dedication of the Plenty Coups Museum on the Crow Reservation in 1974, five veterans formed the honor guard. Left to right: Joseph Medicine Crow, who performed his war deeds—including the capture of a German horse—in World War II; Andrew Bird in the Ground, who earned the Silver Star in World War II; Kenneth Old Coyote, who earned the Bronze Star in Vietnam; Henry Medicine Crow, son of Chief Medicine Crow; and Henry Old Coyote, also a World War II veteran. *Herman J. Viola Collection*

the engagement at Medicine Tail and Big Coulees.) The accounts of White Man Runs Him, Goes Ahead, and Hairy Moccasin from the time Custer divided his troops until the charge down Medicine Tail Coulee were very similar, but once the final action began, confusion quickly set in. Each scout saw things differently. White Man Runs Him, whose account has been regarded as the most reliable, stated: "I cannot remember every detail of the fight, because there were so many things happening during the day and so much excitement that it is hard to remember little things."

Recollections of the three scouts about what happened afterward hang together in the main, but there is some confusion there too. One of them later said that they stopped with the pack horses to help a little bit, and then they took off. Another one said they were up with Major Reno's besieged regiment on a nearby hill. I do not believe that, because, if the scouts were with Reno, they could not have gotten away so easily. They would have still been there when the rescuers arrived later. Even White Man Runs Him seems to have told two stories at one point. Then, of course, later writers came along with their own ideas and theories, adding more confusion.

I think the three scouts did stay for a while until things started getting hot, and then they took off. When a soldier asked them where they were going, they said that

115

Left: White Swan in battle dress, late nineteenth century. His crippled right hand is clearly visible. Photographer unknown.
Hardin, Montana, Photo Services

Below: Proud of his accomplishments as a Crow warrior and scout for the U.S. Army, White Swan rendered a number of drawings depicting his war deeds. Reproduced here is a particularly fine example (now in the custody of the Denver Art Museum) executed in watercolor, ink, and pencil on muslin cloth, measuring 35 by 87 inches— in the lower left corner is the artist's signature glyph, a white swan. The dominant central feature is a large encampment of tipis. White Swan is shown shooting one opponent out of the saddle; he is then chased across the battlefield by enemy warriors, as indicated by a line of red footprints. Amid

a hail of bullets, he receives three wounds to his hand and leg. To the right are three vignettes: At top, he is looking through a telescope. Below, he is taken from the battlefield on a travois led by a soldier with a bugle, which indicates his pride in having been an army scout. The bottom right-hand scene shows White Swan killing a Lakota military society standard-bearer at the Little Bighorn. (According to Douglas E. Bradley, curator of the Snite Museum of Art at the University of Notre Dame and an authority on White Swan's pictographs, the scene at the top right does not relate to the Battle of the Little Bighorn. White Swan is shown wearing a winter capote, which indicates the wrong time of year, and the scouts did not have telescopes when observing the Sioux village from the Crow's Nest.)

White Swan died August 11, 1904.

they were going after water. On hearing that, several soldiers gave them empty canteens and asked the scouts to bring water back for them as well. Once away from the soldiers, however, the three scouts threw away the canteens and lit out for home.

Meanwhile, White Swan and Half Yellow Face had retreated with Reno back across the Little Bighorn River to a defensive position in a depression atop a hill overlooking the river. Later in the day, Reno's forces were bolstered by those of Lieutenant Frederick Benteen, whom Custer had sent on a scouting expedition to the south. During the action with Reno in the valley, White Swan had been severely wounded by bullets that had ripped through his right hand and into his right knee and thigh.

That day and the next were clear and hot, and the soldiers on the hill quickly ran out of drinking water. The thirst of the wounded was unbearable. The only water to be had was in the river about five hundred yards below, down a steep hillside. The Lakota and Cheyenne fired on soldiers to try to keep them from sneaking to the river to get water. Somehow, Half Yellow Face managed to reach the river several times and bring back canteens filled with cool water.

The Crow elders who told me this story—one that has never before appeared in print—said that Half Yellow Face had a special protective power than shielded him from view. Indians had such powers in those days, and he must have had such power because the Lakota sharpshooters never mentioned seeing an Indian going for water.

On one of his trips to the river, Half Yellow Face took a soldier with him to help carry the canteens, and they returned safely. After the Indian wars, this soldier received the Congressional Medal of Honor for going to the river with Half Yellow Face. The Indian's valor was ignored, of course. Apparently he was never interviewed by white historians. Next to nothing is known about his life as a reservation Crow Indian. The records of the Bureau of Indian Affairs do not even have a record of his death.

The Lakota tell a similar story. I heard it from Gerry Conroy, an eighty-three-year-old Oglala Lakota I met in June 1996 at the 120th anniversary of the battle. Conroy told the story through interpreter Vic Runnels: "I am the last living grandson of a participant in the battle that was fought here in June 1876," he said.

My grandfather was called American Boy by the Lakota and John Conroy by the white people. His father was an Irishman, and his mother was a Lakota. American Boy was eighteen years old at the time of the battle. He was one of a dozen Lakota sharpshooters assigned to prevent soldiers from going to the river for drinking water.

They would let the soldiers get to the river and fill their canteens, but when they got close to the top of the hill the sharpshooters would open up and shoot holes in the canteens. Several times this was done. On their last try the sharpshooters allowed the soldiers to carry a large pail of water right up to the top of the hill, and then they blasted it full of holes. They also killed the last soldier as he got to the top.

Apparently, the sharpshooters never saw Half Yellow Face.

But what about Curley, the youngest of the Crow scouts? White Man Runs Him, Goes Ahead, and Hairy Moccasin all later said that Curley had left earlier with some Arikara scouts who left Major Reno before his attack. That is why Curley was the first to bring out the news of what happened. After watching the final moments of the action on "Last Stand Hill" from a distant butte, Curley raced northward. In surprisingly short time he found a boat coming up the Yellowstone River and reported that Custer and his soldiers were killed.

But who killed Custer? Here are two stories.

The first one was told to me in 1965 by John B. Cummins, then the chairman of the Crow tribal council:

> David Hawley was the son of a white military officer and a Lakota woman. He was just a lad at the time of the battle on the Little Bighorn and was still a youngster when the Sitting Bull Band left the refuge in Canada and were incarcerated on a reservation in eastern Montana by 1881.
>
> David Hawley and I were third cousins as our grandmothers were sisters. . . . David's grandmother and my grandmother were sisters of Sitting Bull. Thus, Sitting Bull and Captain Cummins were brothers-in-law and good friends and professional adversaries on the battlefield.

David Hawley asked John Cummins to take him to the so-called Custer Battlefield as he had not seen it since 1909, and he was now over ninety years of age. After looking around, the aged Lakota said to John Cummins that he was now ready to break a secret pact and divulge the name of the Lakota warrior who killed Custer.

He explained that after the battle Sitting Bull had led his band and fled into the Grandmother's Land (Canada) and stayed there for several years. When it became apparent that they were to be returned to the Grandfather's Land (the United States), the people all subscribed to a sacred oath never to mention or divulge the name of the warrior who inflicted the fatal blow on Custer. David added that since all those who took the oath, including Custer's killer, were now all dead except himself, he was ready to break the silence.

He said that he was now very old and felt that he was obliged to pass the secret story on. He wanted his Crow Indian cousin to know the story. It was now his decision to tell the story or let it be forever kept in secret.

David Hawley's statement:

> When the soldiers approached the river to cross it, the Cheyenne and some Lakota counterattacked. Some soldiers fell into the swollen river and disappeared; others turned and headed for the ridge. A Lakota warrior named Spotted Antelope caught up with the soldier chief Custer, who now found himself in the rear of his fleeing soldiers, and hit him with a tomahawk. As the soldier chief tumbled off his horse, another warrior named Black Bear came and took the man's horse. As the soldier chief hit the ground, other warriors shot at him. At this point a Lakota Indian, a former hunting and drinking partner of Custer, came and took charge of the body. He rolled his friend's body in his robe and forbade anybody molesting his dead friend's body. About this time it was reported that the last group of soldiers on the hill were all killed and that the battle was over. This man then put the body of Custer on a horse and took it up the hill and left it with the last of the fallen soldiers.

The second story is by a Southern Cheyenne named Brave Bear, whose story has never been transcribed into a written document before. Three languages—English, Crow, Cheyenne, as well as Plains Indian sign language—have been used to record his account of the Battle of the Little Bighorn. It all started this way: In 1909 Rodman Wanamaker, son of the Philadelphia department-store magnate, and Joseph Kossuth Dixon, author of *The Vanishing Race*, visited the Crow reservation as part of an elaborate plan to honor the American Indian in movies and for a national memorial to be built on Lafayette Island in New York City harbor. Wanamaker sponsored what he called "The Last Great Indian Council." He not only filmed the council, but he also arranged a reenactment of the Battle of the Little Bighorn, which he filmed as well. This film, which is in the custody of the National Anthropological Archives at the Smithsonian Institution, was but the first of many film treatments.

Hosted by Chief Plenty Coups of the Crows, the event attracted many Indian veterans of the Custer fight, including Chief Brave Bear of the Southern Cheyennes, who came from Oklahoma for the gathering. Brave Bear was then about fifty-six years of age, still robust and healthy. Wanamaker wanted to learn the name of the Indian who had killed Custer, and he gave Dixon the task of finding out. The Indians wanted to please their generous hosts, so they agreed among themselves to come up with a likely candidate. The one they selected was Brave Bear. When he was named, Brave Bear told his fellow veterans that when the last group of soldiers came to the ridge where he and some other Cheyenne warriors had stationed themselves, they suddenly jumped up and fired point-blank as the soldiers tried to turn around. The soldiers tumbled off their horses, and all perished quickly. Brave Bear said that anybody's bullet could have hit Yellow Hair (another name for Custer) if he was there. Brave Bear added that he himself had never seen Custer and would not have recognized him.

One morning during the gathering of veterans, a Dr. Russell, a physician of Hardin, Montana, asked Robert Yellow Tail to help seek out the reputed killer of Custer. Russell and Yellow Tail entered the Cheyenne camp, where they were met by Fred Last Bull, a friend of my uncle's, who agreed to help. They found Brave Bear and his wife sitting in a tipi. Fred Last Bull spoke the Crow language quite fluently, so through him the visitors inquired if the chief would tell them about his role in killing the soldier chief. When Fred Last Bull repeated the question, Brave Bear replied that he had nothing to say.

Then Dr. Russell pulled out a twenty-dollar bill and tried to give it to the chief. He again refused and told Fred that this white man was trying to trick him into saying or admitting that he had killed Custer—so that the authorities could arrest and perhaps kill him.

At this point Brave Bear's wife, Walking Woman, spoke up. She chided her husband, saying: "What are you afraid of? When you were a young warrior, you fought the white man and were not afraid. You are getting old now and should not worry about dying. Besides, we need the money so we can get back to Oklahoma." She shamed him into taking the money.

The chief sat there for a while and then told Fred Last Bull that he would go to the battlefield with them. The four of them got into a buggy and stopped at the place where the soldiers had tried to ford the Little Bighorn River.

As they stood on the west bank of the river looking across, Brave Bear's reticence vanished, and he eagerly launched into his recollections of the battle:

The soldiers suddenly appeared around the bend of that coulee over there and came towards the river here at a fast trot. Our camp was close, so our warriors rushed to the river right here. Some Lakota warriors joined us. One of our elder Cheyenne chiefs hollered loudly and told us to hold our fire until the soldiers started to cross the river. He said to aim first at the soldier chief riding at the head of the column, next at the bugler who sounds the orders. He also said to shoot at the flag carrier, since the soldiers go where the flag goes.

When the soldiers splashed into the river, we opened fire with guns and arrows. Then we jumped our horses into the river and caught some soldiers milling around in the stream. Some soldiers were knocked off their horses into the fast current and disappeared. The soldiers bringing up the rear now turned and headed for the hills, and the pursuit was on. By now some Lakota had joined us.

As the soldiers retreated up the hill, an elder chief yelled at me. He instructed me to take some men and ride hard and fast northward along the east side of the river, then swing to the right and take a position where the soldiers might try to escape.

Soon we came to a ridge sloping towards the river [where the Little Bighorn Battlefield National Monument museum is now located]. We dismounted and peered over the ridge. We could plainly see a lot of action. Groups of soldiers were surrounded here and there. Then we noticed a bunch of soldiers riding desperately toward our position. When they approached us, we all jumped up in front of them and fired away. As they wheeled and milled around, pursuing warriors caught up to them from behind. In a very short time these soldiers and their horses were all dead or dying on the ground [at Last Stand Hill]. This part of the battle was over. Some warriors then headed toward the other battle over to the south [where Major Reno's forces were besieged].

Reboarding the buggy, the group of four headed for the ridge Brave Bear had described. There he pointed out the approximate place where he had taken his concealed position. He briefly repeated his description of the action. Afterward, the group returned to camp in a solemn mood. No one said very much.

"Dr. Russell was quite touched, as I was, by Chief Brave Bear's vivid account of his part in a great event," my uncle Yellow Tail told me. My uncle had come away with the impression that it was really the Cheyenne, and not the Lakota, who first met Custer and struck the final disastrous blows to him and his men.

Who, then, killed Custer? Spotted Antelope? Brave Bear? No one knows. And if someone knew, he never said, and the answer is gone.

It was my good fortune to know Brave Bear well and hear his story many times. At the fiftieth anniversary of the battle in 1926, Brave Bear, his wife, Walking Woman, and their young grandson Charlie were with the Cheyenne visitors. One afternoon, the host Crows performed the Sacred Pipe Dance. Many Crows and Cheyennes watched, and young Charlie did, too. Soon he came back running all excited and said to his grandparents that he saw his father standing there watching the dance. The grandparents looked at each other and tried to explain to Charlie that his father was no longer living. But the boy insisted and begged his grandparents to come and see.

Charlie led them directly to a Crow man. Walking Woman looked at the man, gasped, embraced the Crow man, and cried. Brave Bear was also shaken but quickly

Uniform, helmet, flag, McClellan saddle, and other memorabilia of the Seventh Cavalry.
Glen Swanson Collection

explained in sign language that he looked like their only son, who had recently died. Charlie kept looking at his father's likeness. He was happy!

The Crow man was John White Man Runs Him, my stepfather. He invited the Brave Bears to his lodge for a feast. After the meal, a Cheyenne interpreter was summoned. He informed John that Brave Bear and Walking Woman wanted to adopt him as their son to "replace" the son they had only recently lost. This was in accordance with Plains Indian tradition.

When the celebration was over, my parents took the Brave Bears to their ranch at the foot of the Bighorn Mountains some twenty-five miles southwest of Lodge Grass, Montana. They stayed with us all that summer, and every summer thereafter they would return to live with us. When little Charlie died, my brother, Arlis, and I were their only grandsons. They loved us, and we would call them grandfather and grandmother in the Cheyenne language. This made them happy!

Many Crow men liked Brave Bear and would come and visit him. They enjoyed his sign-language account of his intertribal war days. Fortunately, a half-blood Cheyenne woman married to a clan relative of ours was generally around to interpret for us. Through her, I heard many good Cheyenne stories, including the Battle of the Little Bighorn.

Grandfather Brave Bear was a kind, friendly, and wonderful man. His last summer with us was in 1931. He died in December of 1932 at his home in Oklahoma.

Grandmother Walking Woman stayed with us for the last time in 1936. Early one August morning that year, just before sunrise, I was putting my suitcase into the car. My folks were about to take me to the Billings railroad depot where I would board a train for Oregon to attend Linwood College. Walking Woman heard the activity and woke up. She came outside and asked where I was going. My mother told her.

The old woman stood there and looked at me intently for a moment. Then she stepped forward and turned me around to face east. As I stood looking across the Little Bighorn River to the horizon, she started to sing. It was a wailing song that I had never heard before. I did not know if she was singing or crying. It seemed to be a mixture of both. At the end of the song, she gave the Cheyenne woman's trill, a high-pitched wavering warble, something like birdsong.

Then she pushed me and said: "Go!"

This was the traditional way Cheyenne women sent their husbands and sons off on the warpath in the old intertribal war days. She pushed me and said: "Go!"

I can still hear her voice to this day. When I got discouraged at college and was ready to quit and return to the reservation, I would remember that my Cheyenne grandmother sent me off as a warrior. I would remember, and I would try again. That memory kept me going through all my school days, and it gave me encouragement even during my duty in Europe as a rifleman in World War II. I could almost feel that dear old lady singing and crying like the day it happened, but I never expected to hear it again.

In June 1996, I was back in school at the University of Montana in Missoula to receive an honorary doctoral degree. The big field house was packed. The candidates for graduation sat in chairs on the floor, and their families were in the bleachers. The students wore the traditional academic black mortarboard caps, but I saw one Indian boy wearing a war bonnet over his black gown.

After the college president handed me my degree and the crowd applauded, I heard that trilling sound of my grandmother again. Four times it sounded. I thought it must be Walking Woman's ghost!

When the ceremony was over an Indian woman came up to me.

"Did you hear me?" she asked, smiling.

"Were you the one who did that trilling?" I asked.

"Yes," she said, and she walked away.

The Crow Scouts After Little Bighorn

JOSEPH MEDICINE CROW

Six of the twenty-nine Crow warriors who volunteered for scout duty with the combined forces of Generals Terry and Gibbon were assigned to Custer as scouts. These young men, aged sixteen to twenty-five, were Goes Ahead, Hairy Moccasin, Curley, Half Yellow Face, White Swan, and White Man Runs Him, my grandfather. I knew all of these men well except White Swan, who died about 1904 before I was born, and Hairy Moccasin (1854-1922), who I think was married to the mother-in-law of Moccasin, a half brother of my grandfather Yellow Tail. They would take sweat baths together and tell stories. But I do not recall any of his stories about the battle.

White Swan (1851-1904)

White Swan, at twenty-five, was the oldest of the six. He was also the first of the scouts to die. Although no interviews with White Swan are known to be extant, he did leave a pictorial record of his activities in the battle. These, and a drawing by Curley at the Karl May Museum in Radebeul, Germany, are the only drawings of the Custer fight known from the Crow and Arikara scouts.

White Swan's pictorial legacy includes four large pieces of muslin featuring from five to thirteen vignettes, three tanned hides with several vignettes, and individual scenes on six sheets of brown paper which he gave to the artist and naturalist Ernest Thompson Seton, who visited Crow Agency in August 1897. Most—but not all—of White Swan's drawings depict his activities at Little Bighorn. The fact that the former scout was deaf and dumb during his declining years and wanted people to know of his exploits at Little Bighorn may explain why he made the drawings.

Indeed, there is no doubt White Swan was in the thick of the fighting. During the Reno phase of the battle, a bullet tore his right hand apart. He was also shot in the right thigh and knee and whacked in the head by a Sioux war club. Although he eventually returned to active duty as a scout, the injuries caused him serious difficulty in his declining years.

Dan Old Elk, grandson of Curley, heading for the Crow Fair Parade on his prized horse, which features a medicine hat—its ears and crown are a solid color. Tied around its neck is the horse-medicine amulet that belonged to Curley and to which Dan attributes his success as a horse breeder.
Glen Swanson

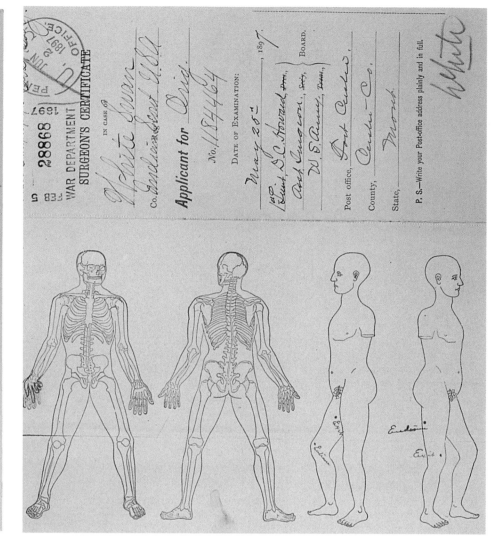

Documents found in White Swan's personnel file in the National Archives of the United States. The two bullet wounds in his right leg are clearly marked, as is the severe injury to his right hand.
National Archives and Records Administration

According to Seton's wife,

the first picturesque figure to catch our eye [upon arriving at Crow Agency] was White Swan, or, to be more accurate, what is left of White Swan after the Custer battle; for now he is chiefly memories and one sound leg. He has, to be sure, a bullet-shattered right arm and two remaining limbs semi-paralyzed, which in his portraits of himself, he very properly disregards. White Swan has passed from a great brave in wartime, to being the chronicler of his tribe in peace.

Artist Elbridge A. Burbank, who painted a portrait of White Swan at this time, left a similar description. The former Custer scout, Burbank wrote, "was deaf and dumb, the affliction having been caused by the blow of a Sioux who had struck him over the head with a war club during the battle. So White Swan had to tell [me] about the Custer fight in the sign language and by drawing rude pictures illustrating features of the battle."

White Swan's infirmities are documented in his pension file in the National Archives. According to his "Declaration for Original Invalid Pension," White Swan suffered from the following disabilities incurred at Little Bighorn: "gunshot wound of right hand & wrist, right thigh and knee and deafness of both ears." The deafness was caused "by being beaten over the head after being found wounded." White Swan's claim for an invalid pension was endorsed by the commanding officer of Fort Custer, Montana, who wrote: "His right hand is entirely disabled by a bullet wound received in . . . [the Custer] campaign; it does not require professional skill to see this; he also received other wounds in the same campaign. He is a very needy and deserving Indian. . . . [I]f any case deserves to be advanced, this one does."

The White Swan drawing reproduced here (see pages 116-17) is in the custody of the Denver Museum of Art. The upper right vignette shows him looking at a large Sioux village with a telescope. Since it is not known that the Crow scouts had telescopes at Little Bighorn, this scene may represent another incident in White Swan's extensive scouting career. The other vignettes are presumably from the Custer fight. Those to the left of the village show White Swan shooting a Sioux warrior and then, after being chased by other Sioux, falling under a hail of bullets which result in wounds to his hand and leg. To the right of the village a soldier is shown taking the wounded scout from the battlefield on a travois.

Of the six Crow scouts with Custer, White Swan is the least known even among his own people. The Crow believe he was evacuated to St. Louis for medical treatment where he remained for some time. When he returned to the Crow Reservation, he did not talk much about his stay in St. Louis or his scouting. The fact that he had made drawings of his war deeds was unknown to me until I received a letter in the 1980s from Douglas E. Bradley, curator of the Snite Museum of Art at Notre Dame University, claiming to have located a pictograph robe made by White Swan, showing his many war deeds. I asked my uncle, Robert Yellow Tail, then in his late eighties, about this. Yellow Tail said White Swan was neither a warrior nor an artist. His only claim as a warrior was his role as one of Custer's Crow scouts. Besides, how could he draw with his deformed hand? At the time, I decided that Bradley had somehow confused White Swan with a Dakota of the same name who had made a fine pictograph painted robe depicting many battle scenes with soldiers.

I have my own unusual story about White Swan. In 1933, when I was a counselor at a Newark, New Jersey, youth summer camp called Camp Wawayanda, one of the boys asked me if I had ever heard of a Crow Indian by the name of White Swan. To my amazement, this white boy said that he was a grandson of White Swan. He told me White Swan had been a patient in a military hospital in St Louis in the summer of 1876. There he met a nurse, or a woman employee of the hospital, and they became lovers. Later, after White Swan left, a son was born, the father of the camper. Apparently White Swan never knew about the son he fathered in St. Louis. I should have asked the camper for more information but failed to do so. I was not interested in Crow Indian history at the time.

White Man Runs Him (ca. 1856-1929)

White Man Runs Him, the son of Chief Bull Chief and Offers-Her-Only-Child, was my stepgrandfather. His given name was White Buffalo Turning Around. At age ten the name of White Man Runs Him—or, more accurately, Chased by a White Man—was given to this boy in accordance with Crow nicknaming custom. The boy's clan uncle was once chased by a white trapper, apparently as a joke, much to the amusement of some Crow men. These men thereupon bestowed upon the man's clan nephew the appellation Chased by a White Man, or White Man Runs Him. He made this a famous name!

White Man Runs Him fasted and sought vision power several times in his youth. He was given power to perform difficult feats. No doubt his "medicine" protected him at the Battle of the Little Bighorn.

This young man, after his service with the U.S. military, traveled around visiting various Indian tribes. He stayed with the Flatheads for a while, married, and had a daughter. To this day, he has descendants living on the Flathead Reservation in north-western Montana. Later, he visited the Hidatsa in North Dakota and again married a woman. He had a daughter called Bachua Tapash, or "Saurvis Berries." Today there are many of his descendants in North Dakota who often come to visit their relatives on the Crow Reservation.

Goes Ahead (1859-1919)

I knew and remember Goes Ahead quite well. His daughter, Helen, was married to my granduncle George W. Hogan. Whenever my grandparents would go to Crow Agency, twenty-five miles away, we would stop at the ranch of Goes Ahead, which was located about halfway between Lodge Grass and Crow Agency. This man and my grandfather Yellow Tail would often take sweat baths together and visit. During these occasions, many good stories were told. His military service as a scout for Custer was well told by his widow, Pretty Shield, in Frank Linderman's book *Pretty Shield, Medicine Woman of the Crow.*

When the agency for the Crow Reservation was established in the Little Bighorn valley in 1884, the Indian Agent Henry L. Williamson required all men to select homesteads and start farming. There was nothing else to do; the hunting days were over. Goes Ahead selected the confluence of Nest Creek and the Little Bighorn River for his homestead. It was about six miles south of the battlefield. He was industrious, raising cattle and horses. He also raised garden produce as well as wheat and oats.

Lawrence C. Wilson, Sr., great-grandson of Goes Ahead, holding the scout's eagle-wing fan. Wilson's Crow name is Man-with-Belt.
Glen Swanson

Goes Ahead liked farming and would refuse offers of help by the young men of the neighborhood, saying that while he was healthy and strong, he would rather work by himself. He was a good farmer and he must also have been a good carpenter because he built a sturdy bungalow near the river that was sort of a retreat for him. After his death, a grandson sold this structure to a neighboring white man and it is still in use as a tool shed.

Goes Ahead was a gentle and quiet man, always kind to all, especially children. His many grandchildren loved him and would gather around him to hear stories. He taught them to be well-behaved.

As a teenager, he fasted on Where-Eagles-Sit, a high hill forming the southernmost tip of the Wolf Mountains. This hill is approximately six thousand feet high and is near the present town of Ranchester, Wyoming. The Crows still regard this high hill as sacred. However, at that time a large one-eyed snake resided there and threatened to attack any Crow young men who went to the hill to fast. Many became frightened and fled, but those who stayed generally received powerful blessings. They became good warriors and eventually great chiefs or medicine men.

Ivan L. Wilson, great great grandson of Goes Ahead, holding the scout's wolf pelt and eagle-claw amulet. Wilson's Crow name is Child of the Stars.
Glen Swanson

Goes Ahead fasted there. On the second night, a strange being appeared to him in a vision and said, "You have come here seeking a gift of power. Your wish is granted." The being then handed him some objects. "Use this pipe, this red paint, and this yellow paint to heal the sick and perform miracles." This is the way Indians got their power in those days. They did not just grab any old paint. It had to be given to them by sacred beings. He got these three things to use from this special being. Goes Ahead was just a young man then. When he volunteered to scout for the U.S. military, he did so with faith that his "medicine" would protect him all the way.

Goes Ahead made a horse medicine, an amulet, which he would tie around his horse's neck to give it stamina and speed. No doubt his horse wore this while Goes Ahead rode with Son-of-the-Morning-Star. Goes Ahead gave this horse medicine to his oldest son before he died. To a grandson he gave an eagle's claw with power to search and hunt. The grandson became an expert rifle shot and a great hunter. He also used the eagle's claw in hand games with great success. These sacred objects are still kept by their families.

A third power gift Goes Ahead received was a snake medicine that could cure rattlesnake bites. This power was represented by a drawing of a snake with wings painted on a slab of wood. It was said that when Custer rode down Dense Ashwood Creek (now called Reno Creek) toward the Indian camp, Goes Ahead stopped long enough to draw this snake symbol on a large cottonwood tree. It could be seen long after the battle until the tree fell and rotted away.

Not long before his death, Goes Ahead accepted the Christian faith by joining the Congregational Church in Crow Agency. At his baptism he gave the snake medicine bundle to the minister for disposal. Two or three other old-timers who joined the church at the same time also gave their medicine bundles to the minister, who piled them on a robe on the ground. A secondhand dealer named A. G. Carter was there. He was always picking things up. He asked the minister if he could have the things the old men were throwing away. "Help yourself," he was told. What Carter did not take was thrown into the Little Bighorn River. Carter may have gotten that snake board, and it is now in some museum or a private collection, or it ended up in the river. No one knows.

Anyhow, from that time until his death in 1919, Goes Ahead always carried the large black Bible he got that day. He took it to church with him every Sunday and everywhere else he went, even though he could not read it. He probably transferred his dependence on his medicine bundle to that Bible. When he died, his family put the Bible in the casket with him.

Crow scout Goes Ahead, who died on May 31, 1919, is buried in the cemetery at the Little Bighorn Battlefield National Monument. Also buried there are fellow scouts White Swan, Curley, and White Man Runs Him, as well as Thomas B. Marquis and Marcus Reno.
David Jeffery

Half Yellow Face (probably late 1850s to early 1920s)

Half Yellow Face and White Swan somehow got separated from the other four Crow scouts with Custer and joined Reno. Despite his serious wounds, White Swan made it to the top of the hill where the soldiers formed their defense. Whereas the other Crow scouts were subjected to repeated interviews by writers and historians, White Swan and Half Yellow Face were ignored or overlooked. The Bureau of Indian Affairs does not even have a record of Half Yellow Face's death.

Shi-shia (Curley) (1858-1923)

At age sixteen, Curley was the youngest of the six Crow scouts with Custer. White Swan, the oldest scout, looked after the youngster. Custer also took a liking to him. Perhaps more has been written about this young scout than all the others put together. Because he happened to be the first person to report Custer's defeat, writers made up all sorts of stories about him. One particularly silly story had him trying to help Custer escape death by giving him a Sioux blanket to wear. He was quoted and misquoted, praised and condemned. He remains one of the most controversial figures from that battle.

Despite his notoriety, Curley tried to live quietly on the Crow Reservation. In 1884, the Crow Agency was moved from the Stillwater River to the Little Bighorn River. At first, Curley joined the Indian agent's police force. Later he was appointed a judge. The agent used the Indian police mainly to enforce his orders, which were often harsh and difficult to obey. The Crow people regarded the Indian police as cruel and guilty of excessive brutality.

Curley soon resigned from his position as a judge in the police force and established a homestead along the Little Bighorn River, just west of the battlefield, about one mile from Custer Hill. His first house was the log cabin which had served as the agent's jail. A new jail had been built, and the cabin was given to Curley. Later, he built a frame house which still stands. His log cabin was purchased by a man from Cody, Wyoming, who moved it there where it is part of a tourist attraction called the Old Trail's Museum, a "frontier town." Curley's cabin is a major attraction in this outdoor museum. It is furnished just as it was the day Curley passed away.

As a rancher, Curley raised a large herd of pintos that were in demand as parade horses. He developed a distinctive line of horses that had black ears regardless of body color. He also raised hay for his horses, farmed, and grew garden produce.

Like other Crow teenage boys aspiring to become brave warriors and perhaps renowned chiefs, Curley had fasted to gain power, or medicine, from the supernaturals. Like the other scouts, he was confident and not afraid to carry out his assignments from Son-of-the-Morning-Star. Like Goes Ahead, he too used an amulet for his horse to give it agility, stamina, and speed.

Dan Old Elk tying Curley's amulet around the neck of one of his horses.
Glen Swanson

After watching the final moments of the action on Custer Hill from a distant butte, Curley raced northward. In surprisingly short time, he found the boat coming up the Yellowstone River and reported that Custer and all his soldiers were killed.

No doubt his horse medicine gave Curley's horse the strength to start from Rosebud Creek early on the morning of June 25, go up to the Crow's Nest and then down the Dense Ashwood Creek to the Little Bighorn, and then later go from the battlefield to the Yellowstone River all in one day and part of the night, covering a distance of nearly two hundred miles of rough terrain during one of the hottest days of summer. Remember, this scout was only sixteen years old at the time: He was a superboy!

Curley received a soldier's funeral when he died on May 22, 1923. He is buried in the battlefield cemetery. Today, Curley's descendants, the Old Elks, are prominent in Crow life. His grandson Dan Old Elk still has Curley's horse amulet.

Whenever these men were interviewed about the battle, they always reminded questioners that in being assigned to Custer, it was understood that their mission was to lead the cavalry to the enemy camp. After that, the soldiers were to do the fighting. Their job would be finished at that time.

Why the Arikara Fought for Custer and the Seventh Cavalry

MELFINE FOX EVERETT

Custer in a characteristic pose that played up to his romantic image: dressed in buckskins, lounging before his tent, hunting hounds at his feet, surrounded by his scouts. Kneeling and pointing to the map is the Arikara scout Bloody Knife, who was killed at Reno's side fighting in the Little Bighorn Valley. Standing in the doorway is the Arikara scout Goose, who was wounded in the battle. The other two scouts remain unidentified. This photograph was taken during the 1874 Black Hills Expedition.
Glen Swanson Collection

lthough we are known as the Arikara, the name we call ourselves is the Sahnish. In the early days, our people were a large, sedentary tribe who built earth lodges and practiced a well-developed agriculture. They cultivated at least twelve varieties of corn, which they grew in large fields. They were the only tribe living on the Northern Plains known to grow melons. Other crops grown were beans, squash (including a large grayish Arikara variety), sunflowers, and tobacco. They lived in the same area for several years, usually until the soil in the fields was no longer fertile.

At one time numbering close to thirty thousand people, the tribe consisted of twelve bands that traveled in distinct groups. Each group had its place and job to do. They traveled together, and when they settled, they separated into four large villages. As they were a very large tribe, they were able to take care of themselves and live in peace most of the time.

Still, warfare was an important part of life. The Sahnish fortified their villages with barricades for protection. Young men were expected to go on the warpath to right wrongs done to the tribe, to rescue their people who had been taken in raids, and especially to gain prestige and earn recognition as honest, strong, responsible, and worthy members of the tribe.

Before contact with the white man, the Arikara had nothing to fear from enemy tribes. However, after coming into contact with the white people, the Sahnish were invaded with foreign diseases: pneumonia, dysentery, and the greatest killer of all, smallpox. The Sahnish people had no previous experience with this disease and consequently had not developed any kind of resistance to it. Repeated epidemics of smallpox were to be the downfall of the Sahnish. Thousands upon thousands of our people were dead within a week after contact with a diseased person on the steamboat *St. Peter.* When whole families died during these outbreaks, knowledge of medicines and our religious ceremonies disappeared with them. Our culture, as we knew it, was erased

133

from the face of the earth. Tragic loss of life was followed by tribal relocation. After the first outbreak of smallpox in 1781, there were only three villages left. Survivors who followed the teachings of their sacred bundles began to move westward along the Missouri River. Always they moved westward. They kept moving until they came to a land where they could live and never have to move again. What was left of the people gathered together into one village. The wise old Chief White Shield said: "It has been prophesied that a people of different skin color would be coming and would change our ways of living. They are here now, so we will have to learn to live with them and learn their language, go to school, so we can live in their world. We know that our way of life will be gone." But the chief also said to the people: "Do not forget that you are Sahnish and the Sahnish way."

Arikara relations with the U.S. government began in 1825 and culminated in the treaties of 1851 and 1866. These treaties placed the tribe on the Fort Berthold

Fort Abraham Lincoln, Dakota Territory. On June 14, 1872, a temporary camp named Fort McKeen was built on the west bank of the Missouri River, near the present site of Bismarck, North Dakota, to protect construction crews of the Northern Pacific Railroad. A few months later it was moved five miles away, and in November 1872 it was renamed for the assassinated president. In June 1873, it became a cavalry and infantry post with a complement of 655 soldiers. The Army abandoned the post in 1891.
Glen Swanson Collection

Reservation and required them to lay down their weapons. The chiefs of the Arikara were true to their word and handed all arms in to the Army post. Thus began a very hard time for the Arikara people. The men did not have weapons to provide food for their families, but the rations that were promised did not come, or the traders took the food before it was distributed to the people. Many children and old people starved to death or got sick because of the lack of healing plants that our medicine people had formerly been able to gather out on the prairies. Now they were required to stay on the reservation.

The treaties also left the Arikaras nearly defenseless. The people tried to live in peace with their old enemy the Sioux (Dakota), but the Sioux took advantage of the situation and would come on horseback and raid the villages and gardens, killing and stealing the women and children. The men were usually out hunting for game, which was scarce, when the Dakota ransacked the villages. The Dakota were well armed, while the Arikara had few guns. Many of the young Arikara warriors wanted to go out and fight, but Chiefs White Shield and Son of the Star would say, "We made our mark, and we have to keep our word."

Our oral historians tell of many desperate fights with our Sioux enemies, who were always lurking around waiting for an opportunity to attack. For example, one day the Sahnish people saw four lone riders on a hill overlooking our villages. They were turning their horses in a sign of challenge. Suddenly, five hundred Sioux warriors swarmed out of the nearby ravines in a wild dash. Following them were a hundred women thinking they would soon be enjoying a victory dance, but they were mistaken. Out of the threatened village rushed our warriors. Even though greatly outnumbered and poorly armed, they were able to stop the Sioux charge.

During a lull in the fighting, Chief White Shield rode onto the battlefield between the two lines of warriors. Prancing his horse back and forth before the enemy, he challenged them. "I am an old man," he yelled. "My teeth are bad. I can't eat corn. I am ready to die. Will my enemy meet me? Will my enemy come?"

As soon as the old Sahnish chief returned to his men, the Sioux made another furious charge. Again our warriors turned them back after terrific fighting. This time the Sioux had enough, and they ran for the shelter of the nearby hills. Before the Sahnish warriors could give chase, however, a torrent of rain and hail began to fall from an almost cloudless sky. White Shield shouted, "Wait, my men, wait! The *neshanu* [Chief Above] warns us to let our enemy go." This act of mercy persuaded the enemy not to kill our wounded.

Although we often prevailed, the situation became so unbearable that Son of the Star took a delegation of chiefs and warriors to Washington, D.C., to ask for assistance. Son of the Star said, "Before, we were able to go out of the village to fight the enemy, and we were able to keep them away. Even though we were a small tribe we could defend ourselves. Now, because of the treaty, we cannot do that. Now we need your help." In response, the government built Fort Stevenson in 1867 and sent soldiers to protect both whites and Indians. The fort remained in operation until 1883.

In 1876, the government asked Chiefs White Shield and Son of the Star if they had warriors who could join the cavalry and help find the hostile Sioux. Son of the Star

Red Bear

Curly Head

Little Sioux

Boy Chief

One Feather

Strikes Two

Sitting Bear

Soldier

Red Star

Running Wolf

Young Hawk

An Indian Wars Service Medal.
Armed Forces History Division,
National Museum of American History

said, "Yes, we do." In fact, our young men were eager to be scouts for the Army. They were glad once again to fight our traditional enemies and earn a name for themselves by performing warrior deeds and proving themselves worthy men.

Our warriors had become tired of their confinement within the reservation boundaries. They looked back to the times when they had the freedom to travel widely over the prairies seeking food and new soil for planting crops. Their villages had become depressing places in which to live. Their children and wives were often hungry and ill-clothed, especially during the long, freezing winters. Many elders and babies died each winter because of improper medical attention and poor living conditions. The rations promised to the Sahnish by the government were either inadequate or spoiled. Our once proud, industrious warriors saw this going on all about them and were helpless to do anything about it. Their families were in great need. That is why so many Arikara warriors willingly accepted the offer to join the Army in its fight against the Sioux. The men would not only get paid for their work and thereby support their families, but also they would once again be able to count coup against their traditional enemies.

The scouts enlisted for six months at a time. They served at Fort Stevenson, Fort Buford, and Fort Lincoln. At least 159 Arikara warriors served as scouts at one time or another between 1867 and 1883.

Arikara scouts were with Custer when he led the Yellowstone Expedition to the Black Hills in 1874. They were with the party that discovered gold. They saw the shiny metal and played with it in their hands, but they did not know its importance. The government people with the Black Hills Expedition told the scouts it was very valuable and warned them not to tell anyone about it. Our relatives on the expedition were told the gold would be packed in buckskin bags and sent to the Great Father in Washington where it would be kept there for them until they got home. The gold was never heard of again.

The Sioux knew we were helping the Army, and it worried them. Probably no one reading this is aware that Sitting Bull himself was part Arikara. His mother was a captured Arikara. In 1874 he sent able delegates to the Fort Berthold Reservation asking that the Sahnish break off their alliance with the U.S. government and join his Dakota confederacy. He made similar efforts to get the Crows into his alliance. His delegates told our people: "You have the key to the door. You can trail us, but the soldiers can't. You can tell the soldiers how to conquer us. If you will join with us, we do not fear the white man. With you to help us, we can hold the land guaranteed to us by the treaty of 1868 and you shall have all you want of this land."

Our chiefs were honor-bound to keep their word to stay on the reservation and not take up arms against the United States. Our tribe was of such a small number now, our leaders knew we would be unable to overcome the great hordes of white people coming into our country. The Sahnish prophets had predicted that strangers would come from the east "like a great wind." That is why, when the Army came again to seek our help for the Sioux campaign of 1876, Arikara warriors went to Fort Lincoln and enlisted.

Forty-one scouts left Fort Lincoln with Custer. Thirty-seven were Arikara and four were Sioux married to Arikara women (see the list of names on page 142). Our warriors scouted ahead of the troops and also supplied them with fresh meat. At Powder River the Army established a base camp. Several of the scouts were left there with the infantry troops assigned to guard the supplies at this camp. Running Wolf, Scabby Wolf, and Black Porcupine were some of those left at the base camp. They were couriers.

As part of their agreement with the Army, the scouts were to provide their own horses. Just before the troops set out from their camp at Powder River in what was expected to be a forced march against the Sioux, Custer announced that he would personally inspect the horse of each scout to make sure it could make the trip and not break down. Black Porcupine told of Custer looking at Howling Wolf's horse and making an unhappy face. The horse was in poor shape and had a large sore spot on its back. "See that gall on his back, it's as large as my hand," Custer said. Howling Wolf wanted to go so badly with the soldiers that he tried to argue with Custer. "You see," he told Custer, "the spot is behind the saddle. It is natural to him and was there when he was born. See, he is sound under the saddle. He can outtravel any horse but yours, and if he fails, I promise you I will keep up on foot."

Custer laughed. He did not believe him, but Howling Wolf was not lying. He knew he could keep his promise. Howling Wolf was known for his fast running and strong lungs. In fact, many of our warriors were able to do this. Once, during a battle with the enemy, Black Porcupine's horse was killed from under him. Howling Wolf rode up to him on his horse and said, "Brother [they were cousins], take my horse and I'll go on foot." Black Porcupine did as he was told, and Howling Wolf was able to keep up with the running horse. Howling Wolf knew he could keep up with the soldiers, so he was allowed to go.

Custer told the Arikara scouts not to fight. His orders to them were just to get the Sioux horses and run them off. Despite those orders, many of the scouts fought during the Battle of the Little Bighorn, and three of them lost their lives: Bloody Knife, Bobtailed Bull, and Little Brave (also known as Bear Trail). Another scout—Goose— was shot in the hand. Bobtailed Bull especially distinguished himself that day. Seeing the man carrying the flag go down, he grabbed the flag. He did not let the flag touch the ground. He took the flag and planted it up a hillside. The scouts knew the flag represented their country, and they protected it.

The Arikara scouts had been told that after the battle, no matter what happened, they were to return to a designated meeting place, which they did with a herd of horses. From there the scouts returned to Fort Lincoln. Most of them were then discharged and sent home.

Despite their willingness to help the Army and their valuable service that day, the Arikara scouts became the forgotten warriors of the Battle of the Little Bighorn. Not until many years had passed did anyone ask the scouts to talk about their part in the battle or to tell how they performed their duty to the United States. By then, most of the scouts had died and the others were old men.

In August 1912, nine survivors of the Arikara scouts who served in the Little Bighorn campaign met at the home of Bear's Belly on the Fort Berthold Reservation. The scouts still alive in 1912 were Boy Chief, Little Sioux, One Feather, Red Bear, Red

Bobtailed Bull, sergeant of the Arikara scouts at Little Bighorn, was killed on the Reno battlefield.
Glen Swanson Collection

Little Brave, killed on the Reno battlefield.
Glen Swanson Collection

Star (Strikes the Bear), Running Wolf, Soldier, Strikes Two, and Young Hawk. The visitors from the North Dakota Historical Society invited the surviving scouts to a barbecue and then asked them to tell their stories about the events of 1876. Their narratives were carefully taken down as interpreted by Peter Beauchamp, a graduate of Hampton Institute in Virginia. Afterward, the narratives were read to the old scouts and corrected by them through their interpreters. Professor Orin G. Libby of the University of North Dakota later edited their narratives, which were published in 1920 by the North Dakota Historical Society under the title *The Arikara Narrative of the Campaign Against the Hostile Dakotas, June, 1876.*

Even as late as 1912, the old scouts clearly remembered many incidents that had occurred during their service with Custer. Although many of their stories were lost, the old scouts were still able to supply Professor Libby with many previously unknown details about the march from Fort Lincoln and their role in the fighting at the Little Bighorn River.

As a result of that meeting, the scouts and their relatives organized a society known as the U.S. Volunteer Indian Scouts. They modeled their society on the Grand Army of the Republic associations that had been formed by Union veterans of the Civil War. The scouts' association still exists on the Fort Berthold Reservation.

A cemetery was also built in their honor at Like a Fishhook village, which we call the "Old Village." The cemetery was named Indian Scout Post No. 1, and the former scouts received proper tombstones from the federal government. In 1953, this cemetery was moved from the bottomlands up to the White Shield area where we all live now. The relocation was necessitated by the Garrison Dam project and the creation of Sacagawea Lake. This reinterment became a very sore point among the Arikara people because the Corp of Engineers placed the graves improperly. It is the Arikara tradition to orient graves east and west, but the relocated graves were running north and south. We also do not know if the artifacts buried with the scouts were transferred to their new graves. When they died, they were buried with their medals and other valued possessions. For example, Ree scout Bear Teeth was buried with his vest, on which all his medals were pinned.

That such a problem arose at all seemed to the Arikara people to be a broken promise. In 1911, North Dakota Congressman L. B. Hanna visited the Fort Berthold Reservation. In his talk to the Sahnish people he referred to the cemetery at the Old Village. "No one," he said, "should go to graves and destroy and desecrate them. There should be a statement in Washington, D.C., to protect the Old Village and the burial grounds. White people do not like their graves tampered with, and there is no reason why Indian graves should be tampered with either." And yet our graves were tampered with and possibly looted.

One good thing is that we finally got the graves facing the right way, even though it took forty-three years to remedy this mistake. Indian Scout Post No. 1 is located seven miles west of White Shield, North Dakota. In addition to the graves of all the Ree scouts, the cemetery is the burial ground for Arikara veterans who fought in all the other wars of our country. Visitors are welcome to come there and pay their respects to these loyal and honored warriors.

The Arikara scouts performed honorably and bravely. Many of them served above and beyond the call of duty. Although the U.S. government forgot them, their memory remains strong among the Arikara people. Every year since the scouts returned home from the Battle of the Little Bighorn, the tribe has honored them. Today, the ceremony takes place on Memorial Day at their cemetery. Although no one living now can understand the precise meaning of the Sahnish words of the Old Scouts honor song, its annual performance is a solemn event full of power and meaning.

The Memorial Day ceremony also includes the singing of a personal honor song for each of the scouts killed in the Battle of the Little Bighorn. There is also an honor song for Custer and for the horses of two of the slain scouts. One of the horses was a pinto that belonged to Bear Trail (Little Brave). Even though its rider had been killed, the pinto made it to the top of Reno Hill. There it was taken by Young Hawk, whose own horse was killed in the retreat. He rode Little Brave's pinto back to Fort Berthold. The other horse that is honored belonged to Bloody Knife. Despite severe wounds, the buckskin somehow found its own way back to Fort Berthold. It lived out its days as a retired warrior, never to be ridden again, its memory kept alive in the oral tradition of the Arikara people, who sing: "This wounded buckskin horse is standing there waiting for his master."

The Arikara people live on Fort Berthold Reservation with two other tribes, the Mandan and the Hidatsa. It is important to note that, despite its small size, the Arikara tribe supplied one of the largest percentages of scouts to the U.S. Army during its wars with the hostile tribes, and that percentage has been maintained by our young men and women who have continued to serve in the armed forces of the United States in our country's times of need.

The purpose in writing this chapter is a matter of justice to the Ree scouts. Their version of the campaign in which they played an important part should have been given to the public long ago. The beginning of the permanent friendship between the Sahnish and the whites came about from a meeting called by A'tipt ("Grandfather," as they called the president) on the Musselshell River in Montana. The Sahnish tribe have made it their duty to serve in the U.S. military from 1867 to the present. There has never been a time since then when there was no Arikara in military service. The

Goose, wounded on the Reno battlefield.
Glen Swanson Collection

Arikara people have always tried to get along with the non-Indians and to honor the U.S. flag, because it represents their country.

Now Indians and whites alike ask: "Why would a tribe of Indians decide to fight on the side of the cavalry against other Indians? After all, you are all Indians." The Sahnish have been called traitors because we were with the Seventh Cavalry. Some whites have even suggested we set up Custer to annihilate him and his command. These critics all overlook facts and miss the point. We were traditional enemies of the Sioux. They came up the Missouri River to defeat us and to take away our hunting lands. Our alliance with the U.S. Army was a matter of survival.

Some Sioux and Cheyenne say they still feel animosity to the descendants of the Ree scouts. Rather than come together as a nation of Native Americans to work for the better good of all our tribes, those with animosities still want to keep us separated tribally. Yes, we keep our customs and traditions separate, but for government, education, and health issues we should come together as one.

We did not tell all the atrocities that were done to us because we would rather not add fuel to the resentment that is still felt today by some people. We chose instead to focus on the strength of our people and the courage of the Ree scouts and their descendants.

THE UNITED STATES VOLUNTEER INDIAN SCOUTS
FORT BERTHOLD RESERVATION, APRIL 1876 TO NOVEMBER 1876
COMPILED BY RHODA M. STAR

BEAR'S EYES, 31. *Detached service at Fort Lincoln.*
BLACK FOX, 29.
BLACK PORCUPINE, 21.
BLOODY KNIFE, 37. *Civilian Scout. Killed in action.*
BOBTAILED BULL, 45. *Sergeant. Killed in action.*
BOY CHIEF, 19.
BULL, 19.
BULL-STANDS-IN-THE-WATER, 29.
CHARGING (RUSHING) BULL, 45.
CHARGING UP THE HILL, 30.
CURLY HEAD (HAIR), 19.
FOOLISH BEAR, 28.
FORKED HORN, 36.
GOOSE, 21. *Wounded in Action.*
HIGH (TALL) BEAR, 45.
HORNS IN FRONT, 42.
HOWLING (BARKING) WOLF, 21.
LEFT HANDED, 45.
LITTLE BRAVE, 27. *Killed in action.*
LITTLE SIOUX, 20.

ONE FEATHER, 45.
ONE HORN, 24.
OWL, 19.
PRETTY ELK (RED BEAR), 23.
PRETTY FACE, 21.
RED FOOLISH BEAR, 28.
RED WOLF, 28.
RUNNING WOLF, 20.
SCABBY WOLF, 19.
SOLDIER, 44.
STABBED, 45. *Corporal.*
STRIKES THE BEAR (RED STAR), 18.
STRIKES THE LODGE, 29.
STRIKES TWO, 29.
WAGON, 20.
WHITE EAGLE, 24.
YOUNG HAWK, 19.

Sioux Married to Arikara Women:

BEAR-RUNNING-IN-THE-TIMBER, 40.
BEAR WAITING, 32.
BUFFALO ANCESTOR.
WHITE CLOUD, 21.

Rhoda M. Star and Melfine Fox Everett at the Old Scouts Cemetery on the Fort Berthold Reservation.
Herman J. Viola Collection

when I was aged about twenty-one years. It was the year of Custer's fatal fight. But I did not get into the battle. Just as they were moving forward to the battle, I was given the mail to take to another camp on Powder River, and there I got mail to take back to Custer's force. I was gone one day. It was the day of the battle, and when I returned the battle was all over. I turned the mail over to a surviving officer. I did not see [the other scouts] that day and not till several weeks after the battle. They were scattered after the battle.

The duties of scouts clearly did not include fighting. Pearl Howard, granddaughter of the Ree scout Little Sioux, recalls that people, often military men, came to visit her grandfather seeking insights into the battle. A frequently asked question was, "Why did the scouts survive, while so many of the soldiers were killed?" According to Pearl Howard, he told them, "We were in the Army, and we had to obey orders. Our orders were to capture the Sioux horses so they could not escape. We were told not to fight but to capture horses. We did that. Unfortunately, we got only the nags and horses they did not value, because they kept the good ones close to camp. We did not have much chance to do anything because the Sioux swarmed out of the village like ants. They were all around us. There was dust and smoke and confusion."

Still other duties of scouts were extremely personal. Pearl tells the story often repeated about Young Hawk, who was assigned to Custer's tent. "He did the cooking and kept things tidy. One of his duties was to keep a large white porcelain pitcher filled with cold water when they made camp. At night, however, Custer used the same pitcher as his chamber pot. Young Hawk then had to scrub the pitcher clean the next morning and fill it with drinking water."

G uiding the Seventh Cavalry through the High Plains and searching for hostile Sioux may have been the chief duties of Crow and Arikara scouts, but these Indians also fulfilled other responsibilities. One was to hunt for fresh meat for use by the officers. Red Star, one of Orin Libby's best informants, told him the Arikara scouts knew Custer's favorite cuts of meat and how he liked to have them cooked. He told them through sign language that he liked to see men eat meat by the fire because if they were full they would be strong.

Another duty of scouts was to carry mail and messages. One old Arikara veteran, Running Wolf, in 1925 recalled his enlistment as a U.S. scout from Fort Lincoln.

George Armstrong Custer with his ever-present
hunting dogs at the entrance to his sibley tent,
in a photograph taken near Fort Dodge in 1868,
during the Washita campaign
Little Bighorn Battlefield National Monument

To all whom it may Concern.

Know ye, That _Whistling Bear (Wa-toch-che-re)_ a _Scout_ of ~~Captain the~~ _Fort A Lincoln detachment_ ~~Company, ( )~~ Regiment of _Indian Scouts_ **VOLUNTEERS**, who was enrolled on the _fifteenth_ day of _June_ one thousand eight hundred and _seventy five_ to serve _6 months_ ~~years or during the war~~, is hereby **Discharged** from the service of the United States this _fifteenth_ day of _December_, 18_75_, at _Fort Abrm Lincoln DT_ by reason of _Expiration of service_ (No objection to his being re-enlisted is known to exist.*)

Said _Whistling Bear_ was born in _____ in the State of _Dakotas_, is _43_ years of age, 5 feet _10_ inches high, _copper_ complexion, _brown_ eyes, _black_ hair, and by occupation, when enrolled, a _Scout_.

Given at _Ft. A Lincoln DT_ this _fifteenth_ day of _December_ 18_75_.

M A Reno
Major 7 Cavalry,
Commanding the Reg't.
Post.

*This sentence will be erased ~~should there be anything~~ in the conduct or physical condition of the soldier rendering him unfit for the Army.

[A. G. O., No. 99.]

Character:
W W Cooke
1. Lt & Adjt. 7. Cavy.
Comdg Scouts

Red Star's Pension

Arikara scouts were to receive government pensions for their service in the U.S. Army, but most of them died before they or their families received any money. According to Melfine Fox Everett, an Arikara delegation went to Washington, D.C., in 1910 seeking the pensions due the scouts for service with the Seventh Cavalry. The delegates were Enemy Heart, Red Bear, and Alfred (Bear) Young Hawk. Louis Benjamin Hanna, a congressman from North Dakota at the time, introduced a bill in the House of Representatives on July 19, 1911, granting pensions for surviving Indians who had served as Army scouts in the Sioux and other Indian wars. "In 1943, there was talk of some monies being found in the State Capitol in Bismarck that belonged to the scouts who had not received pensions because they had died before it was paid out," Everett says. "People still wonder what happened to that money."

Part of the problem was the difficulty for the scouts to prove their military service. At the time of their enlistments, their names were often recorded incorrectly. Other scouts had changed their names since 1876, a common practice in Indian life that seemed beyond the ability of government bureaucrats to either comprehend or accept.

The tedious, repetitive, and time-consuming efforts required of several of the elderly Arikara scouts to obtain their rightful pensions are documented by their pension files in the National Archives. Only the most persistent—and long-lived—scouts managed to overcome the bureaucratic hurdles and see the deeds of their youth finally recognized and rewarded by the federal government.

The scout who seems to have had the most difficult task convincing the Bureau of Pensions that he deserved a pension for his service as a Custer scout was Red Star, who enlisted with several of his friends and relatives at Fort Lincoln in May 1876. His name then was Strikes the Bear, which was recorded on the official roster as "Strike Bear." As late as July 1925, almost fifty years after the Battle of the Little Bighorn, he was still trying to establish his pension claim.

On July 17, 1923, Red Star appeared before E. W. Young, a special examiner sent from the Bureau of Pensions to North Dakota to investigate his claim, which had been rejected as lacking proof of service. Red Star's deposition tells the bare bones of his story.

U.S. Army discharge paper, signed by Major Marcus Reno, of Whistling Bear, an Arikara scout who left federal service in December 1875. The loss of their discharge documents frequently caused serious complications for former Indian scouts who tried to obtain the military pensions to which they were entitled. In the background is the burial ground of the Arikara scouts. Located about seven miles west of White Shield on the Fort Berthold Reservation in North Dakota, it is named Indian Scout Post No. 1.
Herman J. Viola Collection

I served twice as Scout for the United States Army. My first time I went I was aged eighteen years; then I went in two years later again, as a scout for the United States Army, both times as a scout. The first time I enlisted at Fort Lincoln, below Bismarck, then marched up past here but on the other side of the Missouri. General Custer was at the head of the men I was with. We marched, all of us mounted, to the mouth of the Powder Horn, and then across the Powder Horn River we saw a camp of U.S. soldiers. And from where we were we went out to the battlefield on which General Custer lost his life.

We crossed two rivers, and in the evening, instead of giving the orders to camp, General Custer ordered the scouts, I among them, to do scouting duty all the night to find the hostiles. We did so, and in passing some Crows, they told us where the hostile Sioux were, and that by going to a certain high hill we could see them. At daybreak, in the dim light, we saw what we thought was a fog rising. After watching it for a time we concluded that it was the smoke from the hostile camp.

And looking back in the direction from which we came we then saw the smoke of our own camp rising, and we knew then surely that the smoke from the other direction was from the camp of the hostiles. The white man in command of us scouts sent back a note to General Custer, and I was the bearer of that message, the rest of the scouts remaining where they were. I was drinking coffee when General Custer came to me and asked me what I had seen with my own eyes, and whether I had seen tepees. I told what I had seen. He order[ed] the soldiers to break camp, and march. I guided them to the other scouts where I had left them.

General Custer asked the opinion of the Crow scouts as to the best plan of attack. They told him. He thought he would camp there for the day and surround and attack at night. The Crows told him that would be too late, as the enemy had had scouts out, two of whom had passed me on my way but I had not seen them, neither did they see our other scouts, who said they passed so near that they could have shot them.

So Custer concluded to, and did, attack as soon as he could get ready. The U.S. force was divided, and that is how I escaped. Custer was not killed while holding a council. He was killed in battle, and I heard the constant firing from where I was. Before the battle began, we scouts were ordered to advance and get all the horses of the enemy possible, so that they would not be mounted. We crossed a stream and got what we could and were returning with them, when the U.S. command, thinking we were the enemy, began firing and killed one man's horse before we could make them understand who we were. And by that time, the battle was general against the U.S. main force, and it was in that General Custer was killed.

Soon after that, we returned to Fort Buford, and in about forty days after the Custer battle we were back to Fort Lincoln. And as my time was not quite out we then went out in the other direction from [Fort] Lincoln, and then [I] was discharged there and came home that fall. That enlistment was in the name Strikes the Bear. . . .

The same day in 1923, Red Star's fellow warriors Red Bear and Little Sioux supplied corroborating evidence for Young's investigation. Red Bear was only a little older than Red Star, but at Little Bighorn he was a veteran scout in his third term of service.

I went on this enlistment with Custer to the Powder Horn, [during] which expedition he was killed, and was with his command the day on which he was killed. The night before the battle, in the late afternoon or early evening, was seen in the far distance a blue mountain. It was suspected the enemy might be over that way.

Red Star, also known as Strikes the Bear, in an August 1912 photograph taken during interviews with the surviving Arikara scouts by Professor Orin G. Libby of the University of North Dakota. *Glen Swanson Collection*

A scouting party was sent out, one of the scouts being Red Star, here present now. He was then enlisted as Strikes the Bear. After they had gone, the command was ordered to follow. The scouting party was expected to find a lone scout who had been sent out and was expected back before that hour. They were to take food to [him] and to find him. But they missed, as he returned on the opposite side of the river. When he came in[,] the command started after the scouting party. The lone scout was Bobtail[ed] Bull, who was killed in the battle next day. I was with Custer's command in the night march. We camped early in the morning. And as Bull-in-the-Water and I were getting breakfast together, he looked up and saw two men hurrying toward camp along some low bushes. They were this same Red Star and Bull. Red Star had a message for General Custer, who was lying down asleep, but as soon as the messenger was announced he jumped up and received the message, then called Gerard, whom I knew, a man of my own people, as interpreter, and questioned Red Star very closely and told him to be very careful in telling what he knew and what he saw. I know to a certainty that this was the same Red Star who is here before you today. I am now a pensioner under the name Red Bear, so known to the Pension Office, but my enlisted name was Pretty Elk.

Little Sioux's deposition includes similar details:

I had several enlistments of six months each, before my enlistment for the term during which I made the expedition under General Custer to the Powder Horn, on which expedition he was killed in battle on the Little Bighorn. I was camped with Custer's command during the night before the battle, on which night he sent out scouts to scout during the night for the enemy. I was enlisted under the name Little Sioux. Strikes the Bear[,] or Red Star, and I were neighbors and of the same tribe of Indians, and we enlisted that spring together. I know that he was óne of those who were sent out that night scouting for the enemy. I know, too, that the following morning about sunrise we heard a long whoop, which was the imitation of a coyote's call, and it was the signal that a messenger was coming. When they rode up, I saw they were this same Red Star now here present and a young man, also a U.S. scout in Custer's command, named Bull. I was present when they rode into camp. Red Star had a message for General Custer, and I heard then and there Red Star's story that that morning early they had seen from a height what they at first thought to be a fog rising from the river but which they later discerned as smoke from the enemy camp. It was this same Red Star here now present who was that messenger and his enrolled name at that time was Strikes the Bear, my then neighbor at home and the man who enlisted that term with me. Red Star was discharged that time before I was. He and I were both paid by the United States as scouts, $50 for two months of service....

Special Examiner Young was favorably impressed with Red Star's testimony and demeanor. "Claimant is a straight-forward Indian and bears a good reputation," he wrote in his report of July 28, 1923. "His manner was open and frank. I watched his facial expressions, and there was nothing to indicate that he was not telling the truth, and my experience among Indians for thirty years has taught me to note such expression."

Furthermore, Young sought out an outside expert, Professor Orin G. Libby of the University of North Dakota. Libby had talked to the surviving scouts in 1912 in the course of research for *The Arikara Narrative of the Campaign Against the Hostile Dakotas, June, 1876,* published in 1920. "I had a personal interview with Professor Libby," Young wrote:

Not satisfied with what he obtained at the barbecue where all these Indians had gathered, he told me that he took with him this claimant, in whom he has the utmost confidence, by rail to the nearest point to Custer's battlefield, and from there drove to the battlefield, where Red Star pointed out to him the different positions on the day of the fatal encounter, took him to the top of the high hill whence the scouts discovered the smoke in the dim of the morning twilight of the hostile camp which they at first thought to be fog rising from the river, and whence this claimant, accompanied by an eighteen-year-old Indian, hastened back with the message to Custer's camp, apprising the general of the fact that the hostiles had been located and which led to the immediate movement of his troops on that disastrous day to the encounter resulting in his death. Libby is a man of high integrity and ability, and he has no sort of doubt that Red Star was with Custer on that expedition.

Young reported that Red Star at one time possessed the required proof of service, a certificate of discharge:

> Some years ago, when L. B. Hanna was in Congress from North Dakota, the certificates of discharge of all of the Arikara Indians were collected and sent to Hanna. That Hanna got these discharge papers is not denied. He admits it, but what was done with them is not known. Some thought they were left in this Bureau in Washington. That is improbable. Some said they were left in the War Department. It occurs to me that since the purpose of taking them seems to have been to a get a bill through Congress that would grant these scouts a pension, they may have been placed in the hands of the chairman of the proper committee, that on pensions in the House [of Representatives], and that they may have been pigeon-holed with many like papers for such a purpose. Who he was can probably be determined by the Bureau.
>
> Among these discharge papers appear to have been some of this claimant, but what name was in them is not known. A list was kept showing the number of certificates received from each owner but nothing more. The man [who] kept that list is dead and the list cannot be located.

Young was convinced of the merit of Red Star's claim and thought further searches in War Department records would turn up his original enlistment name, Strikes the Bear. Nevertheless, in 1924 and again in June 1925, Red Star and his witnesses went through still more rounds of depositions and statements about his identity and service as a scout with Custer.

The final document in the file, the widow's declaration, shows that Red Star did eventually become, as Strike Bear, pensioner number 12,432. On July 24, 1929, Daisy D. Red Star, age forty-six, applied for a pension as the widow of Strike Bear, who died June 7 that year. The validity of her claim was accepted, and she received her widow's pension with no further dispute.

Edward S. Curtis and Custer's Crow Scouts

James Hutchins

When I answered the telephone that afternoon in 1988 and told the caller
he had reached the National Museum of American History, he identified
himself as Harold P. Curtis, the son of Edward S. Curtis. His father, he
said, was in his day a well-known photographer who specialized in Indian subjects.
Had I ever heard of him? I answered yes, for as it happened, I did know a little about
that brilliant photographer and ethnographer who, in the early decades of this century,
created so many splendid camera studies of Indian life and the multivolume work entitled *The North American Indian,* a priceless written and pictorial record of the traditional lifeways and legends of almost all the Indian peoples of the trans-Mississippi
West.

Harold P. Curtis said that at one time his father had made a considerable study of
the Battle of the Little Bighorn and had uncovered some important facts about it, not
all of which he had ever revealed. Not long before his father died in 1952, he had turned
over to him some papers containing his findings about the battle, charging him to
deposit them at some point in an institution that would see to their continued preservation. Now, at the age of ninety-five, Harold P. Curtis felt that the time had come to
do so. Would the National Museum of American History accept the papers? Of course,
I said yes, and in due time they arrived in the mail. Harold P. Curtis died not long
afterwards.

The fascinating papers proved to be Curtis's personal record of his investigation in
1905-1908 into General George Armstrong Custer's crushing defeat. Curtis's original
intention was to present an account of the battle in an early volume of *The North
American Indian,* one that would be devoted to the Teton Sioux. Typically, he would
seek the stories of Indians who had taken part in the battle, and thus be able to pre-

In 1907, the famed photographer
Edward S. Curtis (inset), who began his
career as a Seattle society photographer,
persuaded Crow scouts White Man
Runs Him, Hairy Moccasin, and Goes
Ahead to reenact for him their activities
of June 25, 1876, until they left Custer at
Medicine Tail Coulee. Here the three
scouts are on the west side of Weir
Point across the Little Bighorn River,
looking toward the village and Reno's
fight in the valley.
*Scouts photo: Museum of New
Mexico/Curtis self-portrait: National
Anthropological Archives*

sent an account of the affair as seen through their eyes. As the account was intended for a white audience, however, it must also give a coherent picture of the battle as a whole.

Curtis commenced his Little Bighorn study in the summer of 1905 with a visit to the battlefield itself, located on the Crow Reservation in remote south-central Montana. On that occasion, he roamed the place alone to acquaint himself with its topography. Later that summer, in the course of fieldwork on the Sioux reservations, Curtis persuaded a number of warriors who had taken part in the battle to give him their recollections. The interviews were not all that he had hoped for. He found that, while the aging warriors could tell of their personal doings in the fight, they seemed unable to give anything like a connected account of the engagement as a whole, at least in terms that white men, starting with Curtis himself, could comprehend. Their verbal descriptions of terrain features that figured in the battle were so vague as to be practically unintelligible. Curtis wished that he could have obtained these eyewitness stories on the battlefield itself, where confusing matters could be cleared up on the spot. Two years later, there came an opportunity to do just that.

In August 1907, Curtis met on the Little Bighorn battlefield with White Man Runs Him, Goes Ahead, and Hairy Moccasin, Crow Indians who in 1876 had served Custer as enlisted Indian scouts—"wolves," as they called themselves—on the expedition that

Hairy Moccasin, Goes Ahead, and White Man Runs Him pose in the Little Bighorn Valley near what appears to be a marker or fenced grave.
Museum of New Mexico

ended so disastrously. They agreed to accompany Curtis on horseback over Custer's route into battle, describing events as they had witnessed them along the way. Here was a situation ideally suited to Curtis's purpose. Moreover, it was intensely thrilling to one of his romantic temperament when, as he wrote of it later, "with our blood all tingling with the swing of our horses . . . we galloped . . . clearing gully and hummock with a clean spring, the Indians singing the medicine songs of that day thirty years ago."

White Man Runs Him, who served as spokesman for the trio, told Curtis that they and three other young Crows, Half Yellow Face, White Swan, and Curley, had scouted for Custer from June 22, 1876, when he left the Yellowstone River to follow the Sioux trail southward along Rosebud Creek, up to the hour of battle three days afterward. Serving as scouts, too, were about forty Arikara Indians. The Arikaras, however, whose homeland lay on the distant Missouri River, were strangers to the country at hand. Thus it fell to the Crows, who knew this region intimately, to range daily far ahead of Custer's column, examining every detail of the Sioux trail.

Every sign told the scouts that Custer's quarry was not far ahead. The Sioux trail grew broader and fresher each day. On the morning of June 24, the day preceding the battle, said White Man Runs Him, he even glimpsed a few Sioux hunters or scouts in the far distance ahead. Riding up the Rosebud late that afternoon, the Crows saw that the Sioux trail swung west toward the divide beyond which lay the valley of the Little Bighorn. Hurrying back to Custer, they reported their find. They told him, too, of a lookout point called the Crow's Nest, high atop the divide. From there, early next morning, they would be able to scan a wide stretch of the country to the west for signs of the Sioux. At once, Custer sent one of his lieutenants with Mitch Bouyer, his famous mixed-blood guide, and a number of the scouts—White Man Runs Him, Goes Ahead, and Hairy Moccasin among them—to ride to the lookout that night and look for the Sioux at dawn.

Now, standing on the Crow's Nest with Curtis, White Man Runs Him related how, at first light on June 25, while the rest of the party were still dozing, he and Mitch Bouyer arose and gazed toward the Little Bighorn Valley, some fifteen miles to the west. There they spotted rising campfire smoke and grazing ponies, sure evidence of the Sioux village, even though the place itself was screened from view by high river bluffs. When Custer joined them later in the morning, they showed him the signs. There was bad news for him, too. A bit earlier, they had spotted a few Sioux watching his soldiers, who were then in bivouac not far east of the divide. Even now, those watchers were probably hurrying to the village to warn of impending attack.

Up to this moment, Custer had intended to conceal his command near the divide all of this day while his scouts sought a better idea of the location and size of the target village. Then, in the night ahead, he would move his troops close to the place and launch a surprise attack at dawn. The Arikara scouts would run off the villagers' pony herds, crippling their power to resist or flee, and his troopers would storm through the encampment itself, shooting right and left, killing or driving off the warriors and capturing the women and children. Now, however, believing his presence discovered, Custer saw no alternative but to advance in broad daylight, hoping to strike the village before its inhabitants could flee.

The scouts were apprehensive about what lay ahead. Their reading of the signs told them that the village must be very large, with warriors far outnumbering Custer's soldiers. They sensed, too, that under sudden attack, the Sioux warriors would put up a desperate fight to cover the escape of their families. But Custer discounted such warnings. As he saw it, the Sioux would think only of flight. And if any of them did choose to stand and fight, his invincible Seventh Cavalry would make short work of them.

Custer led the twelve companies of the Seventh Cavalry—thirty-one officers and some 560 troopers strong—west over the divide toward the Little Bighorn. Just past the crest, he sent Captain Frederick W. Benteen with three companies to scout the country to the left front and then rejoin. Custer himself with eight companies advanced straight ahead, marching down a small tributary of the Little Bighorn, since named Reno Creek. In his wake lumbered the slow-moving regimental pack train, laden with reserve ammunition and food, with the remaining cavalry company as escort.

White Man Runs Him told Curtis that before Custer left the Crow's Nest to put his regiment in motion, he sent Hairy Moccasin ahead with instructions to ride down Reno Creek and seek a closer look at the Sioux village. Now the Crows conducted Curtis along the path they said Hairy Moccasin had followed in his solitary ride. They indicated where he had passed a Sioux tipi containing the body of a dead warrior, and pointed out a pine-clad hill he climbed for a better view of what lay ahead. From there, as White Man Runs Him put it, Hairy Moccasin "saw the Sioux everywhere across the Little Bighorn." Turning back, he met Custer and told him of the size and location of the Sioux village. The Sioux, he said, were not running away as had been feared.

A little later, when Custer arrived at a point on Reno Creek about three miles distant from the Little Bighorn, it began to look as though the Sioux had finally learned of his approach and were commencing to flee. Gazing ahead, said White Man Runs Him,

> we saw a big cloud of dust on the west side of the Little Bighorn. . . Someone said, "What does that dust mean?" One of the Crow scouts said, "The Sioux must be running away." Custer said, "If they are running away I shall send someone to head them off. They are getting foolish and I shall round them up today."

Now, Custer ordered Major Marcus A. Reno, his second in command, to push ahead with three companies, cross the Little Bighorn, and charge the supposedly fleeing Sioux. Reno led his companies toward the river at a fast gait. With him rode the Arikara scouts and two of the Crows, Half Yellow Face and White Swan. The major had been told that he would be supported in his attack by the "whole outfit." He took this to mean that Custer with the five companies still under his immediate command would follow right behind him. But Custer did not ride long in Reno's path. Instead, probably in search of a route that would enable him to attack from another angle and head off the fleeing villagers, he swung his column to the right and led it at the gallop toward the heights that rose up there.

The Crows led Curtis up the slope they said Custer had traveled to reach the heights. Mitch Bouyer and the remaining Crow scouts, White Man Runs Him, Goes Ahead, Hairy Moccasin, and Curley rode ahead of Custer. Close to the top, Custer halted while the scouts went on to the crest. There, they found themselves astride a line of high bluffs that stretched away northward. At their feet lay a broad stretch of the Little Bighorn valley. Looking to their right front, downriver, they saw tipis that marked the southern fringe of the Sioux encampment. Intervening river bluffs, however, still blocked most of the place from view. To their left front the scouts saw Major Reno's command. He had already forded the river and was now preparing to charge down the open valley. The Arikara scouts were racing ahead, intent on running off the Sioux pony herds. A few Sioux warriors maneuvered to and fro in Reno's front, hoping to delay his advance.

The scouts signaled to Custer, who, with some of his officers, hurried up to the crest. Here he paused, as White Man Runs Him put it, "only as a big bird alights and then flies on." Waving his hat to Reno's men, he turned and rode northward along the edge of the bluffs for about a mile and a half to the eminence now known as Weir Peak, one of the highest points in all the adjoining country. From here, Custer could see practically the whole of the sprawling encampment. The Sioux and Cheyenne tipi circles stretched for at least a mile along the river bottom. And they were still in place. Against all the odds, Custer had achieved surprise.

The Crow scouts had traveled somewhat in advance of Custer in his journey to Weir Point. They did not tarry there but continued northward along the bluffs which, beyond Weir Point, descend ever lower toward the river. By this time, said White Man Runs Him, they were only three, Goes Ahead, Hairy Moccasin, and himself. Mitch Bouyer had remained with Custer. Their fellow Crow, Curley, they said, had parted company with them soon after their arrival on the bluffs, when they encountered a party of Arikara scouts driving captured Sioux ponies back toward Reno Creek. Curley had joined these Arikaras, and the other Crows saw him no more.

Now the Crows led Curtis downward along the bluffs to a point about a mile northwest of Weir Point, where the river runs close below. Here, they said, they had halted. Just across the river lay a portion of the great encampment, now in full alarm at Major Reno's approach. Women and children were running about, some of them dismantling tipis preparatory to flight. The Crows dismounted and fired several shots into the village. Then, noting that a number of Sioux had crossed the river and were starting toward them, they rode back to Weir Point. There they found Custer and a number of his officers seated, observing events in the valley below. Custer's command had kept pace with him in his ride along the bluffs. Now, his troopers waited, dismounted, just below the peak.

Looking down from Weir Point, the Crow scouts saw that Major Reno's companies were already in action in the river bottom. Finding himself confronted by more and more Sioux as he charged down the valley, and with the promised support nowhere in sight, Reno had halted his command short of the southern edge of the Sioux encampment. Now, his troopers were formed in a dismounted skirmish line that extended for some distance across the open bottom, and were blazing away with their carbines at the warriors who darted to and fro in their front. White Man Runs Him clapped his hands sharply and quickly in imitation of the crash of gunfire.

To the scouts, it appeared that Major Reno was in sore need of help. Although clouds of dust and gunsmoke rendered the scene somewhat indistinct, they could see

that his thin line was confronted by Sioux and Cheyenne warriors in large numbers and that more were coming up. And they were growing increasingly bold. White Man Runs Him told Curtis that he saw one warrior, mounted on a sorrel horse, ride "right into Reno's men. He was wearing a war bonnet. His horse fell—I think the Sioux was killed."

To the Crows, it was unthinkable that Custer should not lead his companies directly down the bluffs and go at once to Reno's support. Agitated, White Man Runs Him approached Custer and urged him to do so. As he described this episode to Curtis, the dialogue ran thus: "I said, 'Why don't you cross the river and fight too?' I scolded him. Custer replied, 'It is early yet and plenty of time. Let them fight. Our turn will come.'" Then, according to White Man Runs Him, "all the Sioux charged upon Reno's men, and he retreated up the river on foot." At this, as Curtis recorded the story,

White Man Runs Him turned along the bluffs to the south to see if any of Reno's men . . . had crossed the river. . . . He rode along the top of a ridge leading down towards the river. Five men ran out of the point of the "V" formed by the brush and headed for the ridge on which White Man Runs Him sat on horseback. . . . White Man Runs Him shot over the heads of these soldiers towards the pursuing Sioux.

Resting on top of Weir Point. The three former Crow scouts are holding white envelopes that probably contain the payment they received from Edward Curtis for their efforts. Left to right: Goes Ahead, Hairy Moccasin, White Man Runs Him, Curtis, and A. B. Upshaw, the interpreter.
Museum of New Mexico

The five men clambered up to the crest of the ridge, some had no hats and some no trousers. White Man Runs Him conducted them back to Custer's soldiers. He does not know what became of them after that. Custer was sitting on the high point when he went down to rescue the men, and was still there when he returned.

Hairy Moccasin, too, was credited with rescuing one of Reno's men at this time, one who had "many shots through his shirt but was not wounded."

Only after Reno's command had been put to flight, so the Crows' story ran, did Custer finally depart from Weir Point. Now he led his five companies northward, descending from the heights toward Medicine Tail Coulee, a broad creek bed that winds west to the Little Bighorn. Entering the coulee, Custer proceeded down it toward the river. The Crows, aware that there was a good ford in the river opposite the coulee's mouth, expected that Custer would cross there and attack the village. But he did not do so. According to White Man Runs Him, when Custer reached a point about two hundred yards from the river, he came under fire from some Sioux on the opposite bank and halted. While some of the leading troopers returned the fire, the head of the column moved to the right and took a position on the southern terminus of the ridge not far north of the ford, now often referred to as Greasy Grass Ridge. Here, according to White Man Runs Him, some of Custer's men dismounted, lay down, and opened fire on the Sioux. The rest of the command stretched back, "out of sight of the Indians. . . . Scattering Indians were crossing the river, and some stealthily creeping up in Custer's front. He personally while sitting there shot at Indians who were reckless enough to come within range."

At this point Mitch Bouyer, who sat beside Custer, called to the Crows, who had taken cover some distance behind. When White Man Runs Him crawled near, Bouyer told him, "You have brought us to the Sioux village, and have done your duty. The pack train has much ammunition. Go to it and save yourselves." At once, the three Crows mounted and started on the run back up Medicine Tail Coulee, heading for Weir Point. The Sioux were not yet numerous around Custer's force, and the scouts came under scattering fire for only the first few hundred yards of their ride.

Upon reaching the vicinity of Weir Point, White Man Runs Him told Curtis, the three scouts encountered a portion of Major Reno's command. Earlier, after his pell-mell retreat from the river bottom, Major Reno had pulled up atop the high bluffs close to the point from which Custer had first looked into the valley. There he was joined by Captain Benteen with his three companies and, eventually, the pack train. Thereafter, hearing firing from the direction in which it was supposed that Custer had gone, most of Reno's command had made a disorganized advance to Weir Point in an effort to open contact with him. It was these troops whom, according to White Man Runs Him, the Crow scouts now met. As he neared Weir Point, said White Man Runs Him, he

> looked back, and saw Custer and his men moving north toward where he made his last stand. The Sioux were circling around him and his men. When we got near the other [Reno's] soldiers, they shot at the Sioux, and made an opening, so we could join them. I said: "This is a dangerous point. They will shoot us from every side. Let us move up the river." Benteen gave the command to move. Then we moved back. We looked back and saw Custer still fighting. We went toward a

hill where there was a breastwork of mules [the present Reno-Benteen Battle Site]. . . . The soldiers could see the Sioux fighting Custer from the point where they turned around to go to the breastworks. After we were in the breastworks, the Sioux circled around us. We shot so hard the guns burned our hands, and we lay down to clean them among the cracker boxes. Towards evening, we three scouts left Benteen and started east for the pine bluffs.

After leaving Major Reno's beleaguered command, White Man Runs Him continued, he, Goes Ahead, and Hairy Moccasin made a lonely night ride through broken country amid a driving rainstorm. They wept, stricken with grief in the conviction that, from all they had seen, the Sioux must surely have gone on to wipe out the whole of Custer's regiment. Morning found them beside the Bighorn River some miles north of the battlefield, riding west toward their home village on Pryor Creek. Here they encountered a group of Crows who were scouting for a force of white soldiers marching toward the Little Bighorn Valley to link up with Custer's command. After giving these other scouts the dreadful news of Custer's defeat, White Man Runs Him, Goes Ahead, and Hairy Moccasin continued home for a time of rest and renewal. Soon, they learned that the white soldiers wanted them to return for further service as "wolves." When he and his fellow scouts presented themselves, said White Man Runs Him, their hearts were gladdened when they were handed eighty dollars apiece for their previous services. "It was," he recalled, "more than any white man ever paid us for anything."

Setting out to put the Crows' story on paper during the winter of 1907-08, Curtis pondered how to deal with it. He was familiar with such accounts of the battle as were then considered authoritative, one by Captain Edward S. Godfrey, who had fought at the Little Bighorn, and another by Lieutenant Colonel William H. C. Bowen, a close student of the affair. According to these, Custer, after sending Reno ahead to open the attack, proceeded northward by a route so far distant from the river that he was unable to see anything of developments in the valley. Thus, unaware that Reno had fled the field, he launched his own attack only to be met head-on and suffer annihilation at the hands of Sioux and Cheyenne warriors who, with Reno out of the picture, were free to concentrate against him in overwhelming numbers. These accounts confirmed the popular view of Custer as a gallant Indian fighter who, whatever might be said of his judgment in bringing on the battle in the first place, had met death in a manner befitting a hero, battling to the end against hopeless odds after betrayal by cowardly Reno.

The Crows' story turned all that upside down. Here, Reno was the hapless victim and Custer was—well, what to say of a soldier who would callously refuse to go to the aid of struggling comrades in plain view? As Curtis saw it, it would have been a simple matter for Custer to lead his own force down from the bluffs directly to Reno's side. Had he done so, throwing into the balance the weight and firepower of his five companies and his own inspiring leadership, victory surely must have followed. What to say, for that matter, of the mental state of a commander who, according to the Crow scouts, after having seen with his own eyes Reno's utter defeat, persists in making an obviously doomed attack of his own?

Curtis was convinced that the Crows were telling the truth about Custer's actions. His repeated questioning and cross-questioning had not fazed them. But was it wise to present a story that had not a shred of evidence from other sources to support it and that made Custer look so bad? The sure result would be a great furor, with most white Americans branding the story just another Indian lie. And Curtis might well find himself assailed for having sponsored such a tale.

Curtis appears to have reasoned that the best way to deal with the Crows' account would be to secure the appointment of an official investigative body to meet on Little Bighorn battlefield, there hear the Crows present their version of events on the ground itself where there could be no mistaking their meaning, weigh it against all other evidence pro and con, and then render final judgment on how and why the battle turned out as it did. Perhaps his friend President Theodore Roosevelt, after hearing the Crows' story, would be willing to appoint such a body.

Before approaching Roosevelt, Curtis sought to check his own opinion of the Crows' account with that of an experienced professional soldier who was not a partisan for Custer or Reno and so could consider the Crows' story in an objective way. He found just such a person in retired brigadier general Charles A. Woodruff. Woodruff's experience in warfare dated from the Civil War through Indian campaigning, including the Sioux War of 1876, in which he had taken part as a lieutenant of infantry. Upon reading the Crows' story, Woodruff found their account of Custer's doings on Weir Point just as inexplicable and shocking as had Curtis. Even so, he considered that the matter certainly merited further investigation.

Now, Curtis sent the Crows' account, coupled with Woodruff's remarks, to Theodore Roosevelt. Would the president be good enough to look over the papers and advise what his next step should be? Roosevelt's friendship meant much to Curtis, and he placed great value on his counsel. The president was a staunch believer in the importance of Curtis's efforts to record the Indians' vanishing primitive lifeways, and had recently lent his prestige to the undertaking by writing a flattering foreword for *The North American Indian*. Roosevelt's reaction to the Crows' story was one of incredulity coupled with concern that his friend had strayed into a matter he was not equipped to deal with. His written reply, expressed in characteristic thumping prose, speaks for itself.

> I have read those papers thru with great interest, and after reading them I am uncertain as to what is the best course to advise. . . . I need not say to you that writing over thirty years after the event it is necessary to be exceedingly cautious about relying on the memory of any man, Indian or white. Such a space of time is a great breeder of myths. Apparently you are inclined to the belief that Custer looked on but a short distance away at the butchery of Reno's men and let it take place, hoping to gain great glory for himself afterward. Such a theory is wildly improbable. Of course, human nature is so queer that it is hard to say that anything is impossible; but this theory makes Custer out both a traitor and a fool. He would have gained just as much glory by galloping down to snatch victory from defeat after Reno was thoroughly routed as in any other way; and with Reno routed, he must have been obsessed not to see that he was almost insuring his own death. . . . The facts should

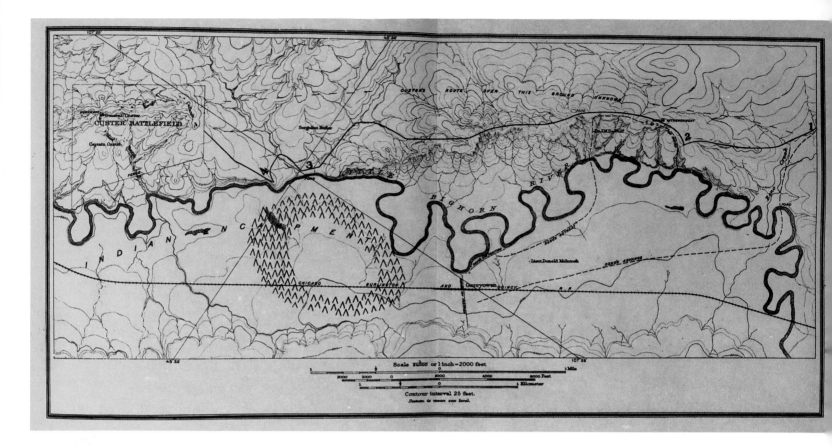

be clearly brought out, and the proof overwhelming, before at so late a day a man of high repute deliberately publishes a theory such as the above.

Meeting with Roosevelt soon afterward, Curtis found him not at all disposed to tamper with Custer's image as a hero, one whom American youth would do well to take for its model. Roosevelt dismissed the idea of creating a board to probe Custer's conduct at the Little Bighorn for no more reason than the claims of a few elderly Indians whose memories were undoubtedly shaky at best. He urged Curtis to abandon this distracting Little Bighorn matter and get on with his really important work. As Curtis expressed it in a letter to General Woodruff afterwards,

> the president's thought is that I am taking too large a responsibility unto myself, also going into a subject which would take considerable of my time, and as I am not strictly a historian it would be better to leave this matter to someone else and cling closely to my Indians.

Although he did not abandon his own belief in the Crow's story, Curtis did as Roosevelt advised. In putting his Little Bighorn text into final form, he omitted everything the Crows had said about Custer's doings on Weir Point. On the map that would accompany the text into print, tracing Custer's route from Reno Creek to the ford opposite the mouth of Medicine Tail Coulee as the Crows had pointed it out, he did show Custer passing over Weir Point but omitted from the legend anything to suggest that Custer might have stopped there. The rest of the account, harmless enough, passed into print in volume 3 of *The North American Indian*.

Opposite:
When Edward Curtis published his account of the Battle of the Little Bighorn in volume 3 of *The North American Indian,* he omitted all mention of what the Crow scouts told him regarding Custer's actions on Weir Point. The legend for this map reads: "This map is a reproduction of a U.S. Geological Survey map made in 1891 by Mr. R. B. Marshall. The notation, 'Custer's route over this ground unknown,' appears on the map as drawn by him. The heavy line beginning at 1, on Reno creek, has been added by the author, and it traces, he believes, the route followed by Custer. 1 is the point where Custer and Reno separated; 2 where Custer was seen by Reno's men to come to the crest of the hill and wave a salutation; 3 where Custer came close to the river, presumably planning to ford; 4 where the Indians made their attack on Custer. Here was the beginning of his battle, and here began his retreat, the course of which is indicated by the line from 4 to the 'fence.' The burying squad found bodies within a hundred yards of this point where the attack was made, and many Sioux participants assert that the first troopers killed were three who fell a few yards from here. It was at 4 also that the Crow scouts left Custer, going back on his trail to join Reno's command. The position and size of the circular Indian encampment are indicated by the A-signs which have been added by the author."
James Hutchins

It was indeed high time that Curtis got on with the business of bringing *The North American Indian* into being. Late in 1906, he had succeeded in obtaining from financial titan J. Pierpont Morgan a beneficent loan to cover the estimated costs of producing the first few volumes, no mean feat in itself. Now, at midpoint in 1908, not a single volume had yet appeared, and it was of vital importance that Curtis get something into the hands of his subscribers without unnecessary delay. Even so, he found it difficult to let go of the Battle of the Little Bighorn. Like many another in the years since, he had succumbed to the almost hypnotic spell that Custer's Last Fight can exert on the mind. Thus, despite a tight schedule that called for his presence elsewhere, Curtis could not resist taking time to ride once more over the Little Bighorn battlefield with the Crow scouts, this time in company with General Woodruff. Then, like the big bird that alights and then flies on, as Crow imagery would have it, he finally pulled himself away.

Never again, so far as the record shows, did Edward S. Curtis take up the subject of Custer's Last Fight in an active way. That he clung to his belief in what the Crows had told him is shown by the care he took throughout the rest of his long life to preserve the papers that contained the whole of their story. Finally, in 1951, old and beset by serious ailments, Curtis reread those papers one last time, perhaps reliving in memory those exciting days with Custer's Crow scouts beside the Little Bighorn so many years in the past. Then he turned the papers over to his son Harold, who in turn, perhaps sensing that his own end was not far away, finally picked up his telephone and placed the call I happened to answer on that memorable afternoon in 1988.

Archaeologists: Detectives on the Battlefield

Douglas D. Scott

Display of items from Sitting Bull's camp found by Jason Pitsch on his family's property, adjoining the Little Bighorn Battlefield National Monument.
Glen Swanson

Every summer, visitors swarm over the almost treeless, rolling countryside of eastern Montana to see Little Bighorn Battlefield National Monument. Battlefields have in modern times become ceremonial sites where people can see, touch, and experience an interpreted version of the past. They evoke drama, sacrifice, glory, and grief. Little Bighorn offers all that, and nearly every visitor arrives with some preconceived notions of what happened there on June 25, 1876. For here is the ground of an event that looms large in a moment of American history still wrapped in mystique, contention, and bafflement.

Little Bighorn seems always to be in the public eye for one reason or another, and that was especially true in 1983 when a range fire burned over the monument's lands. Because the fire cleared the site of vegetation, a new opportunity revealed itself. Between 1985 and 1995 archaeological investigations were undertaken on behalf of the National Park Service, and thousands of artifacts were plotted, analyzed, and recovered. The artifacts and their carefully recorded locations became the basis for a reassessment of the battle story and thereby reduced the bafflement quotient by a significant degree—if not the quotients of mystique and contention.

Spatial patterning of artifacts—recording what they are, where they were found, and studying what their relationship to one another might be—is a central tenet of modern archaeological research. This concept was applied as the fundamental building block for examining the newly unearthed physical evidence of the 1876 battle. The results revealed insights into the movements of individual combatants as well as the overall positions of Indians and Army soldiers.

Evidence to reconstruct the sequence of events at the Battle of the Little Bighorn comes in two forms. First is historical documentation: It ranges from Army reports to oral recollections by survivors and their descendants from both sides of the battle. Second is archaeological data: It is the body of artifacts recovered during the archaeological investigations of the mid-1980s and early 1990s.

165

Aerial view of the Little Bighorn battlefield looking northwest. In the foreground is the parking lot at the site of the Reno-Benteen marker. The road follows the ridge line to Monument Hill and the park visitor center at the top of the photograph.
Larry Mayer

To understand the relative value and relationship of the two forms of evidence, consider a murder investigation. The historical documentation is like the testimony of witnesses, and the archaeological data is like the physical evidence collected at the crime scene. Historians are, in essence, detectives interviewing victims, suspects, and witnesses. Archaeologists are the forensic experts gathering physical evidence for detailed scientific examination in the laboratory. Such analysis is used to either corroborate or refute the testimony of witnesses.

Like detectives, scholars know that individual oral historical accounts—people's stories—should be suspect. Perhaps a witness did not remember correctly, or did not see part of the action, or recounted only what others said they had seen, or was opinionated—or lied. Archaeological data, the physical clues used in forensic analysis, add a wealth of information to the record of the past. Artifacts help form a more complete picture and unbiased view of the situation than oral accounts alone can provide. Artifacts do not lie (although they can be misinterpreted). They are physical evidence of human behavior in the past; they were deposited because of decisions made in that past. It may be that we can never know exactly why those decisions were made nor how, but the results can be interpreted. Archaeological data is the new and previously unstudied evidence. Perhaps, as detectives might say, it can crack the case.

The gathering of physical evidence at the Little Bighorn employed standard archaeological techniques, and was augmented by more than ten years of volunteer hobbyists working nearly 250 metal detectors. The National Park Service–sponsored investigations amassed some five thousand artifacts. Thousands more were collected by Jason Pitsch in his study of the Reno Valley fight and portions of two Indian camp areas (see pages 180–81). The result of these efforts is much new and previously unavailable data on the battle.

The core of the efforts was a metal-detector inventory of the battlefield. Specially selected volunteers, experts in the use of detectors, walked about fifteen feet apart, covering all of the National Park Service–managed lands (the Custer battlefield as well as that of the Reno and Benteen defense) during two five-week periods in 1984 and 1985. In 1994, another 880 acres of Crow tribal lands, lands owned by the Custer Battlefield Land Preservation Society, and some other private lands were scanned with detectors and the artifacts collected in a three-week period. These lands included some battle areas north and south of the main Custer battlefield, as well as lands adjacent to the Reno-Benteen defense site, the area around and below Weir Point, and the lower reaches of Medicine Tail Coulee.

The field methods during each field investigation for more than a decade called for six to eight volunteers to form a detector line and then walk designated zones or transects until a total of more than 1,750 acres was searched. The search or inventory crew did not cover every square inch of the field, nor was that the mission. Rather, tests of metal-detector efficiency coupled with standard scientific sampling procedures allowed us to determine that this spacing was optimal to recover a statistically valid sample of all metallic artifacts left on the battlefield. Some of the site was left intact for future investigators, when newer and better techniques may allow other levels of inquiry into the battle.

The detector operators literally swept the area, swinging their machines across the battlefield. When their detectors beeped, they marked the area with a pin flag. Behind them came the recovery crew, also volunteers, supervised by experienced archaeologists. The crew excavated cautiously, using the archaeologist's tool of choice—a six-inch mason's trowel—to search for the object that caused the detector to signal. When found, the object was carefully uncovered and left in place. Finally, survey crews came along, consisting of an archaeologist transit operator, a person to hold the prism pole, and a volunteer to record, number, bag, and collect each artifact. Before collection, crews set upon a preestablished datum or grid point (using either transits or theodolites), then determined the angle and distance of the surrounding artifacts from that point. This crew made notes on the depth of the artifact below ground surface, and in the case of bullets and cartridges, also noted the orientation (with respect to magnetic north) and the declination (angle up or down from the horizontal) of the piece. Only then was the artifact collected.

Formal archaeological excavations were also undertaken at thirty-seven of the 252 marble marker locations, markers that were erected in 1890 to commemorate the place, it was believed, where officers and men of Custer's battalion had died in battle. Even though the Army had removed the soldiers' remains to a mass grave in 1881, many of their bones were left behind. Studies of those skeletal remains have given us significant new insights into how the men lived, their true ages, heights, physical and oral health, and how they died of wounds from bullets, arrows, knives, and lances, as well as the crushing force of stone-headed war clubs.

The metal-detector survey located the majority of artifacts, including thousands of bullets, expended cartridge casings, and unfired cartridges. It became obvious even before analyses were complete that the Indians were much better armed than had been previously thought. Subsequent firearms analyses using the same forensic techniques employed in modern crime laboratories identified forty-seven different types of guns used by the warriors. Other Indian weapons included bows and arrows (inferred from metal arrowheads), knives, lances, tomahawks or axes, and stone-headed war clubs. All were identified from examination of the artifacts themselves or from marks on soldiers' bones made by the weapons. Crushed skulls, for example, gave evidence of stone-headed war clubs, which of course could not be found by metal detectors.

Indian arms included the .44-caliber Henry, .44-caliber Model 1866 Winchester, and the .44–.40-caliber Model 1873 Winchester, all lever-action repeating rifles that could fire up to sixteen rounds without reloading. The Army did not issue repeating rifles to its troops until 1892, so Custer's troops used the single-shot, .45–.55-caliber Springfield carbine. Although the carbine was more powerful and more accurate than the Indians' repeating rifles, 210 single-shot Springfields were no match for fifteen hundred warriors—at least half of whom were probably armed with guns.

Indian arms also included the Army's Springfield carbine and the Colt Model 1873 cartridge revolver. In some Indian positions that lacked evidence of Army presence, Springfield and Colt cartridge cases were found intermixed. The guns that fired them might have been captured from General George Crook's command during the Battle of the Rosebud eight days before, or in the fight against Major Marcus Reno's battalion earlier on the same day, or even just moments before from men under Custer's immediate command.

Tombstones on Custer Hill show evidence of scorching in this photograph taken several weeks after the fire.
Herman J. Viola Collection

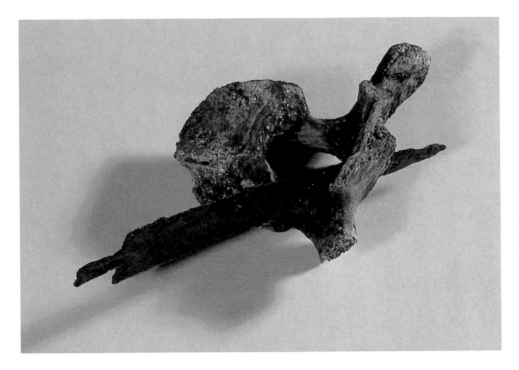

Despite all the recent attention to Indian firepower during the battle, the bow and arrow did their share of destruction, as this relic from the battlefield testifies. Arrows fired by warriors hidden in the heavy brush rained down on the troops and cavalry horses, adding to the general confusion and panic.
Armed Forces History Division, National Museum of American History

By using modern forensic techniques, the number of individual weapons could be determined. Analysis of firing pin marks on cartridge cases indicates that at least 350 different firearms were in the hands of Indian warriors. This estimate is conservative because groups of round balls fired from older muzzle-loading rifles were counted as only one gun per caliber of ball found. With time, oxidation of the lead balls has obscured their individual characteristics beyond the capacity of forensic techniques to determine signatures of individual weapons.

When statistical techniques were brought to bear on this data, a picture emerged of how Indian forces were armed. If we assume that fifteen hundred warriors took part in the entire battle—again a very conservative estimate—about two hundred were

Pieces of metal found by Jason Pitsch on the Reno battlefield and the site of Hunkpapa village. Shown here are unfinished iron arrowheads as well as finished points used in the fighting. Included are two arrows collected from the battlefield by the burial detail.
Glen Swanson

armed with repeating rifles such as Winchesters. Another 375 or so were armed with muzzle-loaders or single-shot rifles such as .40-, .45-, or .50-caliber Sharps and .45- and .50-caliber Ballards. The rest may have been armed with bows and arrows and a few old pistols and revolvers.

Rifles manufactured by Winchester were readily available on the frontier of 1876, and there was no prohibition against their sale to Indians. Those rifles had an effective rate of fire of about twenty rounds per minute under ideal conditions. The Springfield carbines in the hands of the cavalry could fire only four to six rounds per minute. Even using these minimal figures, it is starkly apparent that the 210 men in Custer's immediate command were outmanned at least five to one and outgunned two to one. And the Indians' rate of fire approached an advantage of five to one.

The entire day's worth of fighting is much too complex to discuss in detail here. But one episode of the battle to have riveted many scholars' scrutiny—and the attention of many amateur Custer "buffs" as well—is the critical action at Medicine Tail Coulee. To the average park visitor or the casual reader of Little Bighorn battle history, the most compelling story centers on the last moments of Custer and the troopers with him.

To Custer scholars, however, the canvas is larger, and many diverse and compelling moments in the battle have been studied, dissected, and debated. One of those most-debated elements is the action in lower Medicine Tail Coulee. Some scholars argue that no action occurred near the ford where Medicine Tail Coulee and the Little Bighorn River intersect. Others categorically state that some element of the command did move to the ford in an attempt to hold Indians on the river's west side in check, while Custer moved the remainder of the command to attack the northernmost extension of the Indian village. Richard Fox argues that on June 25, the circular Indian campsites did not extend any farther north than the Medicine Tail Coulee ford, and that some of the left wing of Custer's command was attempting to dash into this end of the village to bolster Major Reno's attack on the south side of the Indian encampment. He has Custer moving with the right wing on a northerly course to cross the river at another ford and circle to the west and create a third attacking force. Such an attack is not unlike the plan Custer executed at the Battle of the Washita some eight years before.

Yet other scholars believe that Custer personally led most of his battalion to the river, and some argue that Custer was wounded or killed at the Medicine Tail Coulee ford, thus depriving the command of its renowned leader and ensuring its annihilation. However one may debate the details, the move north was apparently an attempt to cross the Little Bighorn River and hit the village from the north side in order to divide the warriors' fighting strength. This kind of dividing tactic had been successfully employed by Custer at the Washita some eight years before and had served other commanders well in other battles of the Indian wars.

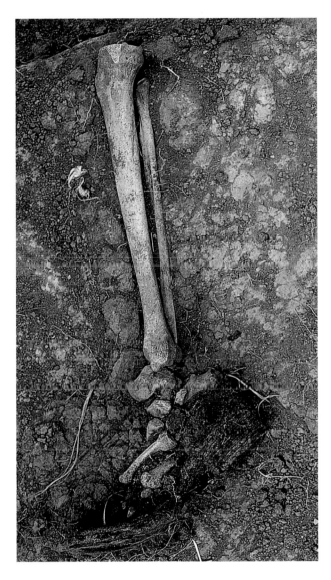

Named "Mike" by the archaeology team, these almost complete remains of a Custer soldier were found during the metal-detecting reconnaissance after the fire. Shown here is the right leg, with the remains of a shoe still on the foot.
Larry Mayer

Historical sources, both written and oral, are the basis of the many conflicting arguments regarding the action in Medicine Tail Coulee. The episode may have been one of short duration, but understanding it and sorting out what truly happened is central to understanding the battle events that followed.

The only source that has not been a factor in the previous analyses is data from a systematic archaeological investigation. That work was done in 1994. Archaeological analysis of this turning point in the fight has not been published before.

In the scheme of battle, the action at Medicine Tail Coulee is an intermediate event between Major Marcus Reno's fight and retreat in the valley of the Little Bighorn River and the destruction of Custer's immediate command (see map, page 18). After Major Reno began his attack on the south end of the Indian village in the valley between 2:00 and 3:00 P.M., the battalion commanded by Lieutenant Colonel George Custer moved north along the river bluffs. From atop the bluffs he, or at least some of his staff, saw evidence of Reno fighting in the valley and were finally able to roughly gauge the enormity of the Indian presence that lay before them. After seeing the size of the Indian encampments, Custer sent two messengers (one with a verbal order and the second with a written order) to try to locate Captain Benteen and order him to join Custer—with instructions to bring ammunition.

As Custer moved his troops from the river bluffs toward the encampments, he descended a small coulee, or "draw," which fed into a larger one called Medicine Tail. At this juncture, Custer sent back trumpeter John Martin with the famous written message to Captain Frederick Benteen to hurry on up and bring the ammunition which was carried by pack mules. Early in the afternoon Custer had sent Benteen scouting to the south to ensure that there were no Indians in that direction, and so Benteen's whereabouts were not precisely known to Custer as he was poised above Medicine Tail Coulee.

The subsequent events in Medicine Tail Coulee were witnessed by many of the Lakota and Cheyenne warriors, as well as by one Crow scout, Curley, based on the analysis of Dr. John Gray in his *Custer's Last Campaign,* and at least a portion of the movement by Trumpeter Martin before he left the column. [An alternative scenario about what the Crow scouts saw is given on pages 152-63. —Ed.] Therefore, we have eyewitness accounts from both combatant groups, and archaeological artifacts found during the investigations of Medicine Tail Coulee in 1994 to compare and contrast for accuracy and validity.

Battle events in Medicine Tail Coulee and the cavalry's movement to Calhoun Hill—as well as the development of Indian opposition to those movements—are some of the most difficult to reconstruct from the historical record given the conflicting views and interpretations held by many interpreters of the battle. It is now, however, fairly well agreed by various scholars that Custer halted in the upper reaches of Medicine Tail Coulee and divided his command into two wings, a right, or northerly, wing under his direct command consisting of Companies C, I, and L. The left, or southerly, wing was commanded by Captain George Yates and consisted of Companies E and F.

A flattened brass trade kettle with pictograph engravings, found by Jason Pitsch. Similar in style to the Red Horse drawings, these pictographs of Indians and cavalry in conflict may well depict scenes from the Battle of the Rosebud, fought a week before the Battle of the Little Bighorn.
Glen Swanson

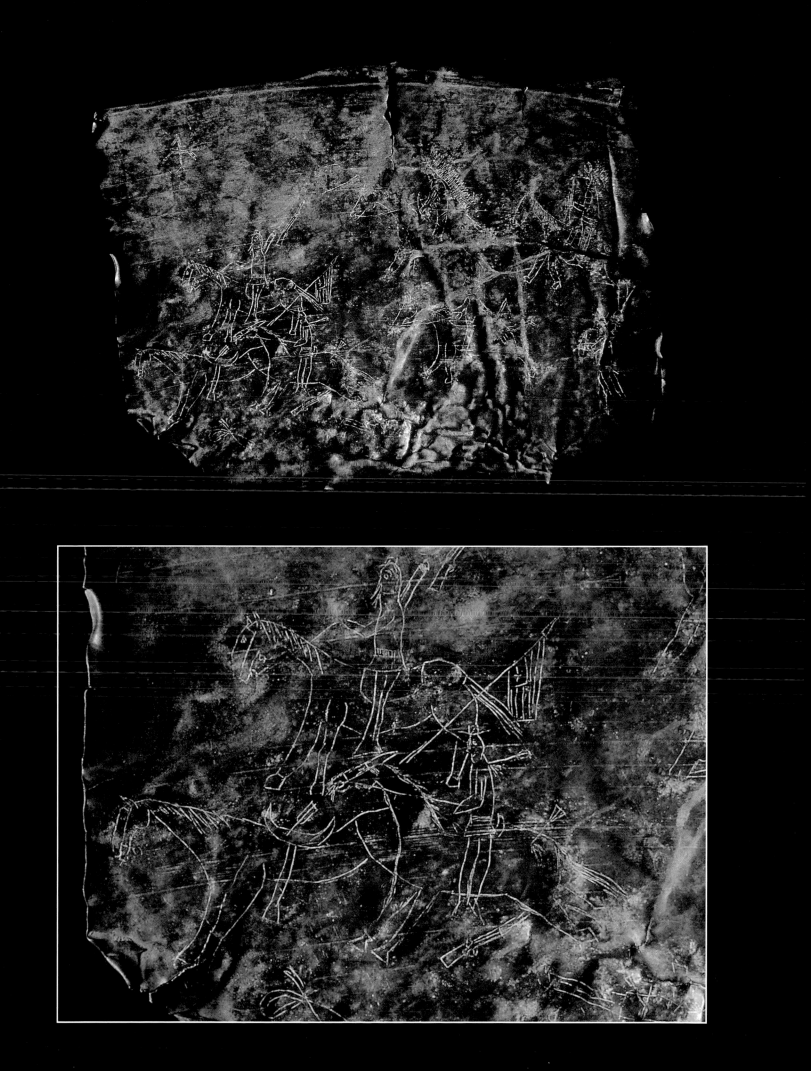

It is historian John Gray's assumption that Custer's strategy in dividing his command was for the left wing to conduct a feint to the mouth of Medicine Tail Coulee, while the remainder of the command was to move along ridges to the north and then descend in an attempt to ford the Little Bighorn and attack the north end of the village (map, page 18). Gray cited the late 1920s work of early battlefield researchers R. G. Cartright and Joseph Blummer and their relic cartridge case finds on Nye-Cartright Ridge as well as cartridge case finds on Luce Ridge. This physical evidence, Gray asserted, supported the idea that Custer moved some element of his command across the ridges between Medicine Tail Coulee and what has become known as Calhoun Hill. Gray also used other Cartright and Blummer artifacts found along a line from Nye-Cartright to Calhoun Hill and from Deep Coulee to Calhoun Hill as evidence of reconvergence of the two wings of Custer's battalion.

The only significant report from the Army's point of view is from the scout Curley. His account suggests that only light firing occurred at the coulee's mouth, which does not contradict other Indian accounts.

Lieutenant Oscar Long, who visited the battlefield in 1877, quizzed a number of his Lakota scouts who had fought Custer only the year before. Long reported that his Lakota informants mentioned only one man killed at the ford at the bottom of Medicine Tail Coulee. The Lakota identified him as an officer who had a compass and field glasses. An Army burial party account identified the man, if he was the same, as a noncommissioned officer found in an unmutilated condition on the west bank,

White Man Runs Him getting a drink from the Little Bighorn River at the ford at Medicine Tail Coulee. Photograph by Edward S. Curtis, 1907. *Museum of New Mexico*

probably trumpeter Henry Dose. Long's informants also reported that to them it appeared as though one company, near the river and mounted on bay horses, tried to run from the Indians but were fired upon by their own men, possibly those on Nye-Cartright Ridge. Perhaps this incident could also be interpreted as a company moving to the mouth of the coulee then retiring with the support of covering fire by another company or group held in a reserve position.

Respects Nothing, an Oglala Lakota, reported that Custer's command came over a ridge (presumably Nye-Cartright) to Calhoun Hill. He has Custer moving there from a southeasterly direction with many Indian warriors following him, most of them having crossed the river at the Medicine Tail Coulee ford. The warriors then enveloped the ridge, including Calhoun Hill and Custer Ridge, from the north, west, and south. Austin Red Bear, Flying Hawk, He Dog (Oglala Lakota), Standing Bear (Miniconjou Lakota), Iron Hawk (Hunkpapa Lakota), and Red Feather all reported that there was little or no fighting at Medicine Tail Coulee. They also recalled that the soldiers on the ridge made an orderly withdrawal to Calhoun Hill, where there was a good fight between the warriors and soldiers.

Other warriors recalled that there was a movement of soldiers down the coulee all the way to the ford. Some said the soldiers fought mounted, while others recalled that at least a few soldiers were dismounted. All remembered that the fight was relatively brief, and when the soldiers began their withdrawal it was along one side of a ravine now known as Deep Coulee. The warriors remembered pursuing the retreating soldiers up the ravine, dehorsing, and killing a few men as they went.

The discrepancies in the Lakota and Cheyenne accounts are of interest in their own right. Some reported that nothing occurred; others recalled only a light action; and yet others speak of a brief fight at the ford but a running fight to Calhoun Hill. Memories are fallible. Not everyone sees an event in the same way, nor does everyone participate in and remember every aspect of the same event the same way—especially not close combat. Native American oral traditions are just as fraught with conflicting recollections as are those of any other group. It is necessary to check and cross-check personal recollections against independent data to help determine which are the most reliable. And it is these conflicting Indian oral testimonies and those of army officers and men of Reno's command and the relief column that have generated the various theories of the action in Medicine Tail Coulee.

Although archaeological evidence for combat at the mouth of Medicine Tail Coulee is meager, it is not missing. In 1958, Don Rickey, then Custer Battlefield National Monument historian, and Little Bighorn battle scholar J. W. Vaughn reported finding a few .45-caliber Army carbine cartridge cases, some horse equipment, and bullets and Indian cartridge cases, as well as personal items at or near the ford. Jerome A. Greene's 1986 summary of prearchaeological investigation relic finds listed in his *Evidence and the Custer Enigma* demonstrated that lower Medicine Tail Coulee had been heavily collected. The firearms artifacts found include at least twelve .45/70 carbine cases, a cartridge, twelve .45 carbine bullets, an unidentified revolver case, two otherwise unidentified bullets, a .45 Colt bullet, two .50/70 cases, three .44 Henry cases, three Spencer cases, a .44 rimfire revolver, and a Winchester rifle. He also lists a number of nonfirearms artifacts including a tent pin, an arrowhead, two buttons, two knives, two tack buckles, a file fragment, an iron screw, a brass grommet, four brass cavalry insignia, a human skull fragment, a human finger bone, two other human bone fragments, and a human skeleton found in the same area.

The coulee has also seen many other uses over the years, primarily as grazing land, but at least one motion picture, *Little Big Man,* starring Dustin Hoffman, was filmed along the park tour road at the coulee's mouth.

During the 1994 archaeological investigations, the eastern side of the ford yielded two pieces of a broken model 1874 Army mess knife, a period butcher knife of the type that might have been carried by either a soldier or a warrior as a belt knife, a lead rifle ball, the cylinder pin to a model 1873 .45-caliber Colt Army revolver, and a .30-caliber Remington Smoot revolver cartridge case. These artifacts and the relic finds report by Rickey, Vaughn, and Greene are consistent and support the historical accounts that describe a small action with only limited weapons firing.

Rickey and Vaughn also found cartridge cases, bullets, and pieces of military equipment in their 1958 research around the south side of Deep Coulee. Jerome Greene reports at least eighteen .45/70 cases, forty-two .50/70 cases, four Spencer cases, ten .44 Henry cases, one .32-caliber rimfire case, two .45-caliber carbine bullets, one .50-caliber bullet, one Henry rifle, three military General Service buttons, a carbine sling swivel, a curry comb, an unidentified skull fragment, and several horse skeletons with associated cavalry equipment have been found over the years in this area. The 1994 archaeological inventory recovered Army spurs, picket pins (an iron stake used to tie horses at night while on campaign), and a curry comb, as well as a large quantity of cartridge cases and bullets. The Army equipment is scattered along Deep Coulee up to Calhoun Hill, which suggests a hurried movement in which there was enough haste to cause the loss of items from saddle bags or individual soldiers or both. Or the artifacts may also represent loss from wounded or killed men or horses. Some support for this comes from skeletal remains. At least one nearly complete human skeleton was found in 1928, and reports locate several more in the Deep Coulee area. The 1928 skeletal find was recently analyzed by physical anthropologist P. Willey of California State University, Chico. He found the man to be about thirty-five years old and about five foot, eight and a half inches tall. He was shot in the back of the head and had been stuck by a blunt instrument after the gunshot wound was administered. In addition his skeletal remains bore the evidence of at least ninety-eight cut marks, indicating probable castration at or about the time of death. These cut marks are consistent with the cutting and slashing of victorious Lakota and Cheyenne so as to mark their vanquished foe so he could not enjoy the spirit world to its fullest. Skeletons of four cavalry horses still partially outfitted with saddle gear were also found, although the horse remains could represent wounded animals that got loose elsewhere on the battlefield before wandering to Deep Coulee to die.

Overall, artifact patterning and distribution gives the impression of soldiers moving up Deep Coulee toward Calhoun Hill. The distribution of spent Army cartridge cases indicates some firing as the withdrawal continued, but it appears light. The distribution of Indian bullets also gives the distinct impression that the Army was under fire as it moved toward Calhoun Hill. And some of those bullets took their toll as demonstrated by the skeletons of soldier dead that have been found over the past seventy-five years.

In any case, archaeological and relic evidence is consistent with observations made by the Crow scout Curley, and the majority of Lakota and Cheyenne warriors who remarked on movement of soldiers to the ford and then a retreat under fire. In summary: A group of soldiers, perhaps a company of about forty men, moved down Medicine Tail Coulee to its mouth. There, a light and probably brief action pitted soldiers on the east bank against warriors on the west bank of Little Bighorn River, with perhaps some combat in the river itself. After this skirmish, the cavalrymen withdrew under relatively light fire and moved up the east bank of Deep Coulee to reunite with the rest of the command. Shortly thereafter, the command was overwhelmed and annihilated.

There is no end to speculation regarding the events at the Little Bighorn. Conspiracy theories abound, as do apology theories that seek to blame someone other than Custer for the epic defeat. Like any criminal investigation, the Little Bighorn battle has many witnesses and many suspects. The witnesses and the detectives point fingers at likely suspects based on their interpretation of the oral testimony and historical accounts. With the addition of the physical data from the systematic archaeological investigations, an unbiased data set is now introduced into the equation. The artifacts were in the ground at Medicine Tail Coulee and along Deep Coulee. This physical evidence of the event allows us to carefully evaluate the witness accounts and critically analyze the detectives' theories. The archaeological evidence validates a number of oral testimonies and historical accounts. It also clearly refutes others. While not excluding the possibility that Custer himself may have been in direct command at the ford, there is no evidence to support it either. The physical evidence and the validated testimonies and accounts combine to support the position that the left wing did make the movement to the river ford at Medicine Tail Coulee, while Custer and the right wing were engaged on Nye-Cartright Ridge. The withdrawal from Medicine Tail Coulee along Deep Coulee and a reconvergence of the command at Calhoun Hill is clear in the archaeological record, and further validates those eyewitness sources whose recollection of the events were gathered over the years.

The Little Bighorn battlefield may be a ceremonial site to many today. Native Americans view it in one context, an epitome of victory in an otherwise lost war for cultural survival. Other Americans see the battlefield in ways that evoke drama, sacrifice, glory, and grief. The archaeological evidence does not change those images and meanings; rather, it places the different meanings on a solid ground where each visitor can begin to truly understand a past where cultures were met in brief and deadly conflict.

After the Battle, by J. K. Ralston, depicts warriors and family members collecting arms, clothes, and other items belonging to the soldiers who fell with Custer. *Photo by Dennis Sanders, Hardin Photo*

One of the Indians' souvenirs is a notebook that belonged to First Sergeant Alexander Brown, G Troop, who died during Reno's initial attack. On this page Brown listed the "best shots" in his troop. His last entry, June 24, 1876, reads: "McEagan lost his carbine on the march while on duty with the pack train." Cheyenne warrior High Bull and several friends reused the pages to depict their war deeds. Here a warrior named Little Sun is shown counting coup with his banner lance on two Shoshone enemies. High Bull survived Little Bighorn by only five months. On November 25 he died in Colonel Ranald Mackenzie's raid on Dull Knife's village, where this notebook was found.

National Museum of the American Indian, photograph courtesy National Geographic Society

From the numerous soldiers' boot bottoms, such as these found by Jason Pitsch in his archaeolgical survey of the Hunkpapa village site, it is evident the Indians cut off the tops for various purposes. Shown at right is an example, a leather pouch that Dr. Thomas B. Marquis obtained from White Moon, a Northern Cheyenne who fought in the battle. It is now in the museum (catalog no. 39) of the Little Bighorn Battlefield National Monument.

Little Bighorn Battlefield National Monument

179

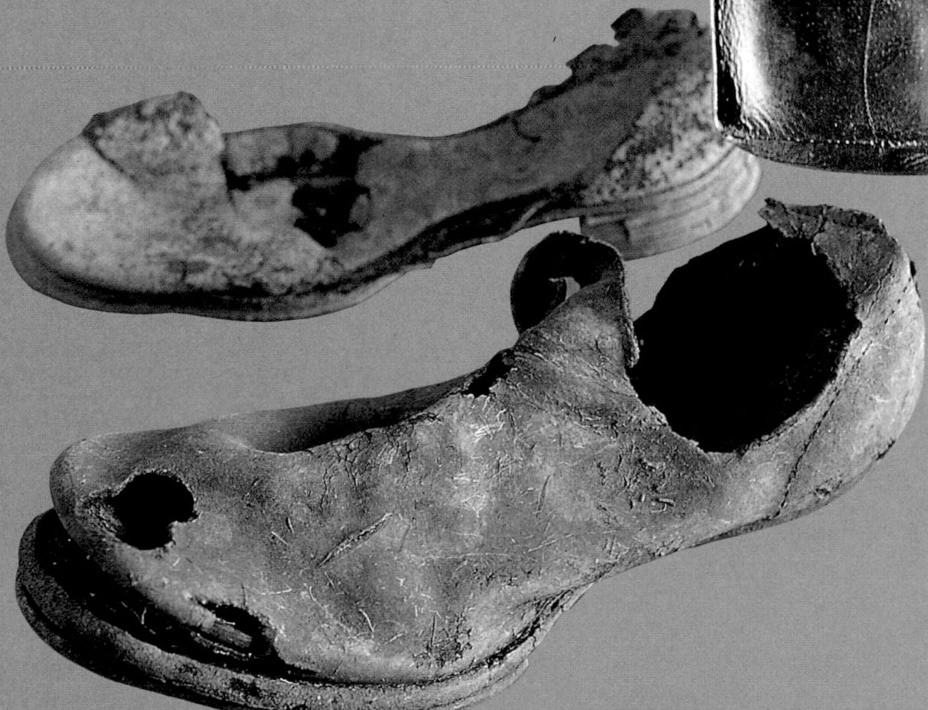

Reno's Retreat

Glen Swanson

Lieutenant McIntosh's ring and (opposite) a button like the one that was used by his brother-in-law, Lieutenant Francis M. Gibson, in identifying the badly mutilated body.
Glen Swanson Collection

As Douglas Scott indicates, the metal detector has clarified some of the mystery surrounding the action at Medicine Tail Coulee. Use of the metal detector is also helping to resolve some of the mystery at another site, this one a full four miles away from Custer Hill. It is along the Little Bighorn River where Major Marcus Reno and companies M, A, and G fought a brief but violent action before retreating to the bluffs above the Indian village.

The plans that Custer laid out that day included sending Captain Benteen with three companies to circle the village to the south, and sending Major Reno with three companies to attack the village at its nearest point. Custer took five companies farther down the river, presumably to attack the village from the rear, but this scenario is pure speculation since he did not reveal his own plan to anyone.

Reno opened the action as ordered, but when hundreds of mounted warriors rushed to block his advance, he chose to dismount his troops and fight on foot. Finding his position untenable, Reno then called retreat to a nearby stand of timber where cover was better. Not hearing from Custer and now being pressed on all sides, Reno chose to charge through the Indians and retreat to higher ground. Although the retreat quickly became a rout, Reno and his badly mauled command managed to reach the bluffs across the river where, joined by Benteen, the combined force made a successful stand.

In their rush to escape, Reno's troops left hundreds of metal items in their wake. These included buttons torn from shirts and jackets, accoutrements of all types, cartridges and shell casings, and spent bullets and arrowheads of every description. Virtually everything hurled at one another or lost by soldier and warrior during that life-or-death struggle was left behind after the dead were collected and buried. As the years passed, the relics of the Reno fight sank deeper and deeper into the soil as the former battlefield became pasturage and cropland.

Meanwhile, few historians paid much heed to the Reno fight. Speculation was offered concerning lines of combat and the movement of troops and Indians, but little data was available to support the various theories. Not until 1990, thanks to a young man's fascination with metal detecting, did hard evidence begin to surface. The detective was Jason Pitsch, whose father and uncle own the land that had been the site of Sitting Bull's Hunkpapa camp circle, the target of Reno's ill-fated attack.

Jason's job on the family farm was irrigating the fields close to the Little Bighorn River. In his spare time, while walking the fields with his metal detector, he began to find lost relics of the Reno fight. Aware of their importance, he carefully recorded his finds on a map.

Eventually, his fascinating finds attracted the attention of the National Park Service. With its help, the finds were plotted and published by Douglas Scott. The result brought some of Reno's movements into focus. Although the old ideas of Reno's fight in the timber still remained unchanged, his main line of attack was changed by the new information.

Further changes resulted from the discovery of maps drawn in the 1930s by historian Charles Kuhlman. Kuhlman's ideas of the battle were often thought imaginative but totally unreliable. His maps indicate that the timber fight took place a full 90 degrees farther to the right than generally believed. With Kuhlman's maps, Jason began to search the area and immediately reaped fantastic results. Scores of shell casings, cartridges, and personal effects torn from Reno's troopers clearly revealed a previously unknown line of battle that was confirmed by a reanalysis of published eye-witness accounts. Almost miraculously, particular land-marks and distances began to fall into place. Scout Charlie Reynolds, for instance, did not die two hundred yards away from Reno's line as previously believed but within twenty feet of it.

As Jason's study continued, more and more artifacts were discovered, recorded, and filed away. Hundreds of items were found on the Reno site and retreat and in Sitting Bull's camp. These included camping gear and personal items belonging to Indian families evidently lost in the hasty breakup of their camp, as well as an amazing quantity of material taken from slain troopers and their horses.

These relics not only open a window onto a little-known aspect of the Custer fight, they also highlight specific individuals such as John Sievertsen, who was a private in Company M when Major Reno led his unit to attack that hot summer day. Private Sievertsen, born in Norway, was thirty-four years old, a blacksmith, and the tallest man in his troop. During the fight, he became separated from his horse and was left on foot as his companions retreated across the river. Private Sievertsen spent a harrowing night alone in the valley until he managed to rejoin his troop the following day. Sievertsen's horse was not seen again until 1994, when Jason uncovered its remains. Killed by a .30-caliber bullet to the brain (the bullet was still in its skull), the horse evidently fell into heavy brush as the battle raged, and there it remained, covered each year by the spring floods but otherwise undisturbed for more than a century. Jason recovered all metal parts of the horse's accoutrements and even some pieces of leather—saddle, bridle, and saddlebags crammed with the standard fifty rounds of 45-70 carbine ammunition and such personal items as shirt and pants buttons, shaving cup, razor, pocketknife, eyeglasses, harmonica, and the tools of Sievertsen's blacksmithing trade. The most amazing artifact given up by the horse's grave, however, was a simple ivory toothbrush, still intact, with the initials J.S. neatly carved into the handle. It is one of the few personalized items ever found on the Little Bighorn battlefield.

Of the many spurs Jason found in the Indian village, one stands out. Deeply carved on its inside surface is the inscription "W 'I.'" Since John Wild was the only trooper in Captain Keogh's I Company whose last name began with a W, it is a safe assumption that the spur belonged to him.

Another Reno soldier identified through personal effects found on the battlefield was Donald McIntosh, First Lieutenant of Company G. The part-Chippewa officer was killed coming out of the timber during Reno's rush to the bluffs. His body had been badly mutilated and also burned in the prairie fire the Indians set as they left the area. His remains were identified by his brother-in-law, a fellow officer in the Seventh Cavalry, only through a button given to McIntosh by his wife before leaving Fort Lincoln. Buried where he fell, McIntosh's body was later reinterred, but when it was moved the graves detail left behind one of the most important artifacts found on the Reno battlefield—his wedding ring. With it was one of the very same sleeve buttons originally used to identify his body. Victorian in style, the ring bears the inside inscription D.M. & M.M. '66. Donald and his wife, Mollie, were married in October 1866.

Another remarkable find was a hammered brass kettle (see page 173) with finely drawn etchings of a battle with soldiers. Strikingly similar in style to the drawings by Red Horse (see pages 83–103), they most likely depict the fight with General Crook at the Rosebud a week earlier.

Since Jason Pitsch began his odyssey, thousands of Indian and cavalry artifacts have been cataloged and dozens of stories have come to light. Many more remain to be discovered. The finds have contributed greatly toward answering some of the lingering questions about one of the most controversial battles ever fought on American soil.

Reily's Ring

HERMAN J. VIOLA

"**M**y dear Sir, May I beg your interest in trying to recover the ring worn by my son, Lieutenant William V. W. Reily, Seventh Cavalry, USA [who was] sacrificed with Custer, June 25, 1876?. . . I am a widow, and my poor boy was my idol; being in every way, all a most exacting Mother could desire." With her appeal to the Commissioner of Indian Affairs, Ellen Roche Reily Johnson enclosed a drawing of the ring's crest, which featured a griffin with a key in its mouth. "You can readily understand how anxious I am to get it—being on his finger when he was killed. By exerting yourself in my behalf, you will have the lasting gratitude of a most afflicted Mother."

This touching plea brings into focus another dimension of Little Bighorn, its impact on the families of those who rode with Custer into the valley of death. At Fort Lincoln alone (headquarters of the Seventh Cavalry), more than a score of women, most of them the wives of officers, became widows that day. Custer's sister Maggie, wife of Lieutenant James Calhoun, lost her husband, three brothers, and a nephew.

The impact was not confined to Fort Lincoln. It affected friends, relatives, and loved ones across the country. It also cast a pall over the nation's centennial celebration that year in Philadelphia. At one end of the country, Americans were thumping their chests over their rise to world power, while half a continent away supposedly disorganized and poorly armed "savages" destroyed one of the nation's most glamorous and elite military units. Adding to the humiliation and horror was the knowledge that the Indians had ravaged and pillaged the bodies of Custer's men after the battle.

It was a sad moment for many Americans, but few could have been more anguished at the news than the mother of Lieutenant Reily. The death of her "beloved Willie" haunted the bereaved woman the rest of her life because she held herself responsible.

Willie was the son of Lieutenant William Reily, a naval officer who died in 1853 when the U.S.S. *Porpoise* was lost at sea with all hands. The elder Reily never saw his son, who was born after the *Porpoise* left on its final cruise. Willie's mother wanted him to be a naval officer like his father. The boy

eventually did receive an appointment to the Naval Academy in Annapolis, but he was not destined for a naval career. After failing to make satisfactory grades his first year, he was asked to repeat the course. When his second effort proved no better, he resigned. Reily spent the next eight months in Nicaragua on a surveying expedition before returning to Washington, where for two years he supervised the demolition of old ironclads left over from the Civil War. Meanwhile, his doting mother took matters into her own hands. Concerned that his future prospects did not seem very promising—how long could he support himself demolishing Civil War monitors?—she petitioned President Ulysses S. Grant in May 1875 to give her son a commission in one of the cavalry regiments. She did not neglect to point out that his father had died at sea "in the discharge of his duty as a naval officer."

Grant responded favorably. On the reverse of the letter he jotted: "War [Department]—Bring up when apt's come to be made—" That fall, the president appointed Reily a second lieutenant in the U.S. Army, contingent upon his passing the written examination. This must have given the aspiring officer a few anxious moments, but he passed—barely. The examination covered five areas of general knowledge: arithmetic, grammar, geography, history, and constitutional and international law. The maximum grade possible was 44; he scored 28. What Reily could not know, of course, is that next to his name on the list of applicants for a commission someone had recorded: "The president directs special attention. Son of Navy officer who was lost with U.S. Brig *Porpoise*."

Of the eight applicants who took the exam that day, Reily placed seventh. The best score was recorded by John Jordan Crittenden of Kentucky. He, too, died at the Battle of the Little Bighorn.

Reily received an appointment as a second lieutenant, but it was to the Tenth Cavalry, a black regiment of "Buffalo Soldier" fame. This did not please his mother, who immediately began agitating for his transfer to a white regiment, citing concerns for her son's health. Meanwhile, the strikingly handsome young man, now twenty-two years old, dutifully reported to Jefferson Barracks in St. Louis, where he spent the winter on garrison duty before receiving a transfer—"at Doctor's request"—to the Seventh Cavalry.

He left for Dakota Territory on March 3, 1876, with eleven musicians assigned to the Seventh Cavalry band. By May he found himself part of the army being assembled at Fort Lincoln for the forthcoming campaign to force Sitting Bull and his militant followers onto reservations.

Despite the fact that he could not ride very well—not unusual for cavalry

Lieutenant William Van Wyck Reily was wearing a family heirloom ring when he died with Custer at Little Bighorn. His grief-stricken mother eventually recovered the ring, which today is in the custody of the Smithsonian Institution. Preceding pages: William Van Wyck Reily's ring (Armed Forces Division, National Museum of Natural History); a letter by his mother, including a drawing of the ring, sent to the Commissioner of Indian Affairs (courtesy of Jonathan Wallen) with her photograph. This page: Reily's letter to his mother, May 15, 1876, with his carte de visite. On the reverse of the photograph she wrote: "My own darling boy sent me this from St. Louis." The Reily family photographs and the three letters he sent to his mother remain with the family.
Ellen T. White Collection

recruits—the earnest young officer anticipated a grand and glorious adventure. His enthusiasm is evident in a brief letter to his "dear ma" written on May 15. Fort Lincoln, he told her, was bustling with activity and thronged with excited friends and relatives awaiting the Seventh's departure. In fact, only the wives of his fellow officers were apprehensive about the expedition. "They were very much affected," he was surprised to discover, when saying good-bye to them the day before, even though their husbands were seasoned veterans with considerable campaign experience. No matter. He certainly was not worried and, like Custer, predicted a quick and successful exercise. In fact, a reporter for the *New York Sun* was accompanying them into the field. "You had better take the paper if you wish to receive glowing descriptions of our adventures."

The first day, the regiment covered fourteen miles. That afternoon, as supper was being prepared, Reily learned that an Indian scout was about to take some dispatches back to Fort Lincoln, and he took the opportunity to send his mother another note. It was hard to write, he grumbled, because so many of the officers were doing the same thing, and they kept asking him for the correct date.

Although a little sore after his first day in the saddle, he was otherwise quite pleased with his performance. "I was very much afraid that I would have trouble learning to ride," he admitted, "[but] I have made out very well." One incentive was the Seventh's standing rule that an officer thrown from his horse had to open "a bucket of champagne." "I have ridden some of the most vicious animals in the command," he boasted, "and with the little practical & theoretical knowledge I have gotten along as well as any." Reily urged his mother to write frequently, care of Fort Lincoln, because couriers would be in continual communication with the regiment. "No signs of any Indians yet," he joked.

Reily's last letter is dated June 21, 1876, only four days before the Seventh's rendezvous with Sitting Bull. Already, Indian fighting had lost some of its luster. His company had just returned to the main command from a fourteen-day scout along the Powder River and was about to leave on a fifteen-day scout to the mouth of the Little Bighorn. "Our horses are almost played out, [and] we lost two in route," he reported. The country was desolate and barren, "with cactus & sagebrush the only things for one's eyes to rest upon, and [they] make a country to march through so bad that it can only be imagined and not described." Moreover, after almost six weeks in the field, the command had yet to see its first hostile Indian, although Custer was promising "a fight" inside of four days. "We have pretty hard times," he confessed, "but I assure you that I am satisfied, and am not complaining." He was nonetheless looking forward to September—"if I live through this campaign"—when he planned to meet his mother in Philadelphia at the fair. Meanwhile, he closed, "Pray for your devoted son, Willie."

Custer kept his promise, but Sitting Bull altered the script. According to Lieutenant Charles DeRudio, Willie's body— "shot full of arrows"—was found lying next to that of Custer within the circle of dead troopers and horses that gave rise to the notion of a "last stand."

Reily's mother was inconsolable. Immersed in remorse, she sought to learn everything she could about the circumstances of his death. She corresponded with survivors of the fight, and she befriended the widows of his fellow officers, among them Mrs. Custer, Mrs. Calhoun, and Mrs. Yates, whose husband had been her son's superior officer. Writing to Mrs. Yates in October 1876—"my darling boy wrote me how fond he was of his captain"—she described a recent visit to St. Louis and a week of "painful pleasure" spent with the mother of Lieutenant James Sturgis, whose son had also died that day. "Mrs. Sturgis and my loss are so nearly alike—our boys being the same age." She asked Mrs. Yates for a photograph of her husband and offered one of Willie's in return. "Do write me— tell me anything you may have heard concerning the fearful slaughter, and can you tell me anything of the remains being brought in?"

Since the ring was not on her son's body when it was buried, Mrs. Johnson made its recovery her all-consuming passion. She appealed to army officers, Indian agents, and the editors of western newspapers. All her appeals included drawings of the ring with its distinctive crest, which was of the distinguished Key family of Georgetown, for young Reily on his father's side was a member of that prominent family and related to Francis Scott Key, author of the national anthem.

Doubtless, most of those Mrs. Johnson approached warned her it would be a hopeless quest, like seeking the proverbial needle in a haystack, but she never lost faith. Eventually, an Indian agent in Montana informed her that a Sioux Indian to whom he had shown the drawing recalled seeing the ring in one of the hostile camps. This news inspired her in April 1877 to ask the Commissioner of Indian Affairs and the Secretary of War to send a circular to each of their western stations, a request that they promptly honored.

Meanwhile, the ring had already been recovered. Earlier that month, Lieutenant William Philo Clark, Second Cavalry, obtained the ring from a Northern Cheyenne who surrendered at Fort Robinson, Nebraska. Clark, assuming that the ring had been taken from one of the dead soldiers at Little Bighorn, notified the editor of the *Army and Navy Journal*. Shortly thereafter, it was presented to Reily's grateful mother. In 1944, the family donated it to the Smithsonian Institution. Reily's letters from the Little Bighorn campaign remain with the family.

Custer: The Making of a Myth

JOHN P. LANGELLIER

If I were an Indian, I often think I would greatly prefer to cast my lot among those of my own people who adhered to the free plains, rather than submit to the confined limits of the reservation, there to be the recipient of the blessed benefits of civilization, with its vices thrown in without stint of measure.

—GEORGE ARMSTRONG CUSTER

In July 1857, seventeen-year-old George Armstrong Custer reported to the United States Military Academy at West Point to don the cadet gray. The ruddy-faced youth brought with him enthusiasm, ambition, pride, a penchant for practical jokes, and a zest for life.

During his days along the banks of the Hudson River, Cadet Custer spent considerable time in extracurricular activities including, according to historian Robert M. Utley in *Cavalier in Buckskin*, "many an all-night excursion to Benny Haven's, the already legendary off-post drinking establishment." There, "Fanny," as his classmates called him for his flowing, curly hair, indulged himself in pleasures far from military discipline. Poor grades and an incredible number of demerits, even for such relatively harmless pranks as throwing snowballs from his barracks late at night, contributed to his graduation as the "goat" (last) of his class. As one of his fellow cadets said, Custer "is always connected with all the mischief that is going on, and never studies any more than he possibly can help."

Although Custer did excel in several martial subjects at West Point, in others he was more a dreamer and romantic than a practical or deep thinker. For a course in ethics he wrote an essay, "The Red Man," in which he demonstrated more knowledge of James Fenimore Cooper's popular fiction than anything even vaguely based on fact.

In the essay, young Fanny wrote: "When we first beheld the red man, we beheld him in his home, the home of peace and plenty, the home of nature." Custer continued his noble savage motif, blustering that American Indians were "favored sons of nature" who "stood in their native strength and beauty, stamped with the proud majesty of free born men, whose souls never knew fear, or whose eyes never

This highly dramatic and fanciful lithograph entitled *Custer's Last Fight* established the popular image of the Battle of the Little Bighorn. Published in 1881 and distributed by Anheuser Busch, it hung in saloons across the country. It was one of the many drawings that generated false ideas about the battle, such as Custer's long flowing hair and saber. (Custer had cut his famous locks years earlier, and the sabers issued to the cavalry had been left in the wagons.) The artist actually visited the site—hence the terrain is rendered rather accurately—but the Indians, with their shields and spears, resemble Zulu warriors and bear little resemblance to Plains Indians.
Armed Forces Division, National Museum of American History

The stuff that legends are made of: George Armstrong Custer and his beloved "Libbie," the former Elizabeth Bacon. They married on February 9, 1864. Later that year Custer gained a second star, being promoted to major general in command of the Third Cavalry Division. After the Civil War, his permanent rank reverted to lieutenant colonel.
Glen Swanson Collection

**Custer and Libbie on April 12, 1865,
three days after Appomattox.**
Glen Swanson Collection

quailed beneath the fierce glance of men." This state of near-perfection had ended because those "monarchs of the west" had become "like withered leaves of their own native forest, scattered in every direction by the fury of the tempest . . . on the verge of extinction . . . [on] his last foothold, clutching his bloodstained rifle, resolved to die amidst the horrors of slaughter. . . ." But such resistance would prove futile, and the Indian soon would "be talked of as a noble race who once existed but have now passed away."

Indians were abstractions to Custer then; he'd never seen one.

More pressing matters occupied his thoughts during the final days at West Point as the threat of the Civil War loomed. When fighting erupted in 1861, Custer concentrated on the immediate task of making his military mark.

As a newly commissioned lieutenant of cavalry, Custer was in a position to do just that. In March 1862, he led a daring charge at Cedar Run, Virginia, where he drove away Confederate pickets. Less than two months later, he saved a key bridge from being destroyed by the enemy, and on the same day captured a Rebel battle flag, the first instance in the Army of the Potomac's history.

Custer's exploits soon brought him to the attention of important superiors. General George B. McClellan appointed Custer to his staff, describing him as "simply a reckless, gallant boy undeterred by fatigue, unconscious of fear; but his head was always clear in danger and he always brought me clear and intelligible reports of what he saw under the heaviest fire."

McClellan judged rightly because Custer truly seemed to be "without fear," constantly cool in combat, often in the thick of things even as a staff officer. He killed an enemy major and took the dead man's "Toledo blade," inscribed "Draw me not without provocation," as a trophy of personal combat. Eleven times Custer had his horse shot from under him; once he narrowly escaped capture. By the age of twenty-three his heroics had earned him promotion to brevet brigadier general of volunteers, an exalted but temporary rank. This youngest general in the Union Army began to dress the part of a cavalier, the streaming locks now set off by flamboyant custom-designed uniforms, prompting one contemporary to label him "a circus rider gone mad!"

Genuine hero or fashion plate dandy? Two views of Custer had already begun to emerge. Some saw him as a grandstander; others viewed him as a *beau sabreur* whom youths could emulate and fair maidens admire. Custer's lofty rise gained him considerable stature and laid the foundation for yet more achievement and fame. With the silver stars of a brigadier general winking brightly from his shoulder straps, "Custer's luck" was riding high.

With his newfound stature, Custer took leave in the winter of 1862–63 to return to his hometown and pursue Judge Daniel S. Bacon's daughter, one of Monroe, Michigan's most sought-after young women. At first, Custer gained little ground in his campaign for Elizabeth Bacon's affection. From a higher social stratum than Custer, whose father was a blacksmith, she probably would not have met the youthful officer had it not been for the circumstances of war.

Dissimilarity in backgrounds was but one obstacle to his courtship. Elizabeth, or "Libbie," as she was known to her intimates, had one afternoon witnessed George staggering his way home from a drinking bout. That did not sit well with the religious, morally motivated young woman. Nor did Custer's insistence on wooing others. Yet "Autie" persisted. (This nickname dated from childhood when

In the study of their quarters at Fort Abraham Lincoln, Dakota Territory, "Autie" (Custer's boyhood nickname) and Libbie appear intent at their literary pursuits. On the wall hang portraits of two of their favorite military leaders: Phil Sheridan and George Custer. Photographer unknown, 1875. *National Park Service, Little Bighorn Battlefield National Monument*

he couldn't pronounce "Armstrong.") Tenacity, when coupled with brashness, had often brought him victory. Libbie's defenses began to wear thin. Custer's luck was still on a roll.

His romantic campaign was aided by his growing renown as an officer bold and reckless in battle. And as Robert M. Utley put it: "Newspaper reporters saw him as superb copy . . . and headlines extolled the deeds of a dashing youth they labeled the 'Boy General.'"

Whatever her reasons, Libbie began to give way to "Dear C—." And although she worried that "a thousand doubts come into my mind like tormenting devils and I doubt that I love him," she decided that "I someday will be his 'little wife.'" That she did, but she was anything but a mere ornament during their dozen years of marriage, which began on February 9, 1864, at the First Presbyterian Church in

Monroe. Elizabeth Custer soon became a driving force in George's personal life and career.

By February 28, just after their honeymoon, Custer was back in the field raiding into Confederate territory in the direction of Charlottesville, Virginia. Toward the end of March, he was given leave and met Libbie in Washington, D.C. They looked for a suitable residence for her and attended the theater and various social functions, often with high-ranking officials. The pair even met Abraham Lincoln, who knew of Custer's military exploits and teased Libbie about them.

After this whirlwind of activities, the young general reported on March 31 to his new superior, General Philip H. Sheridan, who was to exert great influence on Custer's career. Within days the "Boy General" was back in the field. More victories came his way. Both his good fortune and bravado led to appointment as major general of volunteers in command of the Third Division of the Army of the Potomac's Cavalry Corps. Custer's younger brother Tom, who had transferred to Autie's staff as an aide-de-camp, had himself earned remarkable laurels: He was twice decorated with the Medal of Honor—a rare distinction in U.S. military annals then, or since.

No slacker himself, Major General Custer more often than not charged in the front of his troops, but not without the cost of casualties to those who followed his lead. All the conspicuous glory-gaining came to a halt after Robert E. Lee's surrender in April 1865. With the war over, the Custers went to Richmond, where they lodged for a short time in Jefferson Davis's former residence. Soon after, they settled into a new command at Hempstead, Texas. Custer's father, Emmanuel, and brother Tom joined them, the latter once more posted as Autie's aide, the former as a civilian forage master.

Whatever the advantages of nepotism, the new assignment turned sour. Custer proved less successful as a peacetime leader than as a wartime commander. He seemed poorly equipped to deal with the problems of disciplining citizen-soldier troops anxious to return home. Instead of according him respect, many of Custer's troops held him in low esteem. To make matters worse, by 1866 the Army faced a considerable reduction in force. Custer received news that he would revert to his permanent rank of captain in the Fifth Cavalry.

Once again, Custer was off to Washington, this time to meet Secretary of War Edwin Stanton to petition for Regular Army commissions for himself, his brother Tom, and his comrade George Yates. Custer explored alternatives in civilian employment, including a visit to Wall Street. He also considered an offer of $16,000 a year—double his major general's pay—to join Benito Juárez's forces as adjutant general of the Mexican Army. Ulysses S. Grant, still the senior officer of the U.S. Army, and the secretary of war both gave their blessings, but the plan fell victim to diplomatic politics.

Then Custer joined President Andrew Johnson's tour to rally the nation around Reconstruction policies at odds with the punitive goals of the Radical Republicans. Custer considered politics, especially Congress, as another avenue for his aspirations. But on July 28, 1866, he accepted a commission as a lieutenant colonel of the Seventh Cavalry. By October, Autie and Libbie left the grand circle of the president and his entourage for their new home at Fort Riley, Kansas.

In March 1867, Custer left his quiet life in garrison to taste his first campaign against Indians, the former subjects of his ethics paper at West Point. General Winfield S. Hancock gathered forces, including the Seventh Cavalry, for an expedition against Cheyennes and other groups of native people residing within the boundaries of his command. Custer recorded that Hancock's intentions were to convince the Indians that the government had the power to punish any who raised their hands against whites. Custer expressed these intentions succinctly. The combined force of cavalry, artillery, and infantry was "by its imposing appearance and its early presence in the Indian country to check or intimidate the Indians."

Theodore Davis, a newspaper reporter, met Custer as he joined Hancock. Davis commented that the Seventh Cavalry's lieutenant colonel was "endowed by nature with a confidence in himself which was never boastfully exploited, and a believer that the future would surely unfold a continuation of the successful past—Custer's luck, his talismanic guard was trusted by him all too blindly. . . ." Now, as before, Custer had attracted the press, which continued to keep him in public view, a place where he seemed quite comfortable.

Custer later set down his own version of what he and the expedition faced as they prepared in order to promote the impression that he was a seer when it came to Indian campaigning. He grandly described his efforts:

> . . . to seek what? fame and glory? How many military men have reaped laurels from Indian campaigns? Does he strive to win the approving smile of his countrymen? That is indeed in this particular instance, a difficult task. For let him act as he may in conducting or assisting in a campaign against Indians, if he survives the campaign he can feel assured of this fact, that one half of his fellow citizens at home will revile him for his zeal and pronounce his success, if he achieves any, a massacre of poor, defenseless, harmless Indians; while the other half, if his efforts to chastise the common enemy are not crowned with satisfactory results, will cry, "Down with him. . . ."

Davis noted Custer's growing depression during his less than successful Kansas field service in the spring and summer of 1867. Davis wrote that he "never saw him [Custer] so moody, as he increasingly took on a 'somber mien.'" One of Custer's company commanders, Captain Albert Barnitz, who at first shared Davis's favorable impression of Custer, described a man who had "become 'bilious'" perhaps because he was "mad about something. . . ."

Soon after Barnitz posted his May 15, 1867, letter, Custer's own actions tended to support the assessment. Autie wrote to Libbie that he was reading *The Anatomy of Melancholy*, an appropriate title given what seemed to be his frame of mind. For remedy, he enjoined his wife: "Do hurry and come to your boy." When,

Tom, one of three Custer brothers to die at Little Bighorn. He is shown here wearing the two Congressional Medals of Honor he earned for his exploits on Civil War battlefields, one of the few ever so decorated.
Glen Swanson Collection

191

on May 12, it appeared that he would not see her "until fall or winter," he wrote to Libbie that he would "try to kill time by killing Indians. . . ."

Though he may have blurted that out of personal disappointment, Custer had certainly shed the sympathetic veneer he once had for the "red man." He had come to view native peoples as little more than game to be pursued and dispatched like antelope or buffalo:

> It is to be regretted that the character of the Indian as described in Cooper's interesting novels is not a true one. . . . So intimately has he become associated with the Government as ward of the nation, and so prominent a place among the questions of national policy does the much mooted Indian question occupy, that it behooves us no longer to study this problem from works of fiction, but to deal with it as it exists in reality. . . . Stripped of the beautiful romance with which we have been so long willing to envelop him, transferred from the inviting pages of the novelist to the localities where we are compelled to meet with him, in his native village, on the warpath, and raiding upon our frontier settlements . . . the Indian forfeits his claim to the appellation noble red man.

With the veil of fiction removed, Custer now saw the Indian, "as he ever has been, a savage in every sense of the word; not worse, perhaps, than his white brother would be, similarly born and bred, but one whose cruel and ferocious nature far exceeds that of any wild beast of the desert."

Even though Custer still had only passing contact with Indians, he fancied himself a specialist on the subject, particularly when it came to issuing orders to subordinates. For instance, in May 1867, Captain Myles Keogh, commander of Company I, Seventh Cavalry, was directed by Custer, through the regimental adjutant, to: "Without regard to age, sex, or condition kill all Indians you may encounter, belonging to the Sioux or Cheyennes except [if] you are convinced they belong to certain bands of friendly Indians, reported as being at the headwaters of the Republican [River]. . . ." Custer closed by ordering Keogh not "to burden" his "command with prisoners. . . ." The intent was total war with a vengeance.

Custer concluded with the warning: "As to pursuing Indians, while it is not strictly forbidden, in doing so, you must exercise the greatest precaution against stratagem and surprise, remembering, that it is the Indians' 'Ruse De Guerre' to decoy small Garrisons away from their position of defense."

Keogh replied (perhaps with a touch of irony): "I never before appreciated the difficulty of pursuing Indians and have concluded that without knowing exactly where to surprise their camp, or having a guide who can track them at a run, it is a waste of horse flesh and time to endeavor to come up with them."

Custer valued guides, particularly those white scouts whom he pronounced "a most interesting as well as useful and necessary portion of our frontier population." Terrible deaths often awaited them, according to Custer, but they were no fools. He found their "most striking characteristics" to be "love of adventure, a natural and cultivated knowledge of the country without recourse to maps, deep hatred of the Indian and an intimate acquaintance with all habits and customs of

Second Lieutenant George Custer (right) and his former West Point classmate Lieutenant James B. Washington, a Confederate prisoner of war captured at the battle of Fair Oaks (also known as Seven Pines), Virginia, share a moment before the camera, May 31, 1862. George was soon to enjoy a meteoric rise in rank, vaulting from junior officer to brigadier general in less than a year.
Library of Congress

the latter, whether pertaining to peace or war, and last but most necessary to their calling skill in the use of firearms and in the management of a horse."

Custer clearly intended to be identified with the type and went to some lengths to be perceived as a "hunter" or "scout." Others responded favorably to the affectation. For example, William E. Curtis, a correspondent for the Chicago *Interocean,* could have been Custer's press agent when he described him as "a great man—a noble man" who was:

> . . . a soldier that neither drinks, smokes, nor swears. But what, some one will ask, are his vices? His soldiers will tell you he has none, unless an almost inordinate love for the higher brute creation may be called such, for General Custer has the best dogs and the best horses he can procure within the limits of search. His leash of hounds is probably as large and well-bred as any in the country, and his own and the horses of his regiment, the Seventh Cavalry, are famous all over the States, while he has the reputation of being the best sportsman and the most accurate shot in the army.

Luther North, who had achieved a certain amount of fame as a scout himself, remarked that "Custer was quite social and did a great deal of talking. He was a very enthusiastic hunter. . . . While General Custer was always telling of the great shots he made each day that he hunted, he didn't seem to care much about hearing of any one else doing good shooting."

Although some scoffed behind his back at his prowess with firearms—Custer once shot his own horse in the head while hunting—he fancied himself with the sharpshooting skills of James Fenimore Cooper's woodsmen and adopted the outward appearance of those heroes of the Leatherstocking tales. Although Custer

After moving west, Custer began to assume the guise of a frontiersman, setting aside his cavalier image for a new persona as "the man who knows Indians."
Glen Swanson Collection

insisted that Cooper misrepresented Indians, he saw no irony in modeling his own persona after Cooper's Hawkeye, Deerslayer, and Pathfinder.

By the autumn of 1868, Custer's flowing locks from his days as the dashing Yankee cavalryman had disappeared. Now, "with his hair cut short, and a perfect menagerie of Scotch fox hounds," Custer added a beard and his first buckskin field jacket to the ensemble. That garment was to become a sort of personal symbol. By donning it, Custer merged a literary figure of the Victorian era, the frontiersman, with another powerful hero image of the time, the soldier-aristocrat. As historian Richard Slotkin has observed, Custer thereby created a hybrid of two prominent heroes of popular lore being promoted by dime novelists and journalists.

Custer was dressed to kill, and that was what his superior, William Tecumseh Sherman, intended. Sherman chose to translate the scorched-earth warfare that he had practiced during the "march to the sea" in the South and apply it to the West. To carry out the subjugation of the various natives of the Southern Plains, including Arapahos, Cheyennes, Comanches, and Kiowas wintering in Indian Territory (Oklahoma), Sherman called upon his faithful Civil War lieutenant, Sheridan. In turn, Sheridan sought out his protégé Custer and wired, "Generals Sherman, Sully and myself, and nearly all the officers of your regiment, have asked for you, and I hope the application will be successful. Can you come at once?"

On November 11, 1868, attired in an outfit selected to reflect his newly cultivated persona, Custer led his command southward. Two weeks had passed when he drew his command up to attack Black Kettle's village along the Washita River. This Cheyenne chief had advocated accommodation with whites, but during the Civil War, Black Kettle's peaceful overtures had been rewarded by Colorado Volunteers, who attacked his encampment at Sand Creek. Now he and his people were again to suffer.

To the strains of "Charge" and the opening notes of "Garry Owen," the tune that ever after was associated with the Seventh Cavalry, troopers descended on the sleeping Cheyenne. Men, women, children, and animals were thrown into chaos.

Ten minutes later, the din stopped almost as quickly as it had begun. The enemy was subdued. At first it appeared that the fray had cost the Indians dearly while leaving the soldiers nearly unscathed. However, it was soon learned that Major Joel Elliott had been killed. Nineteen others who volunteered to follow Elliott's call of "Here goes for a brevet or a coffin!" shared his fate when they pursued a retreating Cheyenne group out of the camp area only to be ambushed, surrounded, and killed to a man.

Some blamed Custer's poor handling of the battle, charging that he should not have divided his force or withdrawn from the field until he had found Elliott and reunited the command. An existing rift between Custer and some of his officers widened, never to close. Tensions among the Seventh Cavalry's officer cadre twisted another turn tighter. Those in Custer's inner circle enjoyed his favor. Others—such as Captain Frederick Benteen, in many respects the most outwardly anti-Custer officer in the regiment—were kept at arm's length.

Perhaps Custer sought to ease the pain of Washita by an offer that Benteen claimed was made to the officers. After returning to garrison with prisoners, Custer invited those who were interested "to avail themselves of the services of

Within weeks of Custer's death, renderings of "the last charge" or "the last stand," lionizing him as a valiant martyr, became popular sales items.
Autry Museum of Western Heritage

PUBLISHED BY CURRIER & IVES Copyright, 1876, by Currier & Ives, N.Y. 115 NASSAU ST. NEW YORK

CUSTER'S LAST CHARGE.
BREVET MAJOR-GENERAL GEORGE A. CUSTER, LIEUTENANT-COLONEL 7TH U.S. CAVALRY.
Killed in the battle with the Sioux, June 25th, 1876.

a captured squaw" by coming "to the squaw round-up corral." Benteen contended that Custer secured the most attractive prize in the group for himself, a matter that supposedly was "common camp gossip in military circles" of what was then "a not uncommon practice of the frontier military."

Custer frequently mentioned the one Cheyenne woman who, others averred, shared his bed during the winter of 1868–69. She was Monahsetah, daughter of Chief Little Rock, an important Cheyenne who was killed at Washita. Custer described her as about twenty years old, comely, bright, intelligent, and possessed of "a disposition more inclined to be merry than one usually finds among Indians." Custer sang her praises loud and often in his later public writings, referring to her "as belonging to the aristocracy, if not royalty itself. . . ." He even brought the appealing young woman home to Fort Hays, Kansas.

At first, Libbie Custer seemed to view the Cheyenne woman as savage, fearing Monahsetah would stab her on their meeting. Libbie was soon "disarmed" by the charms of the woman's baby, a child born just a few months after her mother's captivity began, timing that squelched rumors that the infant had been sired by Custer. If Monahsetah had been Lieutenant Colonel Custer's mistress, Elizabeth Custer may have known about it. Yet given racial views of the period, military wives probably could not conceive of Indian women as rivals for their husbands.

If the action at Washita might be counted a victory of sorts, the U.S. Army's activities farther west had taken a different turn. From 1865 through 1867, Red Cloud, an Oglala Lakota, had led Lakota, Cheyenne, and Arapaho warriors in a series of fights to preserve traditional hunting grounds threatened by a trail being built to goldfields in Montana Territory. Hostilities were ended by the 1868 Treaty of Fort Laramie, where Northern Cheyennes, Northern Arapahos, Crows, and Lakotas "touched the pen" to an agreement with the federal government. In return for the U.S. Army abandoning three military posts built after the Civil War along the Bozeman Trail, Indian signatories were to take up life on reservations. The government's theory was that once the Plains peoples were so located and confined, the foundation would be laid "to turn the nomadic warriors into peaceful farmers."

Few Indians who signed the pivotal document fully understood its meaning. However grudgingly, many thousands of Indians eventually reported to reservations. Others, however, refused to sign or comply, including Tatanka-Iyotanka, a powerful Hunkpapa Lakota better known to the encroachers as Sitting Bull. He epitomized the so-called nontreaties and chose to continue the life of his ancestors, remaining free to follow the game and pursue the lifeways of his youth. He and others refused to abide by the Treaty of Fort Laramie.

Meanwhile, Custer followed his orders to diverse postings along with several leaves of absence that brought him home to Monroe, as well as on outings to Chicago, St. Louis, New York City, and even a buffalo hunt with Russian royalty guided by none other than William F. Cody—Buffalo Bill. More and more, his time away from strictly military duties caused Custer to pursue the high life of a gentleman of property and position.

This ambition partially accounted for his turn toward literary pursuits between 1867 and 1875. Over that period Custer wrote fifteen accounts under the apt pseudonym "Nomad" for *Turf, Field and Farm,* a sportsmen's magazine published in New York. Most of the pieces had to do with hunting, but three treated Indian campaigns and differed from versions Custer later published.

His efforts to take up the pen did not dissuade Custer from brandishing the sword. He remained active in the field, having transferred westward with his command in early 1873 to the Dakotas. Orders included escort duty for railroad surveyors entering Yellowstone country. In the summer of 1874, he led an exploring expedition in the Black Hills "to see what he could find." From those Black Hills, or "Paha Sapa" in Oglala Lakota, had come rumors of gold.

Black Elk, destined to be a holy man among his Lakota people, was a youth when Custer entered the sacred land. He later summed up the impact of Pe-hin Hanska's (Lakota for "Long Hair") reconnaissance, recalling that Custer's column had discovered "the yellow metal that makes the *wasichus* [whites] crazy; and that is what made the bad trouble. . . ." Custer "had no rights to go there, because all the country was ours. Also, the *wasichus* had made a treaty with Red Cloud that said it would be ours as long as grass grows and water flows." As the leader of those who came to violate the sanctity of the Black Hills, Custer was pronounced the "chief of thieves" by Black Elk and the trail he blazed, the "thieves road."

Many native peoples who faced him could readily accept that judgment because, as had so many other whites, Long Hair had broken faith with them. Years before, Custer had smoked the pipe in a council of Cheyennes and vowed that his intent was not to make war. One of the headmen did not believe him and promised that if he violated his vow the soldier and all his men would be killed. The headman then tapped the pipe's ashes onto Custer's boot to underscore the gravity of the pledge.

After the 1874 expedition discovered gold, Secretary of War William Belknap resolved to crush Sitting Bull and others of his mind-set. To convert his designs into action, Belknap charged the military high command to make preparations for punitive actions that would bring the nontreaty groups into reservations. Custer then prophesied what was to come, when, during an interview with a New York reporter he quipped: "The Indians are quiet now and offering no armed resistance, because they have been told by the military officers that the government will keep its word. But the moment they think that it is not acting in good faith, there will be a rising of every tribe between the Missouri River and the Rocky Mountains."

The time seemed ripe for another diversion to the East. In September 1875, the Custers arrived in New York for an extended holiday. All the while, he concentrated on writing for *Galaxy,* a popular illustrated tabloid of the era that allowed him to reach a broad audience with his self-aggrandizing tales. Between January 1872 and October 1874, he had submitted a series of articles on his western adventures for *Galaxy* that ultimately were compiled into a book, *My Life on the Plains,* published by Sheldon & Company of New York in 1874.

Benteen was quick to dub this "My Lie on the Plains." Benteen's assessment of the book was "readable enough, but to one who was along through the whole series of years which it covers, the falsity of much of it is as glaring as the noonday sun."

Spurred on by his literary aspirations and the enhanced notoriety publication brought him, Autie worked on his Civil War memoirs. Although funds were running low, he and Elizabeth relished their stay in the city. But the two never seemed to have the money to live in as grand a manner as they might have wished. During their New York stay, Custer dabbled in stock speculation, hoping to gain a more secure financial status. He did not succeed.

Then, in March 1876, Custer received a summons to testify before a Senate committee investigating Belknap, who at that point was charged with selling post traderships at garrisons in the West. Custer gave hearsay evidence about efforts by Belknap, who had resigned as Secretary of War, and about his avowed accomplice, Orville Grant, the president's brother. His exposition inflamed President Grant, who nearly denied Custer field command of his unit as it readied for campaign duty. Once again, it took allies in high places, including Generals William Tecumseh Sherman and Alfred Terry, as well as some support from the press, for Yellow Hair to save his career.

Custer was now determined "to orchestrate a dramatic success for himself" because, as he informed some of the Indian scouts who went with him, "this campaign against the Sioux would be his last and he must win a great victory." His future hinged on it.

And so, on May 17, 1876, the Seventh Cavalry, arrayed for combat, set out from Fort Lincoln with Lieutenant Colonel and Mrs. George Armstrong Custer at the head of the column. They often had ridden together, but at the Little Heart River the couple parted. On the morning of May 18, Libbie made her way back to the post, while Autie and his men continued southward where for the next four days they experienced rain and pelting hail, later turning to snow.

Nearly a month of reconnaissance patrols passed before Custer's commander, Brigadier General Alfred Terry, had gathered sufficient information on Indian movement to prescribe a course of action. Calling together his two immediate subordinates, Custer and Colonel John Gibbon, he "communicated to them the plan of operations which [he] had decided to adopt" with Custer being ordered to "Proceed up the Rosebud [River] until he should ascertain the direction in which the trail discovered by [Major Marcus] Reno [Custer's second in command]; that if it led to the Little Bighorn it should not be followed. . . ." Gibbon was ordered to cross the Yellowstone River near the mouth of the Little Bighorn River and follow that stream until June 26. There the two arms would regroup and attack together, unless circumstances made it necessary for Custer to depart from the orders.

Gathering by lantern on the night of June 24, Custer told his officers that the regiment would move in the dark because of the proximity of the Indian encampment. Later in the day of June 25, Custer stopped at the place now called Reno Creek. Again he gathered his officers and divided the regiment into three

Major Frederick W. Benteen, whose disdain for Custer was well known, was always suspected of willfully failing to come to his superior's assistance after receiving this hastily penciled note: "Benteen Come on. Big Village. Be quick. Bring packs. W. W. Cooke. P.S. Bring packs."
U.S. Military Academy, West Point

All of the Benteen memorabilia shown here—field glasses, pocketknife, campaign hat—was used at Little Bighorn.
Glen Swanson Collection

Custer's Last Fight,
woodcut, by William
de la Montagne Cary
(1840-1922).
Library of Congress

battalions: Companies A, G, and M under Major Reno, Companies D, H, and K under Captain Benteen, and the remaining five companies, B, C, E, I, and L, under Custer. The pack train under Captain Thomas McDougall and Company F was to remain in the rear until called upon for deployment.

Custer ordered Benteen "to move well to the left, and sweep everything before him." Custer followed the right bank of the Little Bighorn, or Greasy Grass, as the narrow, winding river was known to Indians. Reno's three companies rode along the left bank before beginning his attack.

Abundant grass, water, and success against General George Crook's forces at the Battle of the Rosebud the week before had brought Lakotas, Cheyennes, and a few Arapahos together that day, where they encamped in unprecedented numbers—thousands of women, children, and warriors.

When or if Custer ever realized what faced him is unknown. It seems that he ignored the exclamations of his Ree scouts earlier in the day when they warned, *"Otoe Sioux! Otoe Sioux!"* ("plenty" or "too many" Sioux). By turning a deaf ear to those true Indian experts, Custer essentially pronounced his own death sentence. Had he really been an authority on Indians, he would have been more cautious than to charge the village in broad daylight. Such arrogant action supposedly prompted a Lakota warrior named Bad Soup to deliver an emphatic epitaph after the so-called "Last Stand" of June 25, 1876. "That man there was Long Hair Custer. He thought he was the greatest man on earth, but he lie [*sic*] there now."

While Bad Soup's words about Custer may have expressed a common opinion among many American Indians, others then and later saw the vanquished Seventh Cavalry lieutenant colonel in a different light. Despite his defeat—indeed because of it—Custer became a larger-than-life figure, and remains so generations after his death along the Greasy Grass. Why was this so?

For one thing, because not a single white soldier survived to tell the Army's story of what happened to Custer's immediate command, the "mystery" that surrounded their deaths gave rise to an American legend. With the passage of years, a faithful following arose. They gathered stories and preserved relics to pass down from one generation to the next. Such responses bore the classic stamp of earlier "last stands," as Bruce A. Rosenberg explained in *Custer and the Epic of Defeat:*

> When the details of the popular legend of Custer's Last Stand are abstracted, its similarities to other heroic fiction (and history) is clearer: the few against the multitude, the fight to the death on the hilltop, the lone survivor, the traitor, and the desperate eleventh-hour call for help. Except for the names and a few other changes, the story is the same all over the world. . . .

So it was that Custer and the Little Bighorn offered the very stuff of adventure and romance required to join an elite circle of heroic tales both imagined and real—from Homeric epics to King Arthur's Court at Camelot to "The Charge of the Light Brigade." Custer, the dashing man in his prime bravely going off to his fate, leaving behind the perfect loving wife, meant, as Rosenberg puts it: "For the young hero . . . death is not only the fitting and brilliant end to a short but momentous life, it is the bright star to which the rest of the magnitude is to be favorably compared."

Custer had already primed himself for such lachrymose notoriety by the charisma that had made him such good copy for the press. Much of his rise to glory came from his exposure as both author and subject in the pages of illustrated magazines like *Galaxy* and *Harper's,* which enjoyed great popularity among the growing middle class of the 1860s and 1870s. Both periodicals were representative "of the great urban newspapers and journals, which had developed (since 1850) into a medium for the nationwide circulation of information and opinion," as Richard Slotkin has observed. Custer can be seen as being "an author of his own myth" in that "he recognized early in his career the value of reputation, or what we would call image, as a means of affecting the judgment of his social and military superiors." From those experiences, Custer learned that "he could shape his audiences' attitude by playing a role drawn from the lexicon of popular myth. In maturity, Custer became interpreter as well as actor, through a systematic literary exploitation of his public image."

Right after Little Bighorn some newspapers sloganeered for revenge by tying Custer's defeat to the republic's centennial then being celebrated across the land. They trumpeted: JOHN BULL 1776—SITTING BULL 1876. Besides being useful to boost circulation, Custer served as a vehicle to promote various political agendas of the Gilded Age, with some factions aiming to use the debacle to bring down Grant's corrupt administration.

Others wanted to use the incident as a moral lesson. Custer personified the essence of what legions of grammar school students were being taught in their *Monroe's Fifth Reader,* an 1871 primer which exhorted: "O waste not life on fond delusion!" Instead, the young scholar was told to "Be a soldier! Be a hero! Be a man!"

The most attentive tender of the Custer flame, his beloved Libbie, was more than just his passive admirer. During their life together and after his death, Elizabeth Custer played an active role in the promotion of her spouse's cause. She wore her widow's weeds well. In fact, surviving her fallen husband by more than fifty years, she wore them right to her death, on April 4, 1933. She remained committed to playing the role of the faithful wife and model Victorian woman, as historian Shirley A. Leckie has described in detail. Through her own public appearances and writings, including her trilogy, *Boots and Saddles, or Life in Dakota with General Custer; Tenting on the Plains;* and *Following the Guidon,* the widow Custer ensured that her beloved soldier husband would be remembered as

From the dime novels of the 1870s to the paperbacks and hardbound novels of the twentieth century, Custer and Little Bighorn have provided the background for hundreds of fictionalized stories.
Autry Museum of Western Heritage

Custer's Last Charge,
lithograph, 1876, by
Feodor Fuchs.
Library of Congress

Following pages:
Battle of the Little Big Horn,
oil on canvas, by John
Adams Elder (1833-85).
*State of New York, Division of
Military and Naval Affairs*

a gallant cavalier whose unblemished spirit would live on as a model for young Americans. She likewise influenced the writings of those who were friendly to Custer's memory. And because of her longevity, she simply outlasted those critics who might have written works denouncing Custer had his widow died earlier. In the process, she managed to secure a comfortable lifestyle from her appearances and books, ending her days in a pleasant New York apartment as a respected member of that cosmopolitan city's society much as both she and her late husband had aspired to on their visits there in the century before.

Beyond Elizabeth Bacon Custer's own widely distributed writings, Custerphiles and Custerphobes past and present have taken up their pens to write biographies, histories, and a vast assortment of literature that has come to be known as "Custeriana," a veritable industry based upon what one historian rightly termed "a minor episode in the history of the United States." Many of those works, which purported to be factual studies, were frequently polemical and often self-published tracts. Some among them were—and continue to be—directed to a specific audience of fellow Custer buffs. Much of it has the tone of conspiracy theories, that cottage industry of our own time.

The Custer industry was launched in a miasma that mingled a few facts with imagined heroics. Dime novels and other pulp publications found a far broader audience far faster than articles in military journals or books with a more academic veneer. In August and September 1876, only weeks after Custer's death, no fewer than five dime novels came off the presses chronicling the death of the fallen "Boy General." It was a performance to rival today's supermarket tabloids questing to reveal the personal trials of celebrities—who could themselves study with profit Custer's genius for self-promotion.

But it was more than just words that etched Custer and the Little Bighorn into the public's mind. Indeed, Custer's final moments became the inspiration for "Hundreds of paintings and illustrations and dozens of movies [that] have sought to capture that momentous instant, but writers have felt that a thousand words are worth more than a single picture, or several celluloid frames," as Don Russell has noted in *Custer's Last*.

Starting as early as 1876, melodramas and Wild West shows made much of the tableaux at the Little Bighorn. One of the Wild West shows even supposedly doubled its attendance after adding Custer's final engagement to its bill in 1887.

By 1909, the budding film industry likewise found the Custer saga a suitable subject to attract patrons, and with the passage of time it became one of seven

In 1909, Custer first came to the silver screen as a brave and noble role model worthy of imitation by the youth of America, a depiction well established in other media prior to *On the Little Big Horn*'s premiere.
Courtesy of the Academy of Motion Picture Arts and Sciences

basic plots for Westerns. *On the Little Big Horn; or, Custer's Last Stand* was the original silver screen treatment. This release by pioneer producer William Selig set the ground rules for all future silent and early sound films. In 1909, Selig sent his company on location to Montana, where hundreds of members of the Crow tribe, along with a number of national guardsmen representing the cavalry contingent, assembled as reenactors for this first cinematic interpretation.

The story opened with the arrest of the Lakota warrior Rain in the Face for the murder of two civilians as a prologue to the climactic battle along the banks of the Greasy Grass. Later Custer movies followed Selig's lead but often turned the Rain in the Face incident into a set piece, molding it indiscriminately to fit variations on the plotline. Such films helped perpetuate and further distort the already dubious Rain in the Face anecdote that first appeared in a sensational newspaper article of July 1876. According to this account, Rain in the Face sought to avenge himself on Tom Custer, Yellow Hair's younger brother, for supposed wrongs done him. Henry Wadsworth Longfellow's highly dramatized poem "The Revenge of Rain in the Face" helped fix the purported incident in the public mind. Armed with this popular story, screenwriters hastened to include the element in their plots. With successive telling, the legend gained more strength.

Besides setting the stage for future imitators, Selig adopted a pro Custer stance, depicting him as a soldier of "proven dash, courage and bravery." Moreover, the script blamed Major Marcus Reno for Custer's undoing. The film represented Reno as a coward, a fact that did not escape some of Custer's loyal officers. Reno was not the only one vilified; the Indians were depicted as a "band of naked painted devils," according to one review.

Selig's basic Custer-as-hero and Indian-as-heavy formula was repeated for generations. By the pre–World War I period, three primary uses of the Custer persona had developed. These were to remain the foundation for most subsequent movies and television scripts. First: The scenario that featured Custer as a central character and the last stand as a significant part of the story line. Next: The use of a figure based on Custer as a main character but with a different name, and the "massacre" of whites by an overwhelming Indian force. Finally: Certain pictures included Custer to add "flavor" or authenticity to a costume drama or Western. Custer had become such an icon that he did not even have to appear on screen. His name merely had to be evoked to cue the audience that this tale was set in the "Old West" and would have plenty of action between Indians and whites.

Early films and those that followed portrayed Custer and the events associated with his life in a way that filmmakers thought would be accepted by the moviegoing public—the equivalent of today's stereotype known as Joe Six-pack. What was served up was the "B" Western, where Custer was but one of a number of character types carried over from one film to the next. Although few such movies were high grossing, taken together they long helped fill the film industry's coffers, even as they pounded the same messages over and over again.

The messages were ethnocentric at best and, all too often, outright racist at the core. The Indians usually "were seen as savage, ruthless, treacherous, and pagan;

Custer and his men, by contrast, were brave, valiant, unflinching" men "who fought honorably with firearms—or gallantly, with sabers," exposed on hilltops against barbarian weapons wielded by Indians who "swarmed through valleys and crawled up ravines," according to Rosenberg.

The ultimate film portraying Custer as a noble warrior who fell fighting for a just cause—an archetypical figure who combats the enemies of progress—was Warner Bros.' 1941 production *They Died with Their Boots On*. Warners decided to match a successful pair of costume-drama performers, Errol Flynn and Olivia de Havilland. The result was perhaps the most famous of all the depictions of Custer and his bride. In the film, Flynn–Custer finds time to woo Elizabeth Bacon and hobnob with Phil Sheridan and Winfield Scott between daring charges reminiscent of scenes from Flynn's earlier film *The Charge of the Light Brigade*.

In *Boots*, Flynn–Custer manages to capture Crazy Horse, incurring the warrior's wrath. In so doing, the stage is set for the revenge that once had been the domain of Rain in the Face of earlier movies.

Such liberties with history were more than just poetic license. With World War II threatening to involve the United States, Warners was, according to one film review of the time, "generous to a fault in paying their respects to the hero." The country would presumably need people of this stature to help win the fight against fascism.

The script of *They Died with Their Boots On* was thereby transformed into a patriotic vehicle and a means of strengthening Anglo-American ties. As William R. Meyer writes in *The Making of the Great Westerns*, while early in the script "Flynn speaks [with] all the arrogance incumbent in an egotist like Custer . . . despite the purification of his character," nevertheless, "the celluloid commandant is also an idealist, a man willing to surrender his life for the common good."

On the eve of battle, de Havilland–Libbie begs, "You can't go. You'll be killed. I won't let you go." To this, Flynn–Custer responds, "I must go. It is my duty. I'm an officer in the United States Army."

On the night before the two sides are about to meet, Custer calls his adjutant, an Englishman named Butler, to him. He tells Butler that he wants him to carry an important letter back to Fort Lincoln. Butler declines, for he knows that Custer is attempting to keep his old comrade out of the fray because he is a "foreigner." Butler says that the only real Americans are the Indians, so in a sense he is no more a foreigner than the rest of the regiment.

Custer then prepares for what follows, confiding that he is riding "to hell or to glory. It depends on one's point of view." He then heads his column into the fray, motivated by a noble desire to protect Terry's column. Willing to sacrifice himself for others, he will stand as the last survivor before being killed by Crazy Horse in the climactic battle.

Not long after the end of World War II, a budding antiwar sentiment began to take hold. Custer's screen persona shifted from heroic model to antagonist or even antihero. Films began to vilify Custer and his men, following along the lines of certain publications that already had started to appear in the 1930s. Further, the

They Died with Their Boots On: Errol Flynn stands alone as the heroic Custer, a victim of white greed who will join his valiant comrades in death even though he is a man friendly to the plight of the Indians who are about to kill him. This 1941 Warner Bros. film was the high-water mark of cinematic depictions of Custer as a sympathetic character cut down in his prime.
Autry Museum of Western Heritage

momentum of the civil rights movement contributed to a shift in the depiction of American Indians to a more positive vein.

At first the shift was gradual—even subtle. In 1948, veteran director John Ford made *Fort Apache,* a black-and-white feature adapted from James Warner Bellah's short story "Massacre," and rewritten by one-time *New York Times* film critic Frank Nugent under the working title of "War Party." Although Ford set his drama in 1870s Arizona with Cochise, not Sitting Bull or Crazy Horse, as the enemy and took his company to Monument Valley rather than the Little Bighorn, he nonetheless intentionally drew upon the Custer story.

Ford's originality was the portrayal of the movie's Custer-figure, Colonel Owen Thursday (Henry Fonda). Thursday is a realistic character with flaws. He is all too human but brave. His death along with that of his troops could have been avoided, but the sacrifice was not in vain. Thursday's replacement as commander, Kirby York (John Wayne), a man who had opposed the fallen cavalry officer, now defends him. York maintains, "No man died more bravely nor brought more honor to his regiment," and sets the troops a heroic model to follow.

So Thursday's charge is given meaning, despite his fatal flaw of pride. He dies for his own sins rather than as a sacrificial victim of betrayal. This is not the case when Custer again came to the big screen in Walt Disney's *Tonka* (1958), a fanciful tale based upon David Appel's juvenile-oriented novel of how Captain Myles Keogh obtained his horse "Comanche" and the biography, in effect, of the steed before its service with that officer.

Originally, the horse Tonka belonged to a young Lakota, White Bull (Sal Mineo), but eventually Keogh (Philip Carey) acquires the fine mount. The Irish captain is kind in contrast to his superior Custer, a role assigned to Britt Lomond, the actor who also portrayed the heavy-handed commandant in Disney's *Zorro* television series. In *Tonka* Lomond–Custer takes the characterization to the point of advocating genocide. He bellows: "It is more important to teach these red savages a lesson than to rescue the white women. They [the Indians] must be exterminated."

Custer sends an ultimatum to the Lakota, who by now are preparing to stop the white onslaught. He tells them that his troops "will march and burn every Sioux village to the ground" if they do not return to their agencies. Custer also admonishes Keogh that there is "no way to separate the good from the bad. They burn, pillage; they're all bad." With this notion firmly fixed in his mind, Custer leads his command to their doom.

The Custer character was shelved from features for several years, but returned in the following decade. In fact, four companies competed to obtain Leon Fromkess's script that eventually became *The Great Sioux Massacre* in 1965. In it, Custer (Philip Carey, promoted from his earlier role as Captain Keogh) undergoes changes, but not for the better. Early on, as *Variety Weekly* pointed out, he was "a gruff, outspoken soldier friendly to the Indians and down on politically appointed and grafting Indian agents." His views on the matter lead him to troubles in Washington, D.C., and to his "unofficial exile." An embittered man, he returns to

COLUMBIA PICTURES
PRESENTS
THE TRUE STORY OF
THE
GREAT
SIOUX
MASSACRE
CINEMASCOPE
COLUMBIA
COLOR

STARRING
JOSEPH COTTEN / DARREN McGAVIN / PHILIP CAREY
CO-STARRING
JULIE SOMMARS / NANCY KOVACK with / MICHAEL PATE
Screenplay by FRED C. DOBBS / Story by SIDNEY SALKOW and MARVIN GLUCK / Produced by LEON FROMKESS / Directed by SIDNEY SALKOW

Philip Carey portrayed Custer as a politically ambitious glory-hunter who died for his ambitions in *The Great Sioux Massacre*, Columbia, 1965.
Autry Museum of Western Heritage

the West, but not before succumbing to a powerful senator's schemes to make the officer into a political hero. With dreams of the presidency in mind, Custer is transformed into an ambitious demagogue who will not rest until the Lakota are destroyed and their lands confiscated. This Custer was left with no redeeming qualities, joining the growing number of frontier antiheroes, typified by Clint Eastwood's morally bankrupt character in *The Good, the Bad, and the Ugly*.

It was a small leap to the most bereft Custer of all—Custer in Thomas Berger's *Little Big Man,* adapted to film by director Arthur Penn. Penn rendered a repellent image of the Army, as personified by Custer, reflecting dark sentiments generated during the troubled times of the Vietnam War. Although Dustin Hoffman had the starring role as a much confused adopted Indian, Richard Mulligan, as Custer, turned in a noteworthy supporting performance. Shortly after the film's premiere in 1970, a critic for *Motion Picture Exhibitor* summed up the film's major flaw: "Penn has juggled history to suit his purposes—while purporting all the while to be telling it like it is." Despite that, the message seemed in keeping with the times. Not only did the lunatic leader suffer for his actions, but the "Christian" nation he represented bore equal culpability for condoning such militarism. No longer the lone survivor standing bravely to meet his fate, *Little Big Man*'s Custer is a raving megalomaniac whose ignoble death comes as a just end for his total disregard for human rights and life.

And so Mulligan–Custer's last moment is exactly at odds with Flynn–Custer's. In the ensuing twenty or so years, Custer's image had become so fluid that diametrically opposing views could be presented without seeming contradiction. This explains why the made-for-television *Class of '61* (1993) could offer a devil-may-care Cadet Custer in the mold of *They Died with Their Boots On,* while at the same time the television series *Dr. Quinn, Medicine Woman* drew upon the Custer of *Little Big Man* as the quintessential white militarist and tool of the power brokers.

In yet another guise, Custer becomes a caricature and the punch line for humorous tales. Indeed, as Vine Deloria, Jr., has noted in his *Custer Died for Your Sins,* "The most popular and enduring subject of Indian humor is, of course, General Custer." And so, "There are probably more jokes about Custer and the Indians than there were participants in the battle." The reason: "All tribes, even those thousands of miles from Montana, feel a sense of accomplishment when thinking of Custer. Custer binds together implacable foes because he represented the Ugly American of the last century, and he got what was coming to him."

Will Custer finally be allowed to perish? Now, in mainstream and Indian culture, he is often the butt of humor or satire. His symbolic worth appears to be on the wane, paralleling the decline of the Western's popularity in general. It would seem that the present generation has rejected him and looks to new role models and icons or will require a new definition of the old form. Despite such possibilities, Custer's decades of exposure as a larger-than-life figure assures that he will not be dismissed easily from the public stage. One only has to reflect on the controversy surrounding the elimination of his name from the battlefield so long associated with him to get some inkling of his lasting symbolic status. Even a dozen decades after his death, he can be resurrected as a lightning rod guaranteed to spark highly charged political controversy.

As such, the unsolvable mystery surrounding Custer's final actions has turned him into a pliable metaphor—one that changes periodically, yet can be resurrected when deemed reusable in a former version. And if movies may be said to count as ballots for fame, consider this: Custer or characters derived from him have appeared in seventy feature films, film serials, and television productions. Sitting Bull and Crazy Horse, his antagonists that day at Little Bighorn, have been portrayed twenty-two and thirteen times, respectively.

Custer's transformation from mortal to mythic figure stemmed not so much from the real episodes and exploits of his life but from what he had become at the hands of others working in many art forms. In this, historian Brian Dippie rightly concludes, "the familiar concept of Custer's Last Stand is largely a creation of nonhistorical material, of popular culture, which, omnivorous, feeds upon fact and fancy, history and legend, and, turning cannibal, upon itself."

Custer's invention and reinvention as a symbol offers insight into how legends develop and tells something about the times and attitudes of the nation that gave his legend birth. Understanding Custer and the Little Bighorn opens a valuable

Richard Mulligan, as the insane Custer of *Little Big Man* (United Artists, 1968), raves about the corrupt Ulysses S. Grant as his fate is about to be sealed. In this rendition of the story, the long-haired megalomaniac and the government he serves are both guilty of a racist war of conquest.
Autry Museum of Western Heritage

Following pages:
Custer's Last Stand, oil on canvas, Edgar Samuel Paxon (1852-1919).
Buffalo Bill Historical Center

Custer's Last Stand, oil on canvas, by William Robinson Leigh (1866-1955). This painting marks a change in emphasis: Indians have become heroic; Custer and his troops are dim figures in the background.
Woolaroc Museum, Bartlesville, Oklahoma

window onto the American West and a glimpse into the national character. In an age of sound bites and bumper-sticker slogans, Custer offers an ideal vehicle for a range of opposing messages. So in the end, whether savior or Satan's spawn—or as merely a minor figure who made a monumental mistake—Custer never will die as long as he can be resurrected to provide meaning to a nation self-consciously struggling to define or redefine itself.

The Little Bighorn Chess Set

DONALD BLAINE TENOSO

The Indian king is One Bull, whose muslin drawing inspired Don Tenoso to create the Little Bighorn chess set. One Bull's pipe, which can actually be smoked, is made of catlinite, a red clay also known as pipestone. The pipe is tilted sideways in remembrance of Custer's failure to honor his pledge of peace made during a Cheyenne tobacco ceremony. One Bull's scalp shirt, with its red and blue bird designs, is based on a real shirt that he owned commemorating the battle. "The red birds," Tenoso says, "represented the red nation; the blue ones represented the blue coats. The barely visible yellow zigzag line represented lightning. It meant we struck like lightning at Little Bighorn. One Bull's scalp shirt indicates he is a leader. Originally there were only four scalp wearers. They were like Supreme Court justices, and their shirts were their robes. I was told the shirts were not made with the scalps of enemies, but with hair from relatives, friends, and society members who donated locks of hair for the shirts, sort of like casting their votes for the shirt wearers as leaders. This enabled them to make judgments. Pipe carriers had the right to settle disputes. That's the other reason One Bull has a pipe."
Eric Haase

A gifted artist whose work is in the finest traditions of the warrior-artists who fought against Custer and the Seventh Cavalry is Donald Blaine Tenoso, a thirty-eight-year-old Hunkpapa doll-maker who has created a Little Bighorn chess set. The rawhide chessboard features a pictograph of the battle based on a muslin drawing by his grandfather Chief One Bull, who counted coup on three Custer soldiers with a stone-headed war club. The chess pieces are six-inch-high dolls with movable parts adorned with outfits made with tanned hides, beads, and other authentic materials. Each doll has a story to tell that is best told by its creator, who has reached into family history and placed the Battle of the Little Bighorn in a timeless context. The Tenoso family still retains One Bull's muslin drawing as well as the stone head of the war club he carried into battle that day.

I am the fifth-generation descendant of a man named One Bull, who, with his brother White Bull, was adopted at a young age by their uncle, Sitting Bull. Although White Bull later chose to join his father's family down on Cheyenne River, One Bull stayed with Sitting Bull and was raised by him. At the time of the battle, Sitting Bull was in his forties; One Bull was in his early twenties. When the attack began, Sitting Bull gave One Bull his war shield and a Winchester rifle and told him to fight while he stayed behind to protect the village and the women and children. One Bull rushed to help blunt Reno's attack at the north side of the encampment. On the way, he met a badly wounded friend named Good Bear. He pulled Good Bear up behind him on his horse and, riding double, got him back to camp even though his horse was shot twice. One Bull was so smeared with blood that, upon seeing him, Sitting Bull tried to stop him from going back to the fight. "You're wounded, my son," he said. "Stay back. You're too hurt to go out and fight any more." "Don't worry," One Bull replied. "This blood is not mine. It is from my horse and the man I just helped." By the time One Bull got back to the battle, Reno's troops were trying to escape across the Little Bighorn. One Bull quickly fired the bullets in the rifle, the only ammunition he had, then he dropped the empty gun and for the rest of the day relied on his swinging war club. With it, he struck a soldier on the embankment leading down to the river and then counted coup on two more who were trying to climb to the top of Reno Ridge.

One Bull later documented his exploits in the battle on a white muslin cloth. Before he died in 1946, he gave the pictograph drawing and the club he used that day to my grandfather Eddie Brown with instructions never to let anyone know he had them because so many things like that had been stolen, sold, or just disappeared and had been lost to the family. My grandfather later gave them to my mother, who was the oldest of her generation. She kept them hidden and did not even tell me she had them until I was thirty-three years old.

Seeing this family treasure had a tremendous impact on me. I had grown up with the war stories of One Bull and White Bull, who lived together in their old age. They told the family lots of stories from their warrior days, and my mother and other relatives told those stories to us. For example, One Bull taught my mother to keep her clothes nicely folded and put everything she would need the next morning in the same place when going to sleep at night. This was not to keep the clothes from getting wrinkled. It was to have things close at hand in an emergency such as a surprise attack or other life-or-death situation. He never knew when the cavalry might attack again. He taught the family to always know where their stuff was, even in the dark, so they could grab it all and get out. My mom knew One Bull very well. She had sat on his knee where she was bounced as a baby. She was ten years old when grandfather died in 1946. Most people believe that the Battle of the Little Bighorn was so long ago that it's ancient history, yet One Bull died only in 1946. There are people alive even now, in my lifetime, who knew participants.

I always thought the stories were fascinating, but they were just stories. It was seeing my grandpa's muslin that really inspired me. Seeing something physical like that was profoundly moving. I already had the idea of making a Little Bighorn chess set; when I saw the drawing of what One Bull did at Little Bighorn, it all came together in my mind. Originally, I had thought I would make a regular chessboard with a box and border design and a pictograph scene as the playing field like the Red Horse drawings I had seen. I would show a dead person on this square, a dead horse on that square, Indians riding off with captured ponies on another square. Maybe one square down there would be a lady being humane and putting some guy out of his misery or giving him misery—it could be taken that way too. But after seeing One Bull's drawing, I said to myself, "That's it!"

These dolls are like my kids. You never know where they are going, or what they are saying about you, or to whom. Naturally, you want them to say something nice. You want them to be interesting so people will enjoy their company and not put them away in a box or on a shelf where no one will see them. I also hope people will learn something from them, things that I have learned. That way, information passed to me is passed along.

Each of the Seventh Cavalry pawns has a distinctive look. "The soldiers supposedly all had similar uniforms," Tenoso says, "but like all humans I am sure they modified their outfits to suit their individual tastes— within regulations— so I put little different touches on each soldier.

"One guy was in the latrine when the fighting began. His pants are off, his coat is open, and his gun belt is over his shoulder. He usually is placed in front of the outhouse, which is one of the castles on the soldier side. I like to say that we scared the pants off of him.

"The cook is one of the soldier bishops. He's an old sergeant with white hair who has been around a lot. His sleeves are rolled up. He has his kettle, his ladle, and his fork, which he uses to prod the soldiers pulling KP. His apron is clean because he really does not do any work himself. Tucked in his boots is a pair of aces—the ace of spades and the ace of clubs—because come payday he takes all the money from the privates. In the military, the sarge is the next thing to God, especially in boot camp. That's why he's a bishop. It's a military thing."
Eric Haase

221

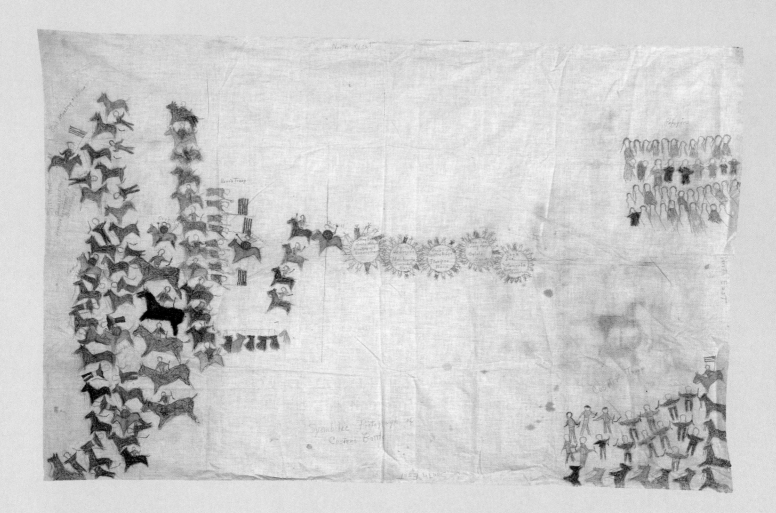

Above: One Bull.
Glen Swanson Collection

Top: One Bull's muslin drawing depicting his actions during the Battle of the Little Bighorn. In the drawing, he is the warrior riding the yellow horse.
Don Tenoso Collection

I teach my kids and I want them to teach other kids. That way the knowledge goes on and on. I send them out into the world with their hands full. Most of them have something in both hands. If you have kids, you want to send them out as prepared as possible. Most of my dolls have weapons because they have to protect themselves out there, like the saloon hall girl with her hairpin. Everybody has to protect themselves, and it's the same with your kids. You give them what you feel they need so they can fend for themselves out there in the world, to protect themselves. They also have to be interesting, knowledgeable, and appealing, because you want people to take care of them, to know their stories. Usually, my dolls go out with complete descriptions. I try to write down everything about them. They go out with what is called documentation. It is something I learned working in museums like the Smithsonian. I try to explain the effort I make to find real materials with which to create the dolls. If I don't write down what I meant to say with them, then a hundred years from now it will be gone. The information will be more than half the value of the doll to those people then.

Does the Battle of the Little Bighorn have relevance today? I think so. Despite the fact that people tried to exterminate us, we are still here. I guess we are meant to be here. Sioux people have been here for over thirty thousand years probably. We were here to greet the other people who came to America. We weren't inhospitable until the other people were bad to us.

222

To me the chess set symbolizes our continuing struggle. The chessboard is a square sheet of rawhide. It is warped and uneven to symbolize the fact that Indians are still playing on an uneven field. The struggle goes on. The Indians still fight the cowboys. Every once in a while we redraw the lines, we group up again, and we go at it. It's like a chess game. We have skirmishes and we have conflicts. Sometimes we win, as we did at Little Bighorn, but usually the Anglo side over-powers us with all its technology and supply lines, their religion, the stuff that spurs them on. Opposed to them are we Indians who used everything from stone clubs and flint-tipped spears to modern guns. We threw everything we had at them. In a sense, the conflict ended in a draw because we are still here and so are they. In fact, I heard there are more of us now according to the 1990 Census than ever before. But, hey, how long have they been counting us anyway?

One Bull and White Bull attending a Sun Dance in 1941. One Bull received the saber in a ceremony honoring the old warrior.
Don Tenoso Collection

Don Tenoso and the rawhide chessboard based on One Bull's pictograph drawing of the Battle of the Little Bighorn.
Herman J. Viola Collection

Left: The complete Little Bighorn chess set. Custer is the king of the Seventh Cavalry. His queen is a dance-hall girl with tarnished silver slippers, "like her reputation." The rooks are an outhouse and a fort with a loose cannon in it. The knights are a mule and a horse. Some of the soldier chessmen wield sabers, even though none were actually carried at Little Bighorn. This is artistic license, taken to give the soldier pawns some individuality, as the chess pieces have no faces. "My grandma told me that traditionally, Lakota dolls did not have faces," Tenoso says. "It was only after our kids saw European dolls that we started putting glass beads on for eyes and mouths."

For the Indian side, the rooks are tipis, the knights are Indian ponies, and and the queen is a woman who carries all the tools a traditional woman should have to make a fully beaded dress, including a knife and an awl. One Indian bishop is a Sun Dancer because, Tenoso explains, "To us, any man can achieve that rank or can be a leader through religion, through visions. Anyway, you can arise to the rank of what you might call a bishop on a chess set. The other bishop is a bear doctor. He's a healer who has the vision of how to use our medicine." Each of the six-inch-high dolls has movable parts, such as pistols and rifles that cock, knives and sabers that can be removed from their sheaths and scabbards, and clothing that can be buttoned or tied.
Eric Haase

Additional Reading

Barnett, Louise. *Touched by Fire: The Life, Death, and Mythic Afterlife of George Armstrong Custer*. New York: Henry Holt and Company, 1996.

Bradley, Douglas E. *White Swan: Crow Indian Warrior and Painter*. Exhibit catalog. Snite Museum of Art, University of Notre Dame, Notre Dame, Ind., 1991.

Custer, Elizabeth Bacon. *Boots and Saddles; or, Life in Dakota with General Custer*. New York: Harper and Brothers, 1885.

————. *Following the Guidon*. New York: Harper and Brothers, 1890.

————. *Tenting on the Plains; or, General Custer in Kansas and Texas*. New York: Charles L. Webster, 1887.

Custer, George Armstrong. *My Life on the Plains; or, Personal Experiences with Indians*. New York: Sheldon & Company, 1874.

Dippie, Brian. *Custer's Last Stand: The Anatomy of an American Myth*. Lincoln: University of Nebraska Press, 1994.

————, and John Carroll. *Bards of the Little Big Horn*. Bryan, Tex.: Guidon Press, 1978.

————, and Paul A. Hutton. *The Comic Book Custer: A Bibliography of Custeriana in Comic Books and Comic Strips*. N.p.: Brazos Corral of the Westerners, n.d.

Fox, Richard A., Jr. *Archeology, History, and Custer's Last Battle*. Norman: University of Oklahoma Press, 1993.

Graham, W. A. *The Custer Myth: A Source Book of Custeriana*. Harrisburg, Penn.: Stackpole Co., 1953.

Gray, John S. *Centennial Campaign: The Sioux War of 1876*. Fort Collins, Col.: Old Army Press, 1976.

————. *Custer's Last Campaign: Mitch Boyer and the Little Bighorn Reconstructed*. Lincoln: University of Nebraska Press, 1991.

Greene, Jerome A., comp. and ed. *Lakota and Cheyenne Indian Views of the Great Sioux War, 1876-1877*. Norman: University of Oklahoma Press, 1994.

Hardoff, Richard G. *The Custer Battle Casualties: Burials, Exhumations, and Reinterments*. El Segundo, Cal.: Upton and Sons, 1991.

————. *Lakota Recollections*. Spokane: Arthur H. Clark Company, 1991.

Katz, D. Mark. *Custer in Photographs*. New York: Bonanza Books, 1985.

Leckie, Shirley A. *Elizabeth Bacon Custer and the Making of a Myth*. Norman: University of Oklahoma Press, 1993.

Libby, O. G. *The Arikara Narrative of the Campaign Against the Hostile Dakotas*. North Dakota Historical Commission, 1920.

Linenthal, Edward Tabor. *Sacred Ground: Americans and Their Battlefields*. Urbana: University of Illinois Press, 1991.

Marquis, Thomas. B. *The Cheyennes of Montana*. Algonac, Mich.: Reference Publications, 1978.

————. *Keep the Last Bullet for Yourself*. Algonac, Mich.: Reference Publications, 1976.

————. *Memoirs of a White Crow Indian*. Lincoln: University of Nebraska Press, 1974.

————. *She Watched Custer's Last Battle*. Privately Printed, 1933.

————. *Wooden Leg: A Warrior Who Fought Custer.* Lincoln: University of Nebraska Press, 1995.

Medicine Crow, Joseph. *From the Heart of the Crow Country: The Crow Indians' Own Story.* New York: Crown, 1992.

Meyer, William R. *The Making of the Great Westerns.* New York: Arlington House, 1979.

Rosenberg, Bruce. *Custer and the Epic of Defeat.* University Park: Pennsylvania State University Press, 1974.

Neihardt, John G. *Black Elk Speaks.* Lincoln: University of Nebraska Press, 1961.

Powell, Peter J. *Sweet Medicine.* Norman: University of Oklahoma Press, 1969.

Rosenberg, Bruce. *Custer and the Epic of Defeat.* University Park: Pennsylvania State University Press, 1974.

Russell, Don. *Custer's Last.* Fort Worth: Amon Carter Museum of Western Art, 1968.

————. *The Wild West ; or, A History of the Wild West Shows.* Fort Worth: Amon Carter Museum of Western Art, 1972.

Scott, Douglas D., Richard A. Fox, Jr., Melissa A. Connor, and Dick Harmon. *Archaeological Perspectives on the Battle of the Little Bighorn.* Norman: University of Oklahoma Press, 1989.

————, and Peter Bleed. *A Look Around the Boundary: Archeological Inventory of the Dyck and Other Properties Adjacent to Little Bighorn Battlefield National Monument.* Report on file, Midwest Archeological Center. Lincoln, Neb.: National Park Service, 1995.

Slotkin, Richard. *The Fatal Environment: The Myth of the Frontier in the Age of Industrialization, 1800–1890.* New York: Atheneum, 1985.

————. *Regeneration Through Violence.* Middleton, Conn.: Wesleyan University Press, 1973.

Smith, Henry Nash. *Virgin Land: The American West as Symbol and Myth.* New York: Vintage, 1950.

Steckmesser, Kent Ladd. *The Western Hero in History and Legend.* Norman: University of Oklahoma Press, 1965.

Tabor, Edward. *Changing Images of the Warrior Hero in America: A History of Popular Symbolism.* New York: Edwin Mellen Press, 1982.

Taylor, William O. *With Custer on the Little Bighorn.* New York: Viking, 1996.

Tuska, Jon. *The American West in Film: Critical Approaches to the Western.* Westport, Conn.: Greenwood Press, 1985.

Utley, Robert M. *Cavalier in Buckskin: George Armstrong Custer and the Western Military Frontier.* Norman: University of Oklahoma Press, 1988.

————. *Custer and the Great Controversy.* Los Angeles: Westernlore Press, 1962.

————. *The Lance and the Shield: The Life and Times of Sitting Bull.* New York: Ballantine, 1994.

Viola, Herman J. *It Is a Good Day to Die.* New York: Crown, 1998.

Contributors

GERARD BAKER, a member of the Affiliated Tribes on Fort Berthold Reservation, North Dakota, received his degree in sociology and criminology from Southern Oregon State University. He has worked for the National Park Service for twenty-three years. In 1998, he became superintendent of the Chickasaw National Recreation Area. Prior to this assignment he served as superintendent of the Little Bighorn Battlefield National Monument.

JEANNE OYAWIN EDER, a Dakota Sioux, was born and raised on the Fort Peck Reservation, Montana. She is named for her great-grandmother Oyawin (Track Woman), a Santee Sioux who, with her brothers, was at Little Bighorn and then escaped to Canada with Sitting Bull's band. Dr. Eder, who holds a Ph.D. in American and public history, is multicultural coordinator at Western Montana College of the University of Montana.

MELFINE FOX EVERETT is a retired schoolteacher living on the Fort Berthold Indian Reservation near Bismarck, North Dakota.

ALBERTA AMERICAN HORSE FISHER has been a bilingual instructor at Dull Knife Memorial College, Lame Deer, Montana. She is currently an administrator of the U.S.D.A. Commodities Program on the Northern Cheyenne Reservation.

MICHAEL HER MANY HORSES is an Oglala Lakota. In addition to teaching courses on Lakota history and culture at Oglala Lakota College, he has been executive director of the Pine Ridge Reservation. He is currently a member of the Pine Ridge Tribal Council.

JAMES S. HUTCHINS is a senior historian at the National Museum of American History, Smithsonian Institution. A graduate of the U.S. Military Academy, he is the author of *Boots and Saddles at the Little Bighorn* (Custer Battlefield Historical Association, 1976) and of the forthcoming *Papers of Edward S. Curtis Relating to the Battle of the Little Bighorn* (Richard Upton & Sons).

JOHN P. LANGELLIER has written more than twenty books and monographs, as well as dozens of articles, on military history, the American West, and American Indian history. He has served as a consultant for motion-picture and television productions and has co-produced two documentaries for A&E's *Time Machine*. He currently serves as director of the U.S. Navy's Civil Engineer Corps and Seabee Museum.

JOSEPH MEDICINE CROW was born in Lodge Grass, Montana, in 1913. He was raised by his grandparents, who knew life before reservation days and from whom he acquired training in Crow ways and customs. The first member of the Crow tribe to graduate from college, he received his M.A. in anthropology from the University of Southern California in Los Angeles, but his doctoral studies were interrupted by World War II. After the war he returned to Lodge Grass and worked for the tribe in various official capacities. In 1996 the University of Montana awarded him an honorary doctorate.

DOUGLAS D. SCOTT is an archaeologist with the National Park Service. He has been an innovator in the study of battlefields and has published extensively. His background has enabled him to assist the United Nations in human-rights investigations in El Salvador, Croatia, and Rwanda, where he has specialized in firearms identification analysis as well as mapping and documenting sites of alleged mass executions and exhumations of mass graves.

ALONZO SPANG, PH.D., is currently the president of Dull Knife Memorial College, Lame Deer, Montana. For many years he was an official of the Bureau of Indian Affairs, and he has served as superintendent of the Northern Cheyenne, Flathead, Salish, Kootenai, and Rosebud Sioux reservations.

HERMAN J. VIOLA is a curator emeritus of the Smithsonian Institution. Prior to joining the Smithsonian in 1972, he worked at the National Archives as an archivist with the records of the Bureau of Indian Affairs, and he served as the first editor of *Prologue: The Journal of the National Archives*. He is the author of numerous books on U.S. history.

THE REVEREND JOSEPH WALKS ALONG, SR., is currently president of the Northern Cheyenne Tribe. In addition, for many years he has been minister of the Mennonite Church on the Northern Cheyenne Reservation.

Index

Page numbers in *italics* refer to illustrations.